New Perspectives
on Robert Graves

New Perspectives on Robert Graves

Edited by
Patrick J. Quinn

Selinsgrove: Susquehanna University Press
London: Associated University Presses

© 1999 by Associated University Presses, Inc.

All rights reserved. Authorization to photocopy items for internal or personal use, or the internal or personal use of specific clients, is granted by the copyright owner, provided that a base fee of $10.00, plus eight cents per page, per copy is paid directly to the Copyright Clearance Center, 222 Rosewood Drive, Danvers, Massachusetts 01923. [1-57591-020-9/99 $10.00 + 8¢ pp, pc.]

Associated University Presses
440 Forsgate Drive
Cranbury, NJ 08512

Associated University Presses
16 Barter Street
London WC1A 2AH, England

Associated University Presses
P.O. Box 338, Port Credit
Mississauga, Ontario
Canada L5G 4L8

The paper used in this publication meets the requirements of the American National Standard for Permanence of Paper for Printed Library Materials Z39.48-1984.

Library of Congress Cataloging-in-Publication Data

New perspectives on Robert Graves / edited by Patrick J. Quinn.
   p. cm.
   Includes bibliographical references and index.
   ISBN 1-57591-020-9 (alk. paper)
   1. Graves, Robert, 1895– —Criticism and interpretation.
I. Quinn, Patrick J., 1946– .
PR6013.R35Z75   1999
821'.912—dc21
                                              99-19629
                                                  CIP

PRINTED IN THE UNITED STATES OF AMERICA

For those who started me on my way: Marilynn Stadtmiller, Ralph Barbaro, Leslie Marshall, and Stuart Hunter: "I thank you for your voices, thank you / Your most sweet voices" Coriolanus II.iii. (79)

Contents

Introduction PATRICK J. QUINN	9

Part I: Criticism

Revising for Reasonableness: Robert Graves as Critic and Poet JOHN BENNETT	19
Captain Graves's Postwar Strategies PAUL O'PREY	36
Robert Graves, Modernism, and the "Poetic Body" PATRICK MCGUINNESS	46

Part II: Poetry

A Measure of Casualness: The Peripatetic in the Poetry of Robert Graves DEVINDRA KOHLI	65
Graves and the Mythology of Desire SIMON BRITTAN	84
The Breaking of the Spell: Graves's Dissatisfaction Poetry of 1937 PATRICK QUINN	94

Part III: Fiction

"Epics Are Out of Fashion": Graves's Short Story as a Model for His Longer Fiction's Narrative Techniques IAN FIRLA	107
Robert Graves and the Historial Novel in the 1930s CHRIS HOPKINS	128
Graves's Milton IAN MCCORMICK	136

Part IV: The White Goddess

"The Nature of the Goddess": Ted Hughes and Robert Graves   149
  NICK GAMMAGE
Robert Graves, the Esoteric Tradition, and the New Religion   159
  DIONYSIOUS PSILOPOULOS

Part V: Influence

Telling the Truth—Nearly: Robert Graves, Daniel Defoe, and
    Good-bye to All That   175
  STEVEN TROUT
Robert Graves, W. B. Yeats, and Dylan Thomas: Poetry, Sex,
    Religion, and Feud   188
  JOHN PRESLEY
The Pastoral Vision of Robert Graves   209
  ROBERT DAVIS

Contributors   220
Index   224

Introduction

PATRICK J. QUINN

1995 WAS THE CENTENARY OF ONE OF THE MOST REMARKABLE ENGLISH WRITERS of the twentieth century. His hundredth birthday was marked by two international conferences: one at St. John's College, Oxford, where he received his undergraduate degree in English in 1925, and the other in his adopted island of Majorca. The conferences brought together scholars from eighteen countries and five continents as well as friends, family, muses, enemies, and interested onlookers, for Robert Graves was fascinating not only as writer but also as a man making his way through personal crises brought about by war, depression, displacement, and unrequited love.

Graves's life and loves have been the subjects of constant criticism and speculation during his centenary year. Martin Seymour-Smith began the trend by rereleasing his 1982 biographical study of Graves, complete with new introduction and several significant revisions. Miranda Seymour's more recent biography, *Robert Graves: Life on the Edge,* provides a useful perspective of Graves's life through the eyes of a female novelist and biographer. Her assessment of Graves's life and loves is fair and provocative, but her work avoids much critical discussion of his writings. The long-awaited third volume of Richard Perceval Graves's biography of his uncle, *Robert Graves and the White Goddess 1940–1985,* also appeared in 1995. R. P. Graves's work is meticulously constructed and well-researched but—like the two previous biographies—lacks pace and energy. The most pleasant surprise of 1995, the year of the Graves biography, was William Graves's insightful portrait of his growing up with a famous father on the island of Majorca. *Wild Olives* weaves a wonderful story of Graves's fame and its immediate disadvantages in the heady paradise of pretourist Majorca.

Unfortunately, the sudden and prodigious output of biographical material on Graves in 1995 was not balanced by an equal flow of scholarly criticism of his literary works. This owes something perhaps to Graves's legendary status (promoted in the 1960s by Graves himself) as a larger-than-life figure dedicated to the service of whichever poetic muse happened to suit at the time, which gave some critics the impression of Graves as an aging hippy who used his literary reputation as an excuse to pursue young women. Three such objects of Graves's passions have confirmed separately in confidence that Graves offered them the "chance to be a Muse," an offer which each of them felt bound to refuse, having no idea what the duties of such a position would entail. In Deia, Graves became a guru to the disaffected youth of several continents who happened to pass through the village; his outspoken attacks on authority and conventional behavior found an appreciative audience in a new generation. Graves's controversial stances on homosexuality, on other English poets, on the occult, and even on the translation of Omar Khayaám's *Rubáiyat*, ensured that he kept his place in the public eye well into the 1970s. Indeed, it was this outlandish public image which he fostered in Deia which kept the writer from being taken seriously by the scholarly community, especially in his native England. Typically, this did not seem to bother Graves.

Controversy and public attention had never been aspects of life which Graves avoided; in fact, he positively courted them. He brought attention to himself as early as 1929 when he embarked upon an autobiography at the age of 33. The result, *Good-bye to All That*, has become one of the most celebrated studies of the Great War ever written, but it also is an insightful polemic against Edwardian family values, against the British public-school system, and against the ineffectiveness of politicians and military strategists. The book has become a classic treatise on the hypocrisy of war and its attendant horrors.

The British critical establishment has never been very comfortable with manifestations of eccentricity in its writers, and Graves certainly was eccentric. Not only did he injure irreparably his reputation by leaving England in 1929, but he doubled his sin in the eyes of his critics (after the end of World War II) by doing the same again in 1946. His un-British behavior and implied criticism of his homeland was never forgotten by British literary circles, and throughout his last thirty years, the most significant studies of his work came from scholars in the United States, Canada, Australia, and Spain.

Since Graves's death in 1985, full-length studies of his poetry and prose have been slow to appear. True, the literary journal *Focus on Robert Graves* (founded in 1972 at Hofstra by Ellsworth Mason) continued to publish articles on Graves until 1995 when *Gravesiana: The Journal of the Robert Graves Society* appeared. Articles on Graves have appeared regularly in journals such as the *University of Toronto Quarterly* or *English Studies;* but comprehensive analyses of his work have been few. Only three critical studies, D. N. G. Carter's *Robert Graves: The Lasting Poetic Achievement* (1989); H. Koike-Ferrick's *Robert Graves: The Poet and the Muse (1992)*, and my own *The Great War and the Missing Muse* (1994) have appeared in the last ten years. One of the objectives of the latter was to address this oversight and bring the light of modern criticism to bear on his varied early works.

The most gratifying element of the two centenary conferences was the number of scholars who were keen to offer papers to large audiences both in Oxford and Palma. In attempting to select papers representative of the quality and variety of those presented for inclusion in this book, however, the pleasure becomes a pain. With over seventy papers from which to choose, many of them revealing original findings and demonstrating first-rate scholarship, it is a bittersweet task to pick out a select few. Because of the limitations imposed by the proposed size of this volume, a number of worthy essays have had to be excluded. The eventual choices for inclusion fell neatly, but not intentionally, under a number of varied headings: "Criticism," "Poetry," "Fiction," "Essays," and "Influences." These five thematic divisions will hopefully guide readers new to the works of Graves and bring some new insights to those already familiar with his numerous works.

John Bennett's opening article in the "Criticism" section of the book, explores Graves's own standards of poetic criticism and discusses whether he practised what he preached in his own writing. Paul O'Prey, the editor of two books of Graves's letters (*In Broken Images* [1982] and *Between Moon and Moon* [1984]), analyses the poetry and criticism which Graves wrote immediately after the end of the Great War and examines the nature of the various therapeutic strategies that he employed during this critical period of readjustment. Patrick McGuinness's *Robert Graves: Modernism and the 'Poetic Body'* focuses on the impact Graves's poetry and literary criticism had on early modernist poets early days of as well as the "Movement" poets in the 1950s.

In the "Poetry" section of the book, Devindra Kohli's illuminating discussion on the use of the peripatetic in Graves's poetry presents a unique way of examining one unifying element of his poetry. Basing his commentary on the insights of Anne Wallace and Roger Gilbert in their critical studies, Kohli shows how meaningful the image of walking is to Graves's work. Simon Brittan's close reading of three of Graves's poems, "Love in Barrenness," "On the Ridge," and "Pygmalion to Galatea," offers an insight into Graves's attitude towards female sexuality. The final paper in this section is my own, which attempts to show by illustrations from Graves's verse of 1937 how the poet attempted to reconcile his own approach to his art with Laura Riding's shifting stance on the role of poetry in the politically conscious 1930s.

If there is one particular area which has been neglected by Graves's critics, it is in the assessment of his fiction. Despite the well-deserved and popular attention lavished upon his Claudius novels, most of his other full-length works of fiction have been seen to be little more than potboilers written simply to make money. Graves himself gave credence to this generalization by stating often that his true milieu was poetry, his true vocation service to his poetic muse. Ian Firla, who opens the "Fiction" section of this collection with an examination of several of Graves's undervalued short stories, demonstrates how the narrative technique in those stories is mirrored in both the Claudius novels and *Count Belisarius*. Chris Hopkins's essay looks carefully at the penchant for historical novels in the 1930s and discovers how the subthemes of the Claudius novels fit well with the concerns of the readers of that particular period. Finally in this section, Ian McCormick's study of Graves's *Wife to Mr. Milton* reveals how Graves's radically different outlook to that of Milton resulted in an unfavorable characterisation of Milton in the novel.

The fourth section of the book is dedicated to essays on the theme of the mythological White Goddess, under whose domination Graves labored for the final thirty years of his productive life. Nick Gammage's opening essay analyses Ted Hughes's interpretation of Graves's *The White Goddess* when he first encounter the text in 1951. Gammage's essay observes the way in which one important English poet was influenced by the muse of another, and how Hughes transformed the raw material which he absorbed from Graves's work to the benefit of his own. Dionysious Psilopoulos ventures into the whole question of the occult tradition in his study of the White Goddess. Psilopoulos presents the essential background of the chthonic esoteric tradition from which Graves's goddess originates and follows the thread into Christianity itself.

The final part of this book, which is entitled simply "Influences," is intended to highlight the literary interactions between Graves and other English writers. Steven Trout's essay on the similarities between *Good-bye to All That* (1929) and Daniel Defoe's *A Journal of A Plague Year* (1721) seems at first glance to be an odd choice of pseudo-fiction to compare. But Trout's deft observations make one wonder why these two books, which seem so dissimilar, have not been examined in conjunction with each other previously. John Presley attempts to answer one of the more difficult questions of Graves scholarship:

that is, why Graves held both Dylan Thomas and W. B. Yeats in such poor regard. Presley's speculations as to the reasons for Graves's often outrageous and ungenerous attacks on his fellow poets are presented with keen insights and observations. In the final article of the book, Robert Davis examines Graves's place in the pastoral tradition; he makes a strong case for examining Graves's poetry in the light of Pierre Borgeaud's pre-Selenic tradition of pastoral poetry, showing clearly at the same time the intentions of a volume such as Graves's *Man Does, Woman Is*.

The fifteen essays collected together in this book cover a broad spectrum of comment on Graves's work. It is hoped that they will spark further interest in one of the most versatile writers of the twentieth century and lead some way to a reappraisal of his work, acting at the same time as a stimulus for further research into Graves's writing well into the twenty-first century.

This work would not have been possible without the kind and generous permission of Carcanet Press, publishers of *The Complete Works of Robert Graves*, for the use of extensive quoted materials. Also greatly appreciated is the permission of A. P. Watt Ltd., on behalf of the Robert Graves Copyright Trust, to reprint sections from *I, Claudius* and *Claudius the God*.

New Perspectives
on Robert Graves

Part I
Criticism

Revising for Reasonableness: Robert Graves as Critic and Poet

JOHN BENNETT

DOES THE TITLE OF ROBERT GRAVES'S LECTURE, "LEGITIMATE CRITICISM OF POetry," refer to all the legitimate ways of criticizing poetry? Or does it refer merely to criticism that is legitimate? Graves probably intends the latter: the title, after all, is "Legitimate Criticism of Poetry," not "*The* Legitimate Criticism of Poetry."

The word "legitimate" suggests a certain defensiveness on Graves's part, a reminder to his audience of his criticism's validity. "You may object to my continuing attacks on famous poets," Graves may be saying, aware that the drubbing he gave Alexander Pope, Ezra Pound, and others in the Clark Lectures had rankled many listeners and readers, "but at least they are legitimate." The author of "Legitimate Criticism of Poetry" seems to be stating his strongly felt case and, in the midst a clamor of objections, stressing the validity of his position.

Is the criticism Graves presents in this lecture the only legitimate variety? Graves never makes this claim for it. Is it legitimate at all? Most of it, by the common standards of logic and reason, is not. Graves, who in his critical writings insisted that poems be logical and reasonable, violates logic and reason throughout his criticism, building his arguments on conjecture and flights of fancy more appropriate for novels than lectures or essays. He demands that all poetry be reasonable, but not rational, and that it conceal layers of meaning, but be immediately intelligible. Having defined good poetry as reasonable poetry, Graves applies this standard inconsistently in this lecture and throughout his critical works. Typically, he invokes reasonableness to belittle English poets he dislikes. Thus, in the essay "Centaurs' Food," he describes, but does not censure, the ritual poetry of ancient Greece, which, uttered in a state of drug-induced ecstasy, could hardly have been reasonable; while in the essay "The Ghost of Mr. Milton," he maligns *Paradise Lost* for being "overpowering." His ideal of reasonable poetry—poems that make sense, probably written about love, and probably written by men—allows him to dismiss most of English poetry as fanciful rhetoric or bombast and to decide, finally, that the English poetic tradition includes only fifteen real poets. His theory of poetry and poetic development is arbitrary, sexist, and inconsistent, rather than logical, impartial, and uniform. Whether he recognized it or not, Graves had reason to defend his criticism even in a lecture's title; houses with the frailest frames have need of the strongest walls.

Confronted with Graves's insistence of legitimacy and reasonableness, it is worthwhile, I think, to examine his critical method and to measure it against the standard of reasonableness he expected of poetry, as well as the standard of logic most critics expect of criticism. How, precisely, did he define his standard? How did he examine poems? What, in his criticism, constitutes evidence? And, finally, what can one conclude about Graves himself and the value of his criticism? I would like to focus on lectures, such as "Legitimate Criticism of Poetry," in which Graves practices an exegetical method he later names analeptic mimesis—writing a poem out by hand to discover its original form and revisionary flaws—because, first, this method is unique to him as a critic (and, as such, allows us to easily distinguish his criticism from that of his contemporaries), and second, because it relates to the methods of discovery he used when working on novels.

Graves delivered "Legitimate Criticism of Poetry" at Mount Holyoke College in Massachusetts in February 1957. Early in the lecture, Graves notes that, as part of their education, the students at Mount Holyoke are asked to appreciate the poetry in some standard anthology. He warns them:

> Be very careful with the word "appreciate," which originally meant "to calculate the quality, or worth, or amount of a thing." Thus Burke wrote in 1769: "Let us calmly appreciate these dreadful and deformed gorgons and hydras." . . . Some such critical judgement as: "This poem is punk, for the following reasons," would also come under the heading "appreciation." (Graves 1958, 33–34)

This definition of "appreciate" and the references to Gorgons and Hydras and a poem being "punk," suggest that Graves is planning to treat the anthology with less awe and reverence than it receives from, say, F. R. Leavis. If Graves appreciates poetry by calculating its worth, what is the standard he uses in his calculations? What is his ideal of poetry?

In this lecture, and in his essays and stories, Graves consistently presents reasonableness, sensibility, and intelligibility as the standard for good poetry. For example, in the Mount Holyoke lecture, he states,

> Poetry (need I say?) is more than words musically arranged. It is sense; good sense; penetrating, often heart-rending sense. . . . How few give any thought to the sense of a poem, though it often has layer after layer of meaning concealed in it! (Graves 1958, 34)

It is unclear what Graves means here by "good sense." Apparently the sense of the poem is not the meaning of it, because the sense contains layers of meaning, yet somehow escapes notice—few readers, he says, give the sense of a poem any thought. A comment he includes in the short story, "A Toast to Ava Gardner," suggests that sense is simply prosaic intelligibility, because, whatever it is, the reader is capable of grasping it immediately. "Really good poetry always makes plain, immediate, personal sense, is never dull, and goes on making better sense the oftener one reads it. 'Poems are like people,' I said. 'There are not many authentic ones around.'" (Graves 1960c, 43). If making plain, immediate sense means making sense the way expository prose is expected to make sense, one can understand, perhaps, why Graves attacked modernist poems, such as Pound's *Cantos* and various poems of Dylan Thomas, for not making sense: these poems frequently dispense with narrative structure and suppress or omit any logical connection among their elements. However, if Graves really does mean that poems should make sense prosaically, one would expect repeated readings of a poem to increase the intelligibility of some other meaning—perhaps the poem's concealed meanings—but not the prosaic meaning, which makes itself known plainly and immediately.

How is the prosaic type of sense "personal," as Graves claims it is? If he means that the reader identifies with the content that makes immediate sense, then that content seems to function as something like an aphorism. The reader must immediately understand the poem and recognize that it applies somehow to his life; otherwise the qualification "personal" is superfluous. (That Graves expects poetry to convince but not, perhaps, persuade, is evidenced from his the final line of his essay, "Rationality:" "All the above may have been sensibly and reasonably written, but not being a poem is unlikely to convince anybody of its truth" [Graves 1973b, 123].)

In several of his critical works, Graves considers the relation of readers to poems. In his book *On English Poetry*, for example, he describes how readers sometimes unconsciously translate the poet's experience into their own:

> Even where a conclusion is definitely expressed in a poem the reader often deceives himself into saying, "I have often thought that before, but never so clearly," when as a matter of fact he has just been unconsciously translating the poet"s experience into terms of his own, and finding the formulated conclusion sound, imagines that the thought is originally his. (Seymour-Smith 1983, 101)

If this is what Graves means by making "personal sense," the reader can only make personal sense of the poem "where a conclusion is definitely expressed," that is, where the poem acts like an aphorism, describing with authority a state of affairs or passing a definite judgement. But this "personal sense" is a delusion, for the reader is mistaken when he "imagines that the thought is originally his." A poem's sense is false, then, even as it is "good sense." Ultimately, the relations among sense, good sense, personal sense, and concealed meaning remain obscure in these passages. When examined closely, Graves's standard for poetry seems confused, a tangle of contradictory definitions.

Another of Graves's definitions is as questionable as it is sweeping. Toward the middle of "Legitimate Criticism of Poetry," he writes,

> I should define a good poem as one that makes complete sense; and says all it has to say memorably and economically; and has been written for no other than poetic reasons. By "other than poetic reasons" I mean political, philosophical, or theological propaganda, and every sort of careerist writing. (Graves 1958, 48)

The parallelism of the second sentence, pairing "poetic reasons" with "political, philosophical, or theological propaganda," suggests that Graves considers all political, philosophical, and theological reasons to be propaganda. This is coarse, and untenable, as well, for how can Graves know absolutely from a poem the motivations (the "reasons") of its author? What he means by "careerist writing," one can infer from a talk he gave at New York University, "The Making and Marketing of Poetry," in 1958:

> The gift of a strong personal rhythm is granted to few poets at birth; still fewer preserve and develop it by a life of integrity. . . . So "integrity," when applied to a poet, should stand for moral principles from which

nothing can deflect him. He refuses to be anyone"s lackey, or ever to write for the wrong reasons (such as fame, fashion, money, patronage, political or ecclesiastical propaganda, idle rhetorical experiment); or ever to behave in a manner inconsistent with the devotion he owes his Muse. (Graves 1960a, 137)

Again political motivations are reduced to propaganda; theological motivations, here qualified as ecclesiastic, are propaganda, as well.

Perhaps by propaganda Graves means any writing that uses rhetoric to persuade its readers. In another essay, "Genius," Graves suggests that logic and rhetoric are used only to deceive a "victim":

Greek logic came to be used as a means of forcing opinions on the listener by arranging words in such a sequence that their conclusion seems uncontradictable; not letting the victim realize how insecure these generalizations were if compared with whatever act, fact, or experience they were verbalizing. From logic developed rhetoric; the art of persuading people by a deliberate slanting of logic that a good cause was a bad cause, and *vice versa*. (Graves 1973a, 8)

Because the rhetorical writer is asking something of his audience, he is not only their deceiver—he is their lackey. A good poem is more likely to be written by someone needing nothing other than the solution to a internal conflict, a solution that rhetoric and propaganda cannot provide. The good poet, in his poetry and probably in his life, is not bound by political or ecclesiastical ties; he is at heart probably a benign apostate, probably with an independent income or at least another job—perhaps someone like Graves himself. And because he is not writing to win favor or persuade his audience to some action, the poet, as Graves remarks elsewhere, "needs no audience." (Graves 1956, 191)

(Graves's friend Stephen Spender may have been objecting to this narrow definition of poetry when he wrote,

For the Romantic, the poet has become the only interpreter of the absolute, and eventually his poetry, and his own being as poet, become absolute. At the same time, he is expected to be a poet in every line he writes. By this test the Romantics themselves of course often fail, yet their successes in writing out of poetic experience in which poetry seems the inevitable language of the Romantic life have caused an impressive confusion of poetry *with* life: so that past acres of worldly, courtierly, witty, scholarly, philosophic, intellectual and religious poetry seem antipoetic, because they contain material or ideas not intrinsic to the fusion of poetry with life. (Spender 1962, 101–2)

Without referring to Graves explicitly, Spender here defends the very categories that Graves consistently dismisses as unpoetic.)

Graves has another important requirement for poets: reasonableness. In the essay, "The Case for Xanthippe," he applies the standard of reasonableness not merely to poems but to poets as well:

> Though I rely on intuition for the writing of poems and for the general management of my life, intuition must obviously be checked by reason whenever possible. Poets are (or ought to be) reasonable people; poems, though born of intuition, are (or ought to be) reasonable entities, and make perfect sense in their unique way. I should not, however, describe either poems or poets as "rational." "Reasonable" has warm human connotations; "rational" has coldly inhuman ones. (Graves 1991, 472)

Graves expects reasonableness (but not rationality) from Milton and from Wordsworth, as well as from *L'Allegro* and the Lucy poems. Without resorting to rationality, poets are to write poetry that makes immediate sense, and Pound is to translate Sextus Propertius accurately.

But even as Graves praises reasonableness and chastises poets for expressing philosophical, political, or theological convictions, he locates the origin of poetry in ritual storytelling and Dionysion dances, in sagas of military and political conquest, and in Druids rhyming rats to death. Were these original poets, the priests and the Druids, so rational and disinterested? Did the Druids raging on heath check their inspiration with common sense? Did they live lives of "integrity," eschewing politics and fame? Graves's definition of poetry is strikingly at odds with the mythic origins he ascribes to poetry. His requirements for poems and poets seem more personal than essential, more prescriptive than descriptive, more useful for censuring contemporaries than for constructing a timeless poetics, applicable to the poetry of all ages.

Through Graves's criticism, one finds him censuring contemporaries and canonized poets, on moral as well as aesthetic grounds, and insisting that aesthetic achievement depends on moral integrity. As early as 1920, according to Peter Quennell, Graves was relating the quality of a man's art to the quality of his morals. Quennell writes: "His view of life, at the time, was still intensely puritanical; and he even asserted that a 'bad man'—bad in the accepted moral sense—could scarcely hope to be a good artist" (Quennell 1989, 4). This view has more in common with Victorian criticism, which treats "great poetry" as the expression of "great men," than it has with New Criticism, which treats poems as autonomous verbal structures. Reading closely like a New Critic, but insisting on the relevance (and existence) of a universal moral code, Graves treats poems as verbal structures whose intelligibility and quality depend on the quality of the poets who wrote them, much as a brass rubbing depends on the features of the brass beneath it.

Influenced by developments in psychoanalysis in the 1910s and 1920s, his criticism attempts to analyze the mind of the poet as it struggles with moral, emotional, and aesthetic problems. According to Graves, a poem is born not merely from a particular period and social class, but from an individual at a particular time and at a particular place, thinking particular thoughts, which the critic, following Graves's method, can deduce. These thoughts have their origin in conflict. T. S. Matthews describes a talk Graves gave at literary club in Oxford in 1923 or 1924, in which he put forward the theory "that a poem is the resultant of a conflict in the poet's mind" (Matthews 1979, 117). Graves assumes he can divine the succession of unrecorded thoughts that passed through a poet's mind during the composition of a particular poem. His criticism seeks to discover this succession, much as a psychologist might seek to discover the case history of a patient; this is the exegetical method he names analeptic mimesis (the imitation of thoughts and sensations that occurred in the past).

In critical essays and lectures such as "Legitimate Criticism of Poetry," Graves describes the mental conflicts that produced a particular poem. In the essay "The Poet and His Public," he writes,

> The pathology of poetic composition is no secret. A poet finds himself caught in some baffling emotional problem, which is of such urgency that it sends him into a sort of trance. And in this trance his mind works, with astonishing boldness and precision, on several imaginative levels at once. The poem is either a practical answer to his problem, or else it is a clear statement of it; and a problem clearly stated is halfway to solution. Some poets are more plagued than others with emotional problems, and more conscientious in working out the poems which arise from them—that is to say more attentive in their service to the Muse. (Graves 1956, 191)

The poem's clarity, its "good sense," is not the problem's "practical answer," but a step halfway towards it. The writing of the poem, or perhaps the poem itself, may be a practical solution, practical perhaps, because the poet "practices" it or performs it.

The conflicts Graves describes in his criticism include not only the conscious and unconscious tensions originating in the poet's personal and social circumstances, but also tensions and choices about word choices and poetic diction. For example, in "Legitimate

Criticism of Poetry," Graves proposes that Milton changed a particular line of a *L'Allegro,* because, upon rereading the poem while composing it, Milton disliked the repetition of the preposition "to" in successive lines.

The critic Graves reads a poem by writing it out in long hand, pointing out the expressions and thoughts he considers to be flaws and offering improvements. His method is similar to the one he and Alan Hodge use in their handbook for prose writers, *The Reader over Your Shoulder,* in which they identify flaws in passages written by their contemporaries and offer revisions—"fair copies"—that aim to improve the logic and expression of the passages examined. As in the handbook, Graves in his criticism concludes with a revised text—improved, he feels, in the areas of sense and form. Graves and Hodge begin their examinations and fair copies by acknowledging their own fallibility, but in his criticism, Graves makes no such acknowledgment. Instead, he justifies his revisions with phrases such as "my little finger told me," and suggests that the faults he finds are discoverable by anyone who troubles to write out the offending poem in long hand. He distances himself from his judgments, presenting his personal prejudices as universal judgments that he has deduced naturally and guilelessly.

(Regarding Graves's reference to his little finger: In his description of the tree alphabet in *The White Goddess,* Graves ascribes divinatory powers to the little finger, which is also called the ear-finger: "The ear-finger—in French *doigt auriculaire*—is based on the two death-letters Ruis and Idho and therefore has oracular power, as they still say in France of a person who gets information from a mysterious source: 'Son petit doigt le lui dit'" (Graves 1966, 196). Graves may be claiming divine inspiration (connection with the Platonic Good) as his source of knowledge about *L'Allegro.* Even if he is not, the references to his little finger and his pen serve to silence debate; if his little finger, in any role whatsoever, is the source of his knowledge, Graves appears to be merely the guileless conveyor of this knowledge.)

In "Legitimate Criticism of Poetry," Graves analyzes Milton's *L'Allegro,* which his daughter Lucia has been asked to memorize.

> I started my appreciation with of the anthology text before me with:
>
>> Haste thee, Nymph, and bring with thee
>> Jest, and youthful Jollity . . .
>
> (There was something awkward about *"youthful* Jollity," I felt at once—it must have been put there for some dishonest reason.)

One way of appreciating a poem is first to write it out in longhand; then to imagine oneself composing the lines, and so creep inside the poet"s skin. The process of getting a rough verse draft into presentable form will be familiar to most of you. And with practice one can often deduce, from some slight awkwardness surviving in the final version, what the grosser faults of the original were. Well, when I tried the longhand test, my little finger told me (and I never argue with my little finger) that Milton had written:

> Hasten, Mirth, and bring with thee
> Jest and Youth and Jollity,
> Sport that wrinkled Care derides
> And Laughter holding both his sides.

Afterwards he had wondered whether the difference between Mirth and Jollity could be justified or, alternatively, the difference between Mirth and Laughter. He shook his head, changed "Mirth" to "Nymph," and kept her anonymous. (Graves 1958, 35)

What follows might belong in a novel, such as *Wife to Mr. Milton*, because no one expects even historical novels to be factual in all their particulars; it certainly does not belong in a critical essay—at least any critical essay that purports to base its conclusions on verifiable evidence. Like a novelist, Graves describes Milton composing *L'Allegro:* he describes Milton shaking his head, crossing words out, and including a reference to Hebe to provide he is a Cambridge graduate. There is no evidence either in the poem or in any of Milton's life records, that any of this actually took place. In fact, there is evidence that some of the details Graves describes are wrong. For example, he describes Milton revising his first draft of the poem to appease his "Puritanical" father, with whom he is living at Horton. At least some biographers of Milton believe that Milton wrote these poems at Cambridge, not Horton. To cite a source from the time of Graves' essay:

> *L'Allegro* and *Il Penseroso* seem to have been written late in Milton's years at Cambridge, before he went to Horton. . . . Their balanced themes surely owe something to the exercises of students on stock themes like the respective merits of Day and Night, or of Learning and Ignorance, as we find them illustrated by Milton's own Prolusions I and VII. (Hughes 1957, 68)

If these other biographers are right, the motivation Graves assigns Milton becomes considerably less credible. Yet one of the revisions Graves attributes to this motivation is paramount: Graves believes that, to appease his father, Milton "dissociated himself from the poem by making it describe *L'Allegro*—the ideal, mirthful man—and not himself, John Milton" (Graves 1958, 38). Since most of Graves conjectures about the poet's thoughts and motivations cannot be confirmed or denied, it is puzzling how he expects one can learn this type of deduction with practice.

(Elsewhere, Graves himself seems to undermine this depiction of Milton's father as a stern, censorius Puritan. In *Wife to Mr. Milton*, Marie Powell describes Milton's father as a "mild, sweet-natured, careful old man" [Graves (1944) 1991, 179]. That he was really a Puritan at all is questionable. Milton's father read the Bible in English, for which he was disinherited by his father, but all that proves is that he abandoned his father's Catholicism. He does not seem to have tied himself to any church or political movement. "As for the old Mr. Milton, there is no reason to suppose that he was of a political cast of mind" [Wilson 1991, 111].)

Graves introduction of his analysis of *L'Allegro* bears other novelistic touches, as well. He begins by describing his "innocent and intelligent" daughter coming to him for help, after finding the poem "a muddle." The commonsense of his daughter, like the commonsense of innocent and intelligent Powells in *Wife to Mr. Milton*, makes Milton look all the more obscure and ridiculous. Graves tries to show us, in his novel and in his lecture, how Milton's rhetorical struttings perplex honest rustics and innocent youth; *L'Allegro*, despite its descriptions of the countryside, appears to be merely another fanciful trapping of a city man, a kind of rhetorical gadget.

Graves criticizes from the point of view of a poet, who is at once himself and the poem's author; his relation to the text is that of leaning over it, sitting at a desk that is not his own. He calls upon his experience with poetic composition, his hours spent revising his own poems, to deduce the revisions other poets have made in theirs; it is this experience he seems to be invoking when he uses phrases such as "my little finger told me" and "my pen told me." A superb craftsman himself, he does not hesitate to point out failures of craftsmanship or translation in any poem he is reading. Sometimes he goes further, revising the poem completely, using the authority of "his pen," for example, to reduce Wordsworth's sonnet praising the leaders of the Commonwealth to a five-line poem that qualifies its praise. In the new poem, the leaders whom Wordsworth praised as "great men," are merely the best of their time, because Graves is not convinced of their greatness. He also questions their friendship with Milton, who was then the Commonwealth's censor. Because they would have benefited from friendship with the censor, Graves suggests that the friendship was not genuine, only one of convenience. Obviously he does not know this.

Graves uses the same method with Wordsworth's sonnet that he uses with *L'Allegro:*

> Recently someone upheld Wordsworth's sonnet "Great men have been among us" as the kind of poem that nobody is great-hearted enough to write in these degenerate days. I refrained from immediate comment, but sat down and copied out the lines in long-hand as though I were composing them myself—a useful technique for testing the integrity of a poem. If my pen runs on without check or hesitation, well and good; if not, I ask myself, "what is wrong?"
>
> This sonnet proved peculiarly difficult to copy out, though I found it had been praised, by educationalists, as "one of that splendid series of generally impressive and universally intelligible poems dedicated to national Liberty and Independence."
>
> At any rate Wordsworth, my pen told me, ought to have qualified his sonorous statement about great men, by defining the period during which there were no better than these available. He could easily have done so by cutting out one miserably prosaic line. (Graves 1960b, 141)

Graves then proceeds to rewrite the poem, changing not only its form, but its politics, as well.

Graves's examination of a poem concludes when his revisions are completed, when, like one of the clumsy paragraphs quoted from government officials in *The Reader over Your Shoulder,* it has become a fair copy. The fanciful rhetoric and bombast, and the Commonwealth politics, have been cleared away to reveal the "real" poem. The real poem is not the text in the canon but the ideal poem, the poem that the poem could always have become if the poet had remained faithful to his Muse, if he had himself revised away more thoroughly the "grosser faults" of the original, if the poet had a true poet, like Robert Graves—I might as well collapse the enthymeme—if the original poet had been Robert Graves. Similarly, for Graves, the real *David Copperfield* is not the text Dickens sent to his publisher, but the revision of that text produced by Graves, which Graves published with the title *The Real David Copperfield.* If only Dickens had been able to wriggle into Graves's consciousness the way Graves wriggles into Milton's, he might have been able to get it right the first time.

Graves's critical method has some features in common with that of Georges Poulet, who writes in *Les lettres nouvelles* (24 June 1959),

> Contrary to what one might expect, criticism must prevent itself from seeing some sort of *object* (whether it is the person of the author seen

as an Other, or his work considered as a Thing); for what must be arrived at is a *subject,* which is to say a spiritual activity that one cannot understand except by putting oneself it its place and causing it to play again within us its role and subject. (Scholes 1974, 7)

Practicing analeptic mimesis, Graves in some sense is causing a poem to play again within him, as it played in the mind of its creator.

Poulet, however, studies works he admires, whereas Graves never practices analeptic mimesis on poems he admires. It is striking that in the numerous lectures and essays in which Graves mentions Skelton, he never practices analeptic mimesis on a poem of Skelton's. Whatever its other purposes, analeptic mimesis provides a rhetorical framework for Graves to censure and even ridicule particular poems and poets. Thus, in "Legitimate Criticism of Poetry," Graves confesses his preference for criticizing poems he dislikes: "I always find it easier to say why a poem is bad, than why it is good. Criticizing a good poem . . . is like trying to scale a tower of such perfectly fitted masonry that one can find neither finger-hold nor toe-hold" (Graves 1958, 50). The climbing metaphor is telling: when Graves criticizes a bad poem, he feels as though he has risen above it; he can survey all of it from his superior position. Accordingly, Graves writes mostly about poets he dislikes.

Later in "Legitimate Criticism of Poetry," he condemns the category of "greatness" and, in doing so, censures the immorality of "great poets."

> Not long ago I denounced a widespread critical plot to make "great" a better epithet than "good." An English critic had written that one becomes "great" by presenting "a diploma piece" of "major form"—such as Eliot"s *Four Quartets,* or Pound's *Hugh Selwyn Mauberly.* I protested that, according to the logicians, nothing is better than the truly good, not even the truly great; therefore, what is not truly good, however great, must be either to some degree evil (an active denial of good) or to some degree bad (a falling short of good). It followed that all truly "great" diploma pieces, unless truly bad, were likely to be truly evil—inspired by ambition, the vice which caused Lucifer"s downfall. (Graves 1958, 50)

Graves is playing the judge here, sorting the good and the great; unmasking greatness, though a perverse play of definitions, as badness or evil; and sending the great to keep company with Lucifer. The valuation of greatness above goodness, regardless of dictionary definitions, is unmasked as "a widespread critical plot," thanks to Graves, who summons disinterested witnesses, "the logicians," to subvert the plot and restore goodness to its proper place in aesthetic and moral hierarchies. Much of Graves's criticism exhibits this playful vindictiveness, as Graves rewrites and repairs cherished poems and twits and teases cherished poets, all in the name of goodness.

A strain of Platonism that keeps poets in the republic runs through much of Graves's thought. The good man, checking his passions with reason (but not smothering them with "coldly inhuman" rationality), can discover the Real, which may be obscured by grosser or lesser faults. The poet discovers the Real by entering an inspirational trance, and then checking his inspiration with reasonable revisions. The critic discovers the Real by rewriting the poem, discovering the faults, and eliminating them. Criticizing the poem, purifies it. The revised poem differs from the unrevised, just as the sun differs from shadows on a cave wall. Treating the unrevised poem as something worthy of reverence or as an autonomous structure, is making the same mistake that Plato's cavedwellers make when they imagine that the shadows they see constitute the world. The true poet is in communion with the Good, and his judgments, which may strike the cavedwellers as confused and irrational, are to be trusted. When the poet writes his own poems, they will partake of the Good. They will be free from rhetoric, and ignore the shadows of politics, religion, and fame. (Platonism may explain Graves's preference for goodness over greatness, and his idealization of "good sense.")

For all his insistence on reasonableness, Graves is quite willing to base his criticism on suppositions, guesses, and imagined scenes; on propositions that cannot be proven. Perhaps because he feels that his genius gives him access to Platonic truth, it suffices for him that a proposition cannot be *dis*proved. In an interview published in *The Paris Review* in 1969, he prides himself on the discoveries he made about Milton during the composition of *Wife to Mr. Milton* and remarks, "I have found out a lot of things about him, heavens knows how, which have never been disproved" (Buckman and Fifield 1989, 99). For "heavens knows how," substitute "using my imagination." Because our knowledge of any poet's life is ineluctably incomplete, we will always lack the evidence to disprove such conjectures. Anyone can make them; no one can refute them. This does not make them true.

In letters, Graves sometimes admitted he was guessing about his subjects. Preparing *I, Claudius* for publication, he confided to T. E. Lawrence in 1933, "I don't want any too great howlers. The book is largely guess-work & imagination but I want it to hold water & have done a great deal of reading to get it passable" (Seymour-Smith 1983, 255). Later, in May 1934, in a note about *I, Claudius,* he recognizes the different standards required of scholars and novelists; nonetheless, he seems pleased that his novel, because it cannot be disproved by other evidence, would be accepted as authentic—that is, as true—if it had been found in antiquity. (That his novel would solve a lot of outstanding historical problems does not render it true; that it is less biased than Tacitus is uncertain.)

> The point is that I have nowhere, so far as I know, gone against history; but wherever authors have disagreed, or there has been a gap or confusion or mystery or they were obviously lying I have felt free to invent, in the spirit of the story, what made sense of the story. . . . If I had written my version of the story in the second century it would now be taken as authentic: it would certainly be less biased than Tacitus and held to solve a lot of outstanding historical problems.
> Needless to say, I'm not a Classical scholar or anything of that sort but there is a story somewhere hidden in that confused and rather dreary history and I have tried to dig it out. If I had been a Classical scholar my historical conscience would not have let me invent a thing. (Graves 1982, 349)

Critics, like classical scholars, require consciences that will not let them "invent a thing." In building his critical arguments on imagined scenes and insupportable suppositions, Graves behaves more like a novelist than a scholar. "Fact is not truth, but a poet who willfully defies fact cannot achieve truth"—Graves makes this point in *The White Goddess,* in a passage comparing the scholar to a quarry man: "All that is required of him is that he should quarry cleanly. He is the poet's insurance against factual error" (Graves 1966, 224). Insurance the poet needs, because intuition is not enough; it must be "checked by reason," as Graves says in "The Case for Xanthippe." Graves knows that the poet needs scholars and scholarship, because, although he may arrive at a surprising truth, he may also arrive at a howler. The poet himself may not be able to distinguish the two.

Consider, then, the oddity of his method in "Legitimate Criticism of Poetry." He neither turns to scholars and scholarship, nor seeks insurance against factual error. Instead, he builds an argument that depends on an imaginary draft of a poem, a draft whose existence is never proved. He builds an argument that depends on Milton misnumbering the pages in one of the few poems he writes in his youth and never correcting the mistake in his lifetime, though Milton remains throughout his life, according to Graves, a careerist poet and a supreme egotist (Graves 1958, 40). He builds an argument that depends almost entirely on hypothetical scenarios. One ought to be suspicious of some of his remarks that are obviously false: his remark at the beginning of the lecture, for instance, that he had never read *L'Allegro* closely before, even though he read all of Milton's poems in preparation for *Wife to Mr. Milton*. It is possible to read Graves's entire lecture as a rhetorical gadget intended to win over his audience and bolster his career. This would be a cynical reading, but one ought to recognize Graves's rhetorical dexterity. He may have been suspicious of rhetoric because he knew all too well its power to deceive, to present a howler, from time to time, as a startling insight.

Graves may have had personal motivations for criticizing poems as he does. His revisions can be considered powerful misreadings of his predecessors. In this light, he contends with the anxiety of influence, with his poetic belatedness, by finding flaws in the poems of others; in the course of the lecture on legitimate criticism, Graves revises and "improves" Milton, Wordsworth, Pound, and Eliot. Along with his dismissal of the category of "great poets," his revisions serve to bolster his own standing as a poet.

T. S. Matthews, in his memoir, *Under the Influence*, suggests that Graves's antipathy toward Milton was at least partially a reflection of his antagonism toward Schuyler Jackson.

> I knew that Robert disliked and denigrated Milton as a "great poet"—a category he equated with "great phony"—but the personal animus he showed toward Milton in this book [*Wife to Mr. Milton*] was more than dislike, it was hatred. I believe that he visited on Milton the bitter detestation he felt for Schuyler: that the Milton he was writing about was Schulyer." (Matthews 1979, 239–40)

In his critical attacks, then, Graves substitutes Milton for Jackson and, by attacking Milton, contends with two rival poets.

But by Graves"s own admission, his antipathy toward Milton preceded his introduction to Jackson. In *The Paris Review* interview, he said, "I'd always hated Milton, from earliest childhood; and I wanted to find out the reason. I found it. His jealousy. It's present in all his poems. . . . Marie Powell had long hair with which he could not compete" (Buckman and Fifield 1989, 99). Rather than form any conclusions about the origin of Graves's loathing for Milton—conclusions that would have to rely on the same intangibles and feats of imagination as Graves's shaky treatment of *L'Allegro*—it is perhaps to sufficient to recognize that the categories Graves derives in his criticism allow him to attack most of the great English poets who preceded him.

Ultimately, Graves's motivation for attacking other poets and poetic categories are not important. If two critics harboring antipathies to Milton both write studies of *L'Allegro*, and one of the studies proves insightful and valuable and the other does not, it is clear that what matters about these studies is contained in the studies themselves, not in the minds of the authors.

Two final considerations. First, regarding good sense. In his criticism, Graves demands that poems make sense, good sense, plainly and immediately. In *The Reader over Your Shoulder,* Graves demands the same of prose. What differentiates poetry from prose, in his scheme, is that poetry conceals meanings—"layers of meaning." But if these meanings are concealed, how can one discover them, and, when one discovers them, how can one distinguish them from nonsense? By insisting that the surface meanings of a poem make sense, Graves may be seeking to limit the types of meanings a poem can have. The poetry of Dylan Thomas and Ezra Pound, then, becomes problematic: without a thread of prosaicness to follow, how can the reader progress through the maze of meanings to find the truth? Faced with modernist poetry that challenged traditional modes of explication, Graves may be retreating to the security of the prosaic.

Second, regarding Graves's achievement. One of the best examples I can cite to counter Graves's thesis that the poet and his nonpoetical activities ought to lumped together, is Graves himself; for, despite shortcomings in the essays and lectures I have cited, Graves remains a superlative poet and novelist and, in essays in which he refrains from rewriting others' works, a shrewd critic. He has an exemplary talent for writing short poems that are as powerful as they are economical; he has, as well, an excellent ear, and a natural ability for storytelling that is rare even among successful novelists. His critical work in no way detracts from his poetry, from *I, Claudius,* "The Shout," or any of his other novels and stories. He said many times that he wanted to be remembered as a poet, and he should be. He was a great poet, and that, not his work as a critic practicing analeptic mimesis, was his "crowning privilege."

Works Cited

Buckman, Peter and William Fifield. 1989. "The Art of Poetry XI: Robert Graves." In *Conversations with Robert Graves,* ed. Frank L. Kersnowski, 92–108. Jackson: University Press of Mississippi.

Graves, Robert. [1944] 1991. *Wife to Mr. Milton.* New York: Book-of-the-Month Club.

———. 1956. *The Crowning Privilege.* Garden City, New York: Doubleday & Company.

———. 1958. "Legitimate Criticism of Poetry." In *5 Pens in Hand.* New York: Doubleday.

———. 1960a. "The Making and Marketing of Poetry." In *Food for Centaurs*, 120–139. Garden City, New York: Doubleday & Company.

———. 1960b. "Pulling a Poem Apart." In *Food for Centaurs*, 140–45. Garden City, New York: Doubleday & Company.

———. 1960c. "A Toast to Ava Gardner." In *Food for Centaurs*, 35–48. New York: Doubleday.

———. 1962. *Oxford Addresses on Poetry*. Garden City, New York: Doubleday & Company.

———. 1966. *The White Goddess*. Amended and enlarged edition. New York: Farrar, Straus and Giroux.

———. 1973a. "Genius." *Difficult Questions, Easy Answers*. Garden City, New York: Doubleday & Company.

———. 1973b. "Rationality." In *Difficult Questions, Easy Answers*. New York: Doubleday.

———. 1982. *In Broken Images: Selected Correspondence*. Ed. Paul O'Prey. Mt. Kisco, New York: Moyer Bell Limited.

———. 1991. "The Case for Xanthippe." In *The Oxford Book of Essays*, ed. John Gross, 472–79. Oxford: Oxford University Press.

Hughes, Merritt Y., ed. 1957. *John Milton: Complete Poems and Major Prose*. Indianapolis: The Odyssey Press.

Matthews, T. S. 1979. *Under the Influence*. London: Cassell.

Quennell, Peter. 1989. "Retreat from Parnassus." In *Conversations with Robert Graves*, ed. Frank L. Kersnowski, 3–6. Jackson: University Press of Mississippi.

Scholes, Robert. 1974. *Structuralism in Literature: An Introduction*. New Haven: Yale University Press.

Seymour-Smith, Martin. 1983. *Robert Graves: His Life and Work*. New York: Hold, Rinehart and Winston.

Spender, Stephen. 1962. "The Romantic Gold Standard." In *The Making of a Poem*. New York: Norton.

Wilson, A. N. [1984] 1991. *The Life of John Milton*. Oxford: Oxford University Press.

Captain Graves's Postwar Strategies
Paul O'Prey

When Robert Graves belatedly took up his classical exhibition at St. John's College, Oxford, in October 1919, he was still physically unfit due to the injury to his lung sustained during the Battle of the Somme. More debilitating even than this was his mental condition. He suffered from an acute form of post-traumatic stress, variously diagnosed at the time as shellshock or neurasthenia. He described his condition in *Goodbye to All That:*

> I was very thin, very nervous, and had about four years' loss of sleep to make up. My disabilities were many; I could not use a telephone, I was sick every time I travelled on a train, and if I saw more than two new people in a single day it prevented me from sleeping. (*Graves* 1929, 353)

In the immediate postwar years, Graves sought to restore his mental stability in three principal ways: through his love for Nancy Nicholson and their attempt to build an idyllic life together in rural Oxfordshire along the lines of the dreams that had sustained him at the front, described in poems such as "Over the Brazier" and "Familiar Letter to S. S."; through applying the new techniques of psychoanalysis to his own case; and through using his writing as a form of therapy. Although none of these was entirely successful as a strategy on its own, the "therapeutic" use of poetry did produce some of Graves's best work of the period and meant that his main contribution to the poetry of World War I was to be in his account of what it meant to survive to reconstruct his life and come to terms with the traumatic memories of the experience which were still to haunt him over sixty years later. The fact that most anthologies of World War I poetry end at or just after the Armistice has meant that the point of view of the survivor, a significant aspect of the literature generated by the war, has been relatively neglected by them, and Graves's importance in the literary history of the war has been understated as a consequence.

The split between engagement and escapism which characterises Graves's wartime writing after 1915 continued to be a major feature of his poetry into the 1920s. He wrote an intense, tortured verse expressive of his neurasthenia—poems like "Rocky Acres," "Outlaws," "Down," "The Pier-Glass"—but this was interspersed with regular retreats into facile sentiment or the nostalgic fantasy of "Country Sentiment." In "The God Called Poetry," written shortly after the war, Graves acknowledges the continued domination of his verse by a schizophrenic muse, which he presents as a Janus:

> Today I see he has two heads
> Like Janus—calm, benignant, this;
> That, grim and scowling: his beard spreads
> From chin to chin: this god has power
> Immeasurable at every hour.

Graves's "calm benignant" muse inspired a small body of light verse during these years. Although technically accomplished and charming, the verse consciously avoids truth rather than illuminates it. The best of his poetry was instead expressive of his nervous state, and he began to fear that his writing would become "dull" and "easy" without the neurosis that fed it (Graves 1929, 381). He therefore resisted psychoanalysis for some time, paradoxically because he thought it might cure him: if his "*Pier-Glass* haunting" ended, he feared he might lose "the power of writing poetry," which was "more important" to him "than anything else" (Graves 1929, 381). It seemed to Graves at the time "less important to be well than to be a good poet" (Graves 1929, 381). This, he realised somewhat tardily, was a self-destructive folly which not only hindered his recovery but put unbearable strains on his marriage. It was an attitude which in another way compromised the integrity of the poetry it was designed to produce, for the inner conflict that generated his poetry could be seen in one sense as being consciously prolonged and sustained. Graves had learned from his visit to Hardy in 1920 what C. H. Sisson has called the important "principle"—that the tensions which produce poetry should be "always accidental" (Graves 1929, 374–5), and Sisson has criticised Graves for what he sees as the latter's wilful continuation of his neurasthenic condition in order to write verse, stating that this displayed an "indifference" to the principle of "accident," as well as "a certain vanity and a certain frivolity in [his] attitude to life" (Sisson 1971, 189). Hardy told Graves that "he had been able to sit down and write novels by time-table, but that poetry was always accidental, and perhaps it was for that reason that he prized it more highly" (Graves 1929, 375). Graves himself seems not to have been aware of any such contradiction in his approach and indeed followed a similar strategy for consciously seeking inspiration in later years, when he deliberately courted danger and suffering through a series of romantic adventures with younger women he deemed to be "embodiments" of the muse, and again placed his need to write poetry above emotional stability and domestic contentment.

In *Good-bye to All That,* Graves explains that he finally came to accept the need for psychoanalysis, but instead of consulting a professional analyst, he immersed himself in the latest theories of clinical psychology with the intention of curing himself (Graves 1929, 381). To try to be one's own analyst is itself perhaps symptomatic of an obsessive personality, particularly as Graves again saw no contradiction in the attempt but presumably considered himself to be following Freud's own example. He did not reveal the conclusions of this analysis, but it did lead to his adopting a view of poetry, expressed in *On English Poetry, Poetic Unreason* and *The Meaning of Dreams,* as a form of therapy which has the aim of consciously resolving internal psychological or emotional conflict by drawing on the subconscious imagination. *On English Poetry* and *Poetic Unreason* are particularly remarkable as early attempts to construct a coherent theory of poetry in the light of modern scientific thought—particularly Freudian thought—and achieve a number of insights into the relation between text and reader as well as into the psychoanalytic interpretation of poetry, which anticipate the developments of later, more sophisticated literary theories.

Theoretical analysis was a radical departure for a member of the Georgian group, and he encountered considerable hostility and opposition from Siegfried Sassoon and other fellow Georgians. However, Graves defended his new approach on the grounds that the old "emotional approach theory" was no longer satisfactory and that in practical terms "analytic thought is the best possible preventative against writing by formula" (Graves 1925, 79). More than anything, however, his analysis in *Poetic Unreason* constituted a call for a poetry which provides an adequate response to the challenges of modern society. To do this it had to come to terms with the revolutionary changes in society and reconcile what he described as "scientific and philosophic theory on the one hand and the old pulse of love and fear on the other" (Graves 1925, 83). He also defined what it should mean to be a poet "in the fullest sense of the word": "The poet . . . must stand in the middle of the larger society to which he belongs and reconcile in his poetry the conflicting views of every group, trade, class and interest in that society" (Graves 1925, 82). Graves's vision is of a form of poetry which consolidates, reconciles, and thereby "heals" the conflicts in society, but which seems to want to avoid engagement in actual issues and events. That this is essentially a nostalgic concept is acknowledged in the acceptance that only Chaucer, Skelton, and Shakespeare have "succeeded memorably" in "representative spokesmanship" (though Skelton's was surely a curious and limited success) and in the conclusion that such a poetry is not realizable in the present context. "Poets, readers, and critics" of the present time were, he wrote, "all equally lost, and few with even the courage of scepticism" (Graves 1925, 85). "Modern society is in such confusion," and in this context, he concludes, "the greatest service a poet can do is to provide a temporary escape to the Lubberland of fantasy" (Graves 1925, 85).

The reference here is to Walter de la Mare's poetry, which Graves had long admired and which is the most significant model for his own escapist verse. However, in noting the irony and paradox inherent in the fact that escape was the "greatest service" contemporary poetry could offer a troubled world, there is an implied awareness that escapism is an inadequate strategy for dealing with his own sense of confusion. Escapism is seen to offer only a temporary, illusory release from the current social and moral turmoil, and Graves's observation that "the walls of Mr. de la Mare's magic garden are beginning to crumble' (Graves 1925, 85), effectively marks a movement in his own poetry away from Georgian fantasy.

In an attempt to restore his artistic equilibrium after the violent social and cultural disruption of the war, he perhaps naturally looked to prewar literature for his models, to Masefield, de la Mare, and in particular to Hardy. When Graves went to see Hardy at his home in Dorchester in August 1920, he had already started to compile the material for *On English Poetry,* and the encounter was important for Graves, whom Sassoon described as Hardy's "poetical grandson" (O'Prey 1984, 153). During their conversation on modern poetry, Hardy had told Graves that, in his opinion, "*vers libre* could come to nothing in England": "All we can do is write on the old themes in the old styles, but try to do a little better than those who went before us" (Graves 1929, 377).

On English Poetry contains a chapter on the "limitations" of vers libre which essentially is a restatement of Hardy's views. Graves recounts approvingly the criticism of Swinburne made "by an elder poet, who asks to remain anonymous" (Graves 1922, 47), who must surely be Hardy, as is the "friend" who "denied that there was such a thing [as vers libre] possible."

To a poet still traumatised by the prolonged experience of mental and physical horrors to which his poetry had on the whole proved unequal, a great poet's advice "to write on the old themes in the old styles," must have been an attractive and consoling suggestion. For a while it encouraged in Graves a nostalgic desire for continuity.

Graves later renounced his early theoretical approach to poetry, commenting wryly that "anything worth preserving" from his poetry between 1922 and 1926 "was written in spite of, rather than by the help of, my new theories" (1938, xxi). This was unjustly harsh, for despite whatever shortcomings the theories perhaps inevitably had per se, the close analysis they entailed proved extremely fruitful in terms of his artistic development. His tendency to use his own work as the "case history" for much of his analysis meant that his work was subjected to a rigorous and prolonged self-scrutiny. Alone among the Georgians at this time, his poetry challenges itself and asks itself difficult questions, and from 1925 onwards a new tone is evident as the poetry acquires a searching edge and abandons to a great extent its previous tendency to whimsy and escapism. Controlled emotion and philosophic enquiry were to become permanent characteristics of his mature work, and it is unlikely they would have been achieved without the preceding process of analysis.

In *A Sinking Island,* Hugh Kenner invokes Stanley Fish's "powerful metaphor of 'interpretive communities' to suggest that "critical activity began to seem so urgent in England around 1930 because *social* fragmentation was being perceived" (1988, 208). Graves's critical writings of the early twenties were, it seems to me, part of a similarly rearguard action against *personal fragmentation,* and part of his search for stability and cohesion. Thus although his selective adaptation of modern scientific method to literary analysis in *On English Poetry* and *Poetic Unreason* suggested exciting new possibilities, essentially he was pursuing through these studies a conservative agenda in which traditional forms of poetry were to be adapted to the demands of a changed society.

On English Poetry was dedicated jointly to W. H. R. Rivers and T. E. Lawrence, the two major influences on Graves at this time. The influence of Rivers as psychologist and anthropologist is well documented, but it is interesting to see Graves during this period pursuing a version of Lawrence's own desperate strategies to reinvent his identity after the war, when he became an ordinary soldier in first the Royal Air Force and then the Tank Corps, seeking anonymity through the persona of T. E. Shaw.

In the poem, "A Letter from Wales," Graves talks of a fundamental change in his character towards the end of the war, which he attributes to his experience of having been left for dead on the battlefield shortly before his twenty-first birthday. It was an incident which became increasingly significant for him as he tried to come to terms with his psychological condition. He came to the conclusion that he had in fact undergone some form of near-death experience, a death-like coma (it was this experience which influenced his later interpretation of the crucifixion, for he believed that Christ had suffered a similar fate). In much of the poetry of the 1920s, Graves describes a process of personal reconstruction and "re-fashioning," and his near-death experience became a central reference point in this. It came to be seen by him as a moment of conversion, which allowed him to establish a new life and personality and enabled him to break free not just from the memories and experiences of the war, but—equally important—of the earlier social and family conditioning, which he now felt encumbered his readjustment to postwar society.

He explained all this in a letter to Sassoon, written in May 1922:

> It boils down to this. . . . You identify me in your mind with a certain Robert Graves now dead, whose bones and detritus may be found in *Over the Brazier, Fairies and Fusiliers,* and the land of memory. Don't. I am using his name, rank and initials and his old clothes but I am no more than his son and heir. (O'Prey 1984, 134)

It would be wrong to dismiss this as a fanciful idea, just as it would be mistaken—if perhaps convenient—to suggest that he never really believed in the existence of the White Goddess except as metaphor. Part of the richness and fascination of Graves's imagination is this rare ability to accommodate supernatural explanations of apparent mysteries and paradoxes, so enthusiastically and wholeheartedly.

In 1929 Graves was joined in his life beyond near-death or, as he called it, living "against kind," when Laura Riding jumped from the window of a fourth-floor flat in St. Peter's Square. Although this was St. Peter's Square, Hammersmith, rather than the Vatican, Riding too underwent a near-death experience and subsequent conversion, her own resurrection even giving her, at least for a time, a quasi-divine status in Graves's eyes. These near deaths constituted a significant shared experience, which joined them closely together in an almost mystical way; in the "Dedicatory Epilogue to Laura Riding," published in the first edition of *Good-bye to All That,* Graves wrote how his lung, which was barometric of foul weather, spoke of "endurance"— (he being the survivor)—while Riding's broken spine, barometric of fair weather, spoke of "salvation" (she being the messiah) (Graves 1929, 446).

The writing of *Good-bye To All That,* and the associated break with family, friends, and literary associates, followed by voluntary exile to a remote corner of Europe, were all parts of another form of death for Graves—a sort of social suicide—which again brought the possibility of resurrection and the refashioning of identity. He predicted a future with Riding of "no more politics, religion, conversations, literature, arguments, dances, drunks, time, crowds, games, fun, unhappiness" (Graves 1929, 446). (Of course, things turned out somewhat differently.) After—as he would have it—dying on his twenty-first birthday, birthdays came to have a large significance for Graves, and it was significant that he should say, in the penultimate paragraph of the 1929 edition of *Good-bye To All That:* "I write these words on July 24th, my 34th birthday; another month of final review and I shall have parted with myself for good" (439). Up until this point his story, he claimed, had been one of "gradual disintegration," of "enduring blindly in time," until he had been released by Riding's jump, when she achieved her "true quality of one living invisibly, against kind, as dead, beyond event," and invited him to join her there.

Graves's attempted break with his past was a form of suicide that Lawrence would have understood, and indeed it has clear parallels with the choice Graves has him make as Alexander in "The Clipped Stater," when he rejects his previous existence and renounces his demigod status to choose alienation and exile: "I must fulfil my self by self-destruction." Graves had fought in the war to preserve that vague construction of social, moral, and spiritual values signified by the notion of what he and others frequently referred to as "England," but by the end of the war it seemed to him that much of what he had thought worth preserving in the notion of "England" had been destroyed by the English themselves, rather than by any foreign army—a view he shared with Wilfred Owen who, in September 1918, attacked the *Daily Mail*'s vision of a victorious nation:

> Nation?—The half-limbed readers did not chafe
> But smiled at one another curiously
> Like secret men who know their secret safe.
> (This is the thing they know and never speak,
> That England one by one had fled to France,
> Not many elsewhere now, save under France.)

The implication of Owen's "Smile, Smile, Smile" is that in sacrificing the younger generation to defend the nation's "integrity," the older generation had irrevocably betrayed the entire notion of "England." A similar bitterness against a society which had betrayed itself was the essential subtext of much of Graves's writing in the postwar period.

Graves was of course not alone in finding it difficult to adjust to the postwar. The survivors—Owen's "secret men"—were to an extent a marginalised group in the immediate years after 1918, still disorientated by the common experience of and stubborn attachment to a war quickly receding in the national consciousness. The writing of such a group was rooted in a world of memory and imagination—of the prewar, of life in trenches and dreams of what a future peace would hold for them. Samuel Hynes, in *A War Imagined*, has Graves (among others) in mind when referring to what he calls the "other meaning of the lost generation":

> Here *lost* means not *vanished* but *disorientated*, wandering, directionless—a recognition that there was great confusion and aimlessness among the war's survivors in the early post-war years, much moving about, much changing of plans, many beginnings without endings, and comparatively little work done. (1990, 339)

One can understand how the decisiveness and dogmatism of Laura Riding could seem attractive at such a juncture, offering as she did a clear new beginning, built on an ending so definite it was claimed by her as the end of historical time itself. Riding's views on the nature and purpose of poetry inspired Graves in the middle and late 1920s and gave his poetry a new sense of direction at a time when he himself had lost his way. She insisted on the inseparability of life and art; "poetry" was "the good existence," and "to live in, by, for the reasons of poems is to habituate oneself to the good existence." (Riding 1991, 413) It was an acceptance of this that led Graves, after 1926, to "struggle" "to be a poet in more than the literary sense" (Graves 1938, xiii). In an essay written before she came to England, Riding set out a view of poetry which was both original and radical and which had a profound influence on Graves's thinking. In "A Prophecy or a Plea" she argued that poetry was a way of giving new birth to "barren life" and providing "meaning" to "experience" by creating "a symbol of peace and reconciliation between the inner nature of a man and the external world without him" (Gottschalk 1925, 7). Graves must have read this essay with some rueful reflection on the present chaos of his own personal life and the lack of "order" in his own "inner being" still racked by the effects of neurasthenia. For Riding the poet should not react passively to the experience of life so much as control and influence experience through his or her art. She rejected the "retreat" into "the penumbra of introspection," the form of "avoidance" that had characterised Graves's previous response to life, and instead "insisted" that the poet faced a "challenge": "the birth of a new poetic bravery that shall exchange insight for outsight and envisage life not as an influence upon the soul but the soul as an influence upon life" (Gottschalk 1925, 3).

In *Poetic Unreason* Graves had defined the ideal poet as a "representative spokesman" of the society in which he lived, using his art to heal the discord on all sides. Under the influence of Riding, Graves rejected this as an ideal and tried to reject society itself. In 1926, in the word-by-word collaboration of *A Survey of Modernist Poetry,* they drew a distinction between "modern-ness," which they defined as a "keeping up in poetry with the pace of civilization and intellectual history," and "modernism," which has nothing to do with the date or with responding to the needs of society (Riding and Graves 1927, 178). Poets such as Yeats who, they felt, tried to "cope" with civilization, and who, "from an imagined necessity of action," adhered to the "social requirements that seemed to be laid on poetry," were misguided and inherently second-rate. The first-class poet, on the other hand, was "something more than a mere servant and interpreter of civilization," "a new and original individual" (Riding and Graves 1927, 163). The creation of poetry originated in such an individual, in his thought and reaction to experience, rather than through any dialogue with the social world which he inhabited. It was an abrupt change of direction for Graves, as he embarked on a new strategy, that of the poet as outsider, of the "fox who has lost his brush" (Graves 1961, 14) as he styled himself in *The White Goddess*—for whom writing poetry, as he claimed in *The Crowning Privilege,* was a fundamentally "anti-social activity" in a fundamentally "anti-poetic world" (Graves 1955, 122).

Works Cited

Graves, Robert. 1922. *On English Poetry.* London: Heinemann.

———. 1925. *Poetic Unreason and Other Studies.* London: Cecil Palmer.

———. 1929. *Good-bye to All That.* London: Cape.

———. 1938. *Collected Poems.* London: Cassell.

———. 1955. *The Crowning Privilege: Collected Essays on Poetry.* London: Cassell.

———. 1961. *The White Goddess.* Amended and enlarged edition. London: Faber.

Hynes, S. 1990. *A War Imagined: The First World War and English Culture.* London: The Bodley Head.

Kenner, H. 1988. *A Sinking Island: The Modern English Writers.* New York: Alfred A. Knopf.

O'Prey, P. G., ed. 1984. *In Broken Images: Selected Letters of Robert Graves, 1914–1946.* London: Hutchinson.

Riding, L. 1991. "1938 Preface." In *The Poems of Laura Riding*. Manchester: Carcanet.
Riding-Gottschalk, L. 1925. "A Prophecy or a Plea." *The Reviewer*, no. 2:7.
Riding, L., and R. Graves. 1927. *A Survey of Modernist Poetry*. London: Heinemann.
Sisson, C. H. 1971. *English Poetry, 1900–1950*. London: Rupert Hart-Davis.

Robert Graves, Modernism, and the "Poetic Body"

PATRICK MCGUINNESS

> If a poet is anybody, he is somebody to whom things matter very little—somebody who is obsessed by Making. Like all obsessions, the Making obsession has disadvantages; for instance, my only interest in making money would be to make it. Fortunately, however, I should prefer to make almost anything else, including locomotives and roses. It is with roses and locomotives (not to mention acrobats Spring electricity Coney Island the 4th of July the eyes of mice and Niagara Falls) that my "poems" are competing. They are also competing with each other, with elephants and with El Greco.
>
> —e. e. cummings, foreword to *is 5,* quoted by Riding and Graves in *A Survey of Modernist Poetry*

> I have often wondered what the term "a poet's poet" meant. Perhaps simply a poet, like Graves, with no definable "message," no "unifying philosophy," no marketable gimmick.... In prose he has defined poetry as "sense: good sense; penetrating, often heart-rending sense."
>
> —D. J. Enright, *Conspirators and Poets*

IN ONE OF HIS CLARK LECTURES, GIVEN IN CAMBRIDGE IN THE ACADEMIC YEAR 1954–55 and entitled "These Be Your Gods, O Israel," Robert Graves takes as his subject the theme of idols and idolatry. The idols in this case are five contemporaries: Yeats, Pound, Eliot, Auden, and Dylan Thomas. The idol worshippers are the academics and scholars who would, along with students and various nonaligned readers of poetry, have been present in force among the audience he was addressing. "The living poet-hero is a modernism," asserts Graves, claiming that the rites demanded by these living idols "are quite incompatible with devotion to the Muse herself" (Graves 1995, 221). But idols cannot be idols without there being someone, somewhere, prepared to defend and organise their idolization. Another "modernism" Graves homes in on his lecture is the academic industry itself, satirizing such thesis titles as *W. H. Auden and the Freudian Theory of Transference* and *T. S. Eliot as Anticipated by Duns Scotus.* Moreover, Graves points out that the so-called discipline of literary studies, and the consequent cult of the contemporary poet, was one that, not yet fully enracinated in the early 1920s, was not able to interfere with his own early poetic formation—it is in this sense that he could call himself "post-Canonical." The canon, such as it then was, was time-delayed by several decades, "the current text-books of English literature stopped at Tennyson and Swinburne," and it is that time-delay—cushioning the poet writing *Now* from an obtrusive pantheon of contemporary idols that enables him to develop unimpeded. He sees the building up of a living canon as an unholy alliance between academic and poet. If Graves had very little time for his Modernist contemporaries, the immediate beneficiaries of "Canonisation," he had even less time for those, like me, who teach and write about them. In Graves"s criticism I have found two of my major preoccupations—Ezra Pound and T. E. Hulme—treated with a healthy disrespect and a good deal of perspicacious harshness, and it is this, and its wider implications, that I want to go into here.

This essay will examine Graves's relations with the Modernists. (The word 'Modernist' is here used with a capital *M* to distinguish it from Riding and Graves's use of it in their 1927 book *A Survey of Modernist Poetry*.) It will end with a very brief look at how his own poetry and criticism provided, or seemed to provide, an alternative direction for English poetry in the eyes of a group of poets—the "Movement"—who themselves sought to bypass not only Pound and Eliot, but also Yeats, Dylan Thomas, and W. H. Auden. Indeed, it appears that Graves's five false gods correspond uncannily with those the Movement were trying to knock off their pedestals, and the date of Graves's lecture—1954—similarly corresponds with the coalescing of the Movement mood. The final part of this essay will open up for discussion the question of what Graves actually represented, and may still represent, for post-1945 English poetry. It will do so tentatively and in the full knowledge that Graves's extraordinary literary and critical independence, his refusal to claim or be claimed by followers, schools, or movements (a refusal which has perhaps worked against him), presents us with difficulties from the start.

In his Clark lecture, Graves describes his place in a popular English text book as follows:

> I am briefly mentioned with the Georgian War Poets of 1914–18 (*see* p. 1), successors to the Imagists (*see* p. 11) and themselves superseded (*see* p. 21) by the Modernist Movement of the "twenties; which merged (*see* p. 111) into the Left Wing Movement of the "thirties; which was suffocated (*see* p. 141) by the 1939–1945 War; which gave pause for reflection, the

new poets being few and inhibited. And for the setting up of five living idols—namely Yeats, Pound, Eliot, Auden and Dylan Thomas (*see separate chapters devoted to each*). (Graves 1995, 223)

More than the cursory mention of his own name, it is the parcelling up of poetic "schools" which swallow individual authors into "isms," and the notion that one school "supersedes" another, that bothers Graves. In *A Survey of Modernist Poetry*, he and Riding had written "No genuine poet or artist ever called himself after a theory or invented a name for a theory" (Riding and Graves 927, 46). The separate chapters devoted to each of the idols comes as the final insult, as well as the prelude to his own debunking of these idols.

Graves's comments on T. E. Hulme in *A Survey of Modernist Poetry* are vital because it is here that he and Riding target what one could call a characteristic Modernist anxiety: analogies between literature and other arts, analogies which are then elevated to the status of *artes poeticae*. One sturdy platform of Gravesian "theory" (I put that in quotation marks for obvious reasons) is the absolute uniqueness of the poetic craft; one of the most rickety, but also most productive, platforms of Modernism is the desire to analogize between poetry and sculpture, poetry and painting. Riding and Graves refuse to allow that this Modernist dissatisfaction with the written medium can actually provoke poetry into a positive, rather than a destructive, crisis, that it can actually plumb and activate its unsuspected resources. But given this initial lack of sympathy for that aspect of the Modernist enterprise—exemplified differently by Hulme, Pound, and Eliot—Riding and Graves nonetheless go to the center of one impetus behind Modernist experimentation. For them Hulme's urge to organize the arts according to a single analogical system is hugely flawed and, beneath all the aggressive machismo of his tone, deeply naive:

The fundamental fallacy in such an attempted co-ordination appears with the difficulty which poetry has to face in entering a new and artificially barbaric era. In painting and sculpture neither colour nor stone had been intrinsically affected by the romantic works in which they had been used. To escape the Renaissance, painting and sculpture merely had to revert to barbaric modes negroid, Oceanic, Aztec, Egyptian, Chinese, archaic Greek creating modern forms as if in primitive times; forms primitive, obedient to conventions which they accepted, therefore final, absolute, "abstract." But poetry could not seemingly submit itself to an *as if*, because its expressive medium, language, had been intrinsically affected not only by the works in which it had been used but also by all the non-poetic uses of which language is capable. This difference between poetry and the more regular arts points to a variance in poetry and suggests the probable falsity of all philosophical generalisations on art. The falsity is the falsity of analogy; yet analogy is the strongest philosophical instrument of co-ordination. Since poetry as an art is not sufficiently regular, not sufficiently professional, it is to become so by being made more sculptural or pictorial, by having grafted on it the values and methods of more professional arts. (Riding and Graves 1927, 273–74)

There exist few better, clearer and more careful diagnoses of the restlessness and anxiety of Modernist literary endeavor than this passage. Indeed, Riding and Graves hit on something which has been frequently observed by critics and historians of the Modernist period: it is almost as if Pound, Hulme, and company wished that literature could be written without words, or at any rate without language. They do not do justice to Hulme's thought—which is infinitely more interesting than Riding and Graves allow for—but the whole extract does exemplify a confrontation between two writers trying to claim a separate and indivisible entity for poetry and a group trying to harness poetry to paradigms leased from other arts. This is a position from which Graves was never to shift, as his subsequent and voluminous criticism shows. We find this confrontation played out in his and Riding's discussion of the imagist movement (where pictorial analogies lead up a false path) and in their discussion of French symbolism (where the musical paradigm misleads equally). The fact that they are actually misunderstanding and misrepresenting both imagism and symbolism is of no concern to us here but important to note in passing. We all know what they are driving at, having at one time or another scrambled for terms like "musical," "painterly," "monumental" to describe poems; but when have we ever called a piece of music, a painting or a sculpture "poetic?"

If poetry, according to Riding and Graves, is *not* susceptible to being accurately measured, described, or evaluated in terms borrowed, however temporarily and however figuratively, from other arts, then where do we look for its own native, home-grown, exclusive, paradigms? Their answer to this question occurs in the course of an earlier discussion of Imagism as a "dead" movement. The force of their objection to Imagist theory and practice, and of Imagism as an exemplum of the notion that poetry "translates" something not in itself pertaining to poetry, comes out clearly in this paragraph:

The ideal modernist poem is its own fullest, clearest and most accurate meaning. Therefore the modernist poet does not have to talk about the use of images "to render particulars exactly," since the poem does not give a rendering of a poetical picture or idea existing outside the poem, but presents the literal substance of poetry, a newly-created thought-activity: the poem has the character of a creature by itself. Imagism, on the other hand, and all other similar dead movements, took for granted the principle that poetry was a translation of certain kinds of subjects into the language that would bring the reader emotionally close to them. It was assumed that a natural separation existed between the reader and the subject, to be bridged by the manner in which it was presented. (Riding and Graves 1927, 118).

The imagists "wanted to be *new* rather than to be poets," they assert, and the claim they make for imagism's failure—over and above the imagists's rebarbative self-promotion—rests on their view of the fallacy that it was enough to bridge the gap between reader and subject through the *manner* of presentation rather than the *matter* presented. Moreover, since they categorically state that the poem presents "the literal substance of poetry, a newly created thought-activity," then the distinction made by the imagists between *matter* and *manner* is wrong from the start, that is, "dead on arrival." What they object to is the breaking up of an organic but disciplined and irreducible poetic process into various subdepartments of mere technique.

Now returning to their treatment of e. e. cummings, it is clear that theirs is an altogether greater plan than a series of local skirmishes with imagism, Georgianism, the 1890s, and so on. Cummings is a poet for whom Graves retained a great deal of admiration, but, as we discover on close inspection, his apparent defence of cummings's formal innovations actually masks a cunning attack on Modernism generally. In the first chapter of *A Survey*—"Modernist Poetry and the Plain Reader's Rights"—cummings is singled out as illustrating "the divorce of advanced contemporary poetry from the commonsense standards of ordinary intelligence" (1927, 9). Granted that Riding and Graves admit that "our common intelligence is the mind in its least active state," they set about justifying cummings's dislocation of syntax, his formal and grammatical liberties, his ellipses, and his disregard for punctuation in his poem "SUNSET." In order to do this, they "rewrite" it as a conventional poem on the same principles, they claim, as those along which "the naturalist Cuvier could reconstruct an extinct animal in full anatomical detail from a single tooth" (Riding and Graves, 1927, 10).

Here is cummings's poem:

Sunset

stinging
gold swarms

>   upon the spires
>   silver
>
>   chants the litanies the
>   great bells are ringing with rose
>   the lewd fat bells
>   and a tall
>
>   wind
>   is dragging
>   the
>   sea
>
>   with
>
>   dream
>
>   —s
>   (Riding and Graves 1927, 12)

And here is Riding and Graves's "reconstruction":

> ### Sunset Piece
>
> *After reading Remy de Gourmont*
> White foam and vesper wind embrace.
> The salt air stings my dazzled face
> And sunset flecks the silvery seas
> With glints of gold like swarms of bees
> And lifts tall dreaming spires of light
> To the imaginary sight,
> So that I hear loud mellow bells
> Swinging as each great wave swells,
> Wafting God's perfumes on the breeze,
> And chanting of sweet litanies
> Where jovial monks are on their knees,
> Bell-paunched and lifting glutton eyes
> To windows rosy as these skies.
>
> And this slow wind—how can my dreams forget—
> Dragging the waters like a fishing-net.
>   (Riding and Graves 1927, 16–17)

The result, according to Riding and Graves, "shows that Cummings was bound to write the poem as he did in order to prevent it from becoming what we have made it." Rather than a case of them rewriting cummings, it is cummings rewriting them. Now is that really true? Is this really the "lost original" behind what Riding and Graves are trying to persuade us is cummings's *re*writing (*re*writing is the crucial point)? Are they not, at the same time as championing the *necessity* of cummings's work, also putting words into his pen to accuse him of inventive bankruptcy in the midst of formal innovation? Well, yes they are, and it becomes clear where their experiment is leading when they write

> the poetry of E.E. Cummings is clearly more important as a sign of local irritation in the poetic body than as the model for a new tradition. . . . Cummings in this poem was really rewriting the other poem we gave into a good poem. But for the rarer poet there is no "other poem"; there is only the one which he writes. Cummings's technique, indeed, if further and more systematically developed, would become so complicated that poetry would be no more than mechanical craftsmanship. . . . Poets, however, do not pursue innovations for their own sake. They are on the whole conservative in their methods so long as these ensure the proper security and delivery of the poem. (Riding and Graves 1927, 20)

"Conservative in their methods *so long as* these ensure the proper security and delivery of the poem"—so: not always conservative? Conservative only when conservativeness *serves* rather than *dictates* the poetic process? Conservative by choice, except when the poetic body needs a kicking? Or perhaps until the *reader* needs a kicking? The reader is an important figure here, since *A Survey* is, among other things, a compendium of guides to *close reading* and is a clear forerunner of what was to become the New Criticism. These questions are all begged by that one rather double-edged line.

So it is not Riding and Graves who are rewriting the poem but cummings— *they* are merely recovering the lost original and showing us, so to speak, the "writer over his shoulder." It suddenly transpires that (a) cummings is falling into the imagist trap of thinking that new forms will make up the thematic shortfall, (b) *rewriting* something old and clapped-out, (c) not a "rarer poet," and, perhaps most importantly, (d) a "sign of local irritation in the poetic body" and not pioneer of poetic novelty. Then, reproducing almost exactly the terms of their attack on Imagism, they continue:

> the virtue of the poem is not in its being set down on paper, as a picture's is in the way it is set down on canvas. Genius in the poet is a sympathy between the different parts of his own mind, in the painter between his paint-brush and his canvas. Method in poetry is therefore not anything

that can be talked about in terms of physical form. The poem is not the paper, not the type, not the spoken syllables. It is as invisible and as inaudible as thought; and the only method that the real poet is interested in using is the one that will present the poem without making it a substitute for a picture or for music (Riding and Graves 1927, 21).

By relegating cummings to the status of formal innovator—a status to which they more dismissively relegate the Imagists—they are actually removing him from any real revolutionary position. We may note that Riding and Graves prove the self-sufficiency of poetry—"prove" in the sense of "test" as well as in the sense of "establish"—by showing how paraphrase *diminishes* the poem in question. If paraphrase *improves* the poem or says the same things more clearly, more memorably, and more economically, then the poem is a bad one. I note this in passing because they use Ezra Pound's "Ballad of the Goodly Fere" as an example of a poem so bad that prose paraphrase actually makes it better. But they do play fast and loose with their terms here—no reader would be gullible enough to believe them when they say that "Sunset Piece—after Rémy de Gourmont" is a poem cummings was avoiding writing, and that his own "SUNSET" is the product of a conscious struggle *not* to write it. Cummings has been, to some extent, "framed," "set up," he has become a pawn in a larger game. What larger game might that be?

I want to pursue this idea of cummings being merely a sign of "local irritation," because here, I believe, is where the key to Graves's view of Modernism lies, and also the key to what Graves may have represented to post-1945 English poetry. By the time he gave his Clark lecture he may, despite his spirited cracks at the five idols, have recognised that what was still to all to play for in the late 1920s—when he and Riding were writing their *Survey*—had been largely lost by the mid-1950s. Pound he considered beneath contempt; Eliot was an adversary to be treated more cautiously (and not without some real fellowship); Yeats was ludicrous and histrionic ("seduced into a period of grandiose literary showmanship"); Auden self-emasculatingly ironic; Thomas a charlatan and "sound-over-sensist" (Pound's phrase). In 1961 Graves succeeded his junior W. H. Auden as Oxford Professor of Poetry (defeating F. R. Leavis in the process)—by then he had watched Eliot become a preeminent critical arbiter and powerful publisher, followed Yeats's accession to international superstardom, Pound's more-than-comeback from lunacy and incarceration, and Dylan Thomas feted as a kind of tragic Welsh Rimbaud. If what cummings represented could be passed off in 1927 as "local irritation," then by 1954 the infection had entered the bloodstream.

But Graves is not finished yet, because something very subtle has been going on in all his dealings with Modernist poets. The notion of "local irritation" is the means by which Riding and Graves use the Modernists as a stick with which to beat a stultifying tradition and then discard the stick in order to *rejoin* a freer and invigorated tradition. By assuming the guise of someone showing us how it improves on another poem, Graves uses the cummings model—the process by which he takes cummings's poem and, under the guise of showing us how it improves on another poem—to squeeze cummings, and by extension Modernism, finally to the point at which it has to give up and say: "OK, it's a fair cop, I'll come quietly—I'm no real danger to anyone." His treatment of cummings and the imagists is a miniature reenactment of a greater enterprise begun with Laura Riding and sustained throughout his later critical pronouncements. He relegates revolution to mere reaction, as if reaction were no more than a kind of *cri de coeur* against the *status quo*. In this sense his admiration for cummings is faint praise, and Modernism was not to be a break or rerouting of poetry but a warning to tradition to develop in a more responsible way, to learn to absorb its own development along its own lines. Modernism was thus more of a bomb scare than a bomb. Graves's subtle co-opting of that most self-styled iconoclastic set of movements has been lost sight of in our anxiety to set him straightforwardly and unsubtly at odds with them, or equally simply to say that he was "open" to Modernism in the 1920s and then changed his mind. Both of these positions oversimplify; he did not simply oppose the Modernists (and let himself get trampled by them and their academic worshippers) but put forward a way of absorbing them, in a kind of damage-limitation exercise, so that they became not the overthrowers of conventional poetry (as they wished to be) but simply an early warning system that all was not right in the "poetic body." Hence the carefully weighted, apparently noncommittal phrase that real poets were "Conservative in their methods *so long as* these ensure the proper security and delivery of the poem." There are ways, suggests Graves, in which Modernism *can* be profitably used to shock a tradition grown either too comfortable or too lazily tyrannical into renewing itself. "In the present confused state of literature, I probably rank as a traditionalist, but not as one who opposes innovations in poetic technique," writes Graves, and it is this delicate balance between encouraging experimentation without damaging the "poetic body" that best captures his stance towards his Modernist contemporaries. It is, therefore, ironic that some of the earliest, most acute, and most sympathetic (and most exactingly close) readings of cummings and Marianne Moore should have come from a poet determined to place these experimental poets as, so to speak, "symptoms" of a greater poetic crisis rather than breakers of new ground.

Some Thoughts on Graves in the 1950s and After

What, then, did Graves represent to those poets, the Movement, for whom the Modernist experiment, the "age of Auden," and Dylan Thomas, and the postromantic 1940s, were to be discarded in favor of a new, old, and more hygienic poetic practice? And can a brief excursion into this issue help us to elucidate Graves's position today? One treads on dangerous ground in ascribing a set of common principles to a group of poets so radically different as Larkin, Gunn, Davie, Enright, or Amis, but the risk of generalization is worth taking. The Movement poets saw, or *tried* to see, Modernism as an interruption of what Robert Conquest claimed, in the preface to the second *New Lines* anthology, was "the main tradition of English poetry." For them, Modernism appeared not as a way forward but as a jolt to a poetic body grown flabby and lugubrious—now that Modernism had had its day it was time to build bridges back to the likes of Hardy. Graves, having been "formed" in a pre-Modernist climate, independently fostered throughout the Modernist "period" and emerging more or less unscathed from its exhaustion, was, with important reservations, claimed for a beacon in the Movement's anti-Modernist crusade: as, precisely, a solitary and uninterrupted link between a "native tradition" and post-1945 poetry. Graves as poet represented the possibility of working outside and largely independently of Modernism but throughout the "Modernist" period; Graves as critic showed a way of taking on the not only the Modernist idols but Auden and Dylan Thomas into the bargain (that is, respectively, the "politicized" 1930s and the neoromantic 1940s).

This comes out most strongly in a lecture given by D. J. Enright and later reprinted in *Conspirators and Poets,* entitled "Robert Graves and the Decline of Modernism." Graves's definition of poetry as "sense; good sense; penetrating, often heart-rending sense" is cited approvingly by Enright, who asserts,

When art is in the doldrums, the outsider, the lone wolf, comes into his own; it may even happen that he—and only he—can help that art to get moving again. As you can trace in the work of one poet, Yeats, the decline of late romanticism and the rise of modernism, a résumé of poetic history between 1880 and 1942, so in the history of Graves's reputation you can trace the rise of modernism and its present decline. Graves's rise coincides with its decline. He was always outside movements; and now that—despite the various contrivings of reviewers, critics, and other interested persons—there are no movements to get into, the contemporary poet turns to Graves for encouragement and advice. (Enright 1966, 5)

Enright picks up on several key points here: first, as if to corroborate Graves's persistent rejection of literary "schools" or "movements," there is his status as "lone wolf" finally coming into his own; second, we have him pitted directly against Modernism and its offshoots as exemplary of a poetic enterprise working confidently *outside* the jurisdiction of self-styled movements; next, we have the idea of Graves—or rather his *reputation*—being actually a *measure* of the decline of Modernism; finally, in words strongly reminiscent of Graves's own attack on critics (and Enright's great bugbear in this and other essays is what he calls the "criticocracy"), Graves is presented as an opponent of the conspiracy of "critics, reviewers and other interested persons" who contrives to form literary taste. Enright follows Graves in deliberately driving a wedge between the academic/literary journalist and the reader of poetry. This is worth remarking on because the appeal is lodged over the heads of the "academy" and aimed directly at another poetry-reading constituency—an appeal which continues to determine a great deal of today's debate on the writing, reading, and marketing of poetry.

Another, though much shorter, appreciation of Graves appeared in *The Guardian* in 1958—Philip Larkin's review of *Steps,* entitled "Graves Superior." The points of contact between this and Enright's article, and between Enright and Larkin and the Graves of the Clark Lectures, are considerable. Both Larkin and Enright note that Graves is unfavorably compared by several reviewers and critics to Pound. Graves notes the same thing. In "The Legitimate Criticism of Poetry," Graves himself was informed by a critic that he had not produced any "diploma pieces." The same critic offered Graves a "major lyric" of Ezra Pound's to illustrate what he meant. The said piece, an extract from Pound's cantos, prompted the following response from Graves: "If this was a major lyric, I said, might I never write one." Apart from showing us that Graves objected to being hounded in the literary press by Poundian comparisons, and that the issue of Graves *and*—or more exactly Graves *or*—Modernism was topical at the time, this common thread shows that Graves serves a dual purpose for Enright and Larkin, allowing them to attack both Modernism and the criticocracy in one swoop. Both poets see Graves as a bulwark against what the Movement perceives as Modernism's second phase, that is, a phalanx not of poets this time but critics. Indeed, it is with some alarm that Enright and Larkin acknowledge that if Modernism is exhausted—that it has, according to Enright, "lost its nerve"—it has once and for all entered the critical realm, that it has taken its place as an orthodoxy: something perhaps more to be feared than its actual literary productions.

Furthermore, both Enright and Larkin stake a claim for Graves as a model, though in both cases this claim comes with the telling caveat that Graves is not among "the greatest" poets currently writing. For Larkin, Graves is "Neither respectful nor vulgar, unlettered nor pedantic, unbalanced nor entirely sane, Mr Graves is as good a poetic mentor as the young are likely to get. His advantage as a scatterer of other people's nonsense resides chiefly in the intimidating quality of his own" (Larkin 1958, 4). While for Enright the "Georgian versifier" had become a sort of father figure (albeit a not wholly respectable father). Both Movementeers acknowledge Graves's crankiness while at the same time seeing it as a useful antidote to prevailing lunacies.

In his review Larkin also captures other facets of the Movement ethos: the refusal of rhetoric and a retreat from grandly coercive poetry. It is with approval that he quotes Graves's attitude to the reading of poetry: "If a poet, called upon to read his poems, chants or croons or declaims, something is wrong. A true poem is best spoken in a level, natural voice: slowly or solemnly, and with a suppressed emotion . . . not the one in which we try to curry favour with children at a party or with an election crowd, or with a traffic cop" (Larkin 1958).

The relative boom Graves enjoyed in the 1950s and 1960s, as if he had been, so to speak, "waiting in the wings," was partly due to the shift of taste represented by the Movement. And yet there were, there still are, considerable problems inherent in Graves's so-called rise, and the Movement flirtation with Graves falls far short of an alliance. As we have seen, though both Enright and Larkin set Graves up as a "poetic mentor" or "father figure," both are equally certain that he is not, to use a loaded but empty term, a "great." There is almost a sense of dissatisfaction on their part that their big guns against Modernism—Graves the critic and Graves the poet—are not of a higher caliber. They are also acutely aware that certain of his ideas are outlandish and of no more use to their own eminently sane, reasonable, and sober poetic practice than Yeats's. Enright is sceptical of Graves's Muse, declaring that "I prefer the dark gods to Graves's 'White Goddess': she sounds like a cross between a shrewish wife and a military dictator, they at least govern by majority rule—or misrule" (Enright 1966, 9).

It was on the question of what Graves represented to the poets of the 1950s that I wrote to Donald Davie. His reply, parts of which I shall quote here, helps to situate Graves in what is, ironically, his native territory on the outside. Davie writes,

> Graves's claim on us was one of the shamelessly many matters on which The Movement refused to accept responsibility. I seem to have written an approving review called "Impersonal and Emblematic," and also a broadcast on "The Toneless Voice of Robert Graves." But in these pieces I spoke only for myself, not for the group of us. Nor did I persist for long. For the Gravesians were not in a mood to receive any olive-branches. The Movement, so far as it represented anything more than a socio-political shift, was "anti-Romantic," whereas Graves and the Gravesians were, in their own quite special understanding of the matter, unashamedly and even belligerently, "Romantic." Graves's Clark Lectures, *The Crowning Privilege*, made it clear, if any one had doubted, that the issue was non-negotiable. A great pity—opposing stances in (not literary theory but) literary history made it impossible for us to acknowledge what we (I, at any rate) owed to Graves in the building of lyric stanzas.

The rifts in this non-alliance are quite clear: a kind of renewed, proud, and seemingly outdated romanticism in Graves stands squarely before the Movement poet, something tacitly suggested by Enright and Larkin, even as they stake their claim for Graves's time as "mentor" having come. Moreover, Davie continues, something of the so-called opposition's values *had* been absorbed by the Movement:

> Though some of the Movementeers (e.g., Amis, Larkin) chose to posture at times as anti-modernists, the alternative to modernism that Graves and the Gravesians offered was not to our liking at all—it was altogether too "unsmart" and fusty; to give us a little more credit, Auden had entered our bloodstream, whereas Gravesians wouldn't give him the time of day.

Coming to the matter of Davie, it should also be pointed out that the case of Robert Graves is one that exposes certain deep rifts in the Movement itself. To say that the Movement did not, except for assenting to a few common principles, move wholly in concert is no news to anyone, but Graves's part in revealing certain inherent incompatibilities between its member poets has not been explored.

In 1957 Donald Davie gave his *Poet in the Imaginary Museum* broadcasts, in which he explores André Malraux's thesis that today's writer is faced with a plethora of exhibits from different languages, cultures, and periods to which he retains—and must take advantage of—a curious and characteristically modern blend of unimpeded access and ultimate alienation. (We are far closer than we think to that alleged new discovery, postmodernism, if it actually exists). Such internationalism, along with its uncertainties, difficulties, and defensive ironies we recognise in the work of Pound, Eliot, Yeats, and others. Davie writes, "before the imaginary museum situation arose, poems could be complete in themselves, self-dependent . . . in the way no modern poem can be. That sort of pleasure can be afforded by modern poems only when they are minor, even provincial achievements" (Davie 1977, 56). Graves in the same essay is posited by Davie as a poet who has not taken account of the imaginary museum situation (this is another thing that distinguishes Graves despite his immense linguistic and historical learning from the likes of Pound and Eliot). Graves's response to Davie can be found in his lecture "The Making and Marketing of Poetry." What is interesting is that Davie's argument sets him at odds with some of his Movement contemporaries and that Graves is one of the bones of contention. In his article on Graves and the decline of Modernism, Enright actually takes up the challenge, attacking the imaginary museum thesis *through* a defence of Graves:

> Behind the creation of much art is the horrified effort to win a degree of order, . . . of mere comprehensibility, out of the surrounding anarchy; to secure a modicum of temporary mercy from the midst of cruelty, to tame one small beast in the jungle of wild beastliness. "Poetry . . . is not the expression of personality," Eliot wrote . . . "but an escape from personality." Perhaps that was an appropriate way of putting it in 1917. Today one would rather say, perhaps, that poetry is not the expression of personality—who wants to *express* it?—but the preservation of it against the forces which in their different ways, whether savage or kindly, are out to kill it. Poetry is written on a battlefield, not in a library, nor in the imaginary museum crammed with objects from the past which you must have fingered carefully one by one, the theory has it, if you wish to be more than a minor and provincial these days. (Enright 1966, 9)

Enright implicitly but unmistakably attacks Davie by contradicting the basic premise of the existence and necessity of the imaginary museum (Davie had claimed that Graves wrote "minor, even provincial" poems), and he does so with recourse to the only living poet of enough stature, enough longevity, and enough cultural breadth to mount the assault: Robert Graves. If Enright is sceptical of Graves's White Goddess, he, nonetheless, firmly prefers Graves's Muse to Davie's imaginary museum (and by extension Eliot and Pound's). Enright goes on to take a far more explicit swing at Davie by excusing the shrillness of Graves's tone in his Clark lectures:

> The objection to these lectures, in which Graves lists a number of things which a true poet is not, is that he displays himself as something which a true poet is not—a nagging old woman. Again, there is a sort of extenuation: the lectures were given at Cambridge, and he must have felt that he was on enemy ground, that he was entrapped in an imaginary museum if not a real one. It was from Cambridge that, as an inveterate non-museumite, he was doomed to minority. (Enright 1966, 11)

Enright, perhaps seeing the "situation rhyme" between himself, a poet-critic teaching and working abroad, and Graves, a poet in perpetual geographical as well as academic "exile," directs us straight to the center of the web of issues that Robert Graves raises: the academy *or* the poetry reader, Modernism *or* tradition, Muse *or* museum, in with *or* out of step with the criticocracy?

Davie's broadcasts underlined his own break from the Movement, which he saw as a stultifying and parochial influence, a group of "cultural teddy-boys," and the broadcasts incurred the wrath of other Movement writers, notably Robert Conquest and John Holloway. This divergence simply brought to the fore certain incompatibilities which were always there, and the literary issues at stake were far wider, but the Graves case makes it easier to follow. We cannot go so far as to split the Movement into two groups—Muse worshippers and museum attendants—but it seems to me that the issue has implications far outside the specifics of Graves's reputation or the present status of the Movement. Nonetheless, it remains central for anyone trying to work out how Graves fits in, and indeed *if* he should fit in. Graves is still, as it were, battling with the same idols he challenged in 1954.

It has often been argued that Graves began *A Survey* with a receptive attitude to Modernism and that this attitude hardened later into overt antagonism (partly out of professional jealousy) of the kind found in the Clark Lectures—he had, after all, planned to write a book called *Untraditional Elements in Modern Poetry* with Eliot. If Graves was indeed more prepared to countenance Modernism in the 1920s, then, it was in the greater context of a need for a more than skin-deep renewal of the poetic body rather than merely the plastic surgery of new forms for their own sake. And besides, as I have suggested, it is more than likely that his receptiveness to the likes of Eliot, cummings, and Marianne Moore was part of an altogether more cunning and prescient investment in an anti-Modernist agenda than he has been credited with.

Reviewing Graves's 1960 *Collected Poems* Donald Davie wrote of "the difficulty we have in seeing where Graves fits in with Eliot and Pound and Yeats, Auden and Dylan Thomas" and concludes that historians "will try to forget Graves." (Davie 1977, 76) For Davie, Graves "seems to be the exception that proves the rule about his time, the case which belies the generalization but cannot disprove it because the case is so clearly a special one." It would be interesting to see how Graves's anomalous position has altered in the thirty-five years since Davie's essay, or how it has developed with regard to the idols he took on in his Clark lecture. To consider this question is to think about a great deal more than Robert Graves.

WORKS CITED

Davie, Donald. 1977. *The Poet in the Imaginary Museum.* Manchester: Carcanet.

Enright, D. J. 1966. *Conspirators and Poets.* London: Chatto and Windus.

Graves, Robert. 1995. *Collected Writing on Poetry.* Ed. Paul O'Prey. Manchester: Carcanet.

Larkin, Philip. 1958. "Graves Superior." *The Guardian.*

Riding, Laura, and Robert Graves. 1927. *A Survey of Modernist Writing.* London: Heinemann.

Part II
Poetry

A Measure of Casualness: The Peripatetic in the Poetry of Robert Graves

Devindra Kohli

Walking is among the most natural human activities, and it has traditionally had a close association with another very basic activity, the creation of poetry. Perhaps the confusion of the peripatetic with the pedestrian is the reason why this link has not been greatly researched by critics in the past. In the 1990s, however, some critics have examined in detail the connection between walking and poetry. The creative and sociopolitical nature of the walk among English writers of the nineteenth century is treated in Anne Wallace's *Walking, Literature, and English Culture,* which looks at the use of walking in both poetry and fiction. Roger Gilbert in *Walks in the World: Representation and Experience in Modern American Poetry* argues for the walk-poem as a distinctive genre and asserts that "the walk uniquely answers the various and often incompatible impulses to redefine and remake poetic representation that have guided American poets over the last century." Among the various things Gilbert discusses is the sexual nature of the relationship between body and earth, in the process of walking, using John Crowe Ransom's metaphor "The World's Body" and Alfred Kazin's from "The Open Street" ("I in my body and the world in its skin of earth" and "blending into a simple act of knowing") as prime examples.

However, neither of these studies offers any comment on Graves's use of the peripatetic. Of course, anyone who met Graves in person would corroborate that he was vigorosly peripatetic. Reporting in 1973 on how she witnessed Graves wholly engrossed in pacing about her room for half an hour in search of the one right word he needed to complete a poem that he had written twenty-three times, Diana Graves remarked, "he . . . thinks best when he's on the move" (1973). William Graves in *Wild Olives* points out that whenever Robert Graves had writer's block, he turned to "Bottling fruit, making jam and jelly, gardening, washing up as therapies" and "sorted out his work in his head as he walked or strode to the Cala for his daily swim." Graves's compulsive habit of revising his poems is well-known, but it is not clearly established that his act of actually composing a poem coincided with the act of walking. However, he has, in his poetry, used the image of walking in significantly original ways.

This is not, of course, to suggest that Graves set the tradition, or may owe nothing to the great body of poetry in English in which walking figures in large and complex ways as in the poems of Chaucer, Spenser, Milton, John Clare, Wordsworth, Arnold, Whitman, Hardy, Yeats, Eliot, Frost, and Wallace Stevens. Yeats's analog of "pacing" and "walking in excited reverie" and Frost's leaf treading readily come to mind. What is significant is that Graves uses walk as image and symbol in a way that is wholly consistent with his poetic mythography. For him, walking is, for one thing, a means of connecting with the life-giving earth, an activity in a natural landscape which resists the mechanization of modern life. Secondly, walking and rock climbing serve as therapy, as self-exhortation to the harnessing of body and mind. Thirdly, walking as homage to the Goddess is a religious ritual of passionate servitude, of humility as honor. Finally, walking as celebration of togetherness in love, or as a mark of liberation from fears and terrors is described in "Gold and Malachite" as, "Let her know by your gait alone that you are free at last."

I should like to say at the outset that while Graves sometimes uses the image of walking without symbolic association as, for example, in "As Jane walked out below the hill, / She saw an old man standing still" (1920, 58), or a purely physical allusion buttressing an element of fantasy in "Finland" (117, 19) where "Feet and face tingle . . . / Legs wobble and go wingle," it is more often the case that his walking imagery permeates his mythology as a whole. For example, there is the "Thirsting and hungering" Christ walking in the wilderness, followed by the weeping loverlike scapegoat "with ragged coat / Gaunt ribs . . . / Bleeding foot, and burning throat" in "In the Wilderness" (1916, 15), the lover in "Oh, Oh!" (1916, 16) who "walk[s] aloof" with "Head burning and heart snarling, / Tread feverish quick"; the lover in "A Lover since Childhood" (first published in *London Mercury,* September 1921): "Walking so miserably, / Wanting relief in the friendship of flower or tree"; and the lover in "Lost Love" (1921, 29) "who is quickened so with grief, / He wanders god-like or like thief / Inside and out, below, above, / Without relief seeking lost love" all seem to anticipate Graves's symbolism of the poet and his cowalker, the Lack character, the weird self, and describe some of the symptoms of love which Graves mythologizes in a poem of the same title from *More Poems* 1961.

Drawing from his analyses of various poems, G. S. Fraser has cogently argued that several of the analogs which Graves uses for the body—analogues such as a ship, a castle, a prison cell, a railway compartment—are inorganic and suggest "a sense of awkward and unwilling attachment to his body" (1959, 139). There is a preoccupation with images of crookedness and physical asymmetry in some of Graves's prose writings, too. In *Good-bye to All That*, for example, we have the well-known passage in which Graves dwells with bemused pride and wry humor on the two "naturally unassorted" sides of his face, the high cheek bones on different levels, the "noticeably crooked" setting of his eyes, eyebrows, and ears, the crooked nose, and the crooked smile. Many of Graves's poems—notably "Brother," "Reassurance to a Satyr," "In Broken Images," and "The Face in the Mirror"—portray or rather celebrate one aspect or another of this crookedness. In "The Face in the Mirror," after two stanzas, which dwell on the unassorted details of his physiognomy, the poet pauses in the final stanza to question, with a degree of self-satisfaction, "the mirrored man" for his readiness to court the Moon-Goddess with "a boy's presumption." The asymmetry seems to be also projected as a measure not only of his own individuality but of the uniqueness of a "true" poet, and of the nature of "true" poetry. The recurrent imagery of body movement and walking reflects the process through which Graves harnessed this sense of crookedness, heightened by the physical and mental injuries received in the war, to an "overriding" but liberating poetic passion. "Mind is the prudent rider; body the ass / Disciplined always by a harsh bit."

> But, dear self, learn to love your own body
> In its full naked glory,
> Despite blemishes of moles and scars—
> As she, for whom it shines, wholly loves hers.
> ("Cock in Pullet's Feathers," 1966)

This process of harnessing had, in fact, started early in Graves's life when at Charterhouse he turned to boxing and to rock climbing in order to disperse his "private terrors." Later, during and after the war, he took up walking on hills as a therapeutic exercise to cure his neurasthenia. "Big words" speaks of the desire

> For winning confidence in those quiet days
> Of peace, poised sickly on the precipice side
> Of Lliwedd Crag by Snowdon, and in War
> Find it firmlier with me than before.
> (1916, 27)

The first therapeutic use of walking is in "Not Dead," (first published in *Goliath and David* [1916]). It concerns the poet's attempt to find relief from the painful memory of David's death: "Walking through trees to cool my heat and pain."

"To Walk on Hills" was published in July 1936 and as such belongs with the group of poems such as "The Legs," "Trudge, Body!," "Nature's Lineaments," and "Certain Mercies." However, its extended use of the image of walking for therapeutic purposes seems to suggest that either it is an earlier poem or a recollection of an experience pertaining to his stay in Harlech. In any case, the poem has not attracted adequate critical attention. Douglas Day in *Swifter than Reason* inexplicably omits a mention of this poem, as does Martin Seymour-Smith both in his monograph and his critical biography. Daniel Hoffman's comment in *Barbarous Knowledge* is confined to an acknowledgement of the use of "a phrasal rather than a metronomic rhythm." Michael Kirkham, who does offer a detailed analysis of the poem, over emphasizes, it seems to me, the comic element at the expense of the more important element of the rhythmic trance, and his Ivor Winters—like preoccupation with poetry as "an evaluation medium" of "moral analysis and judgement," though not entirely irrelevant, leads to a paraphrase such as this:

> Hill-walking which, as the poem goes on to show, connotes looking for picturesque sights to be awed and thrilled by, is an emblem, in other words, for the sentimental-romantic search. "Legs" by walking with no purpose but to exercise the body, and "heart," by sentimentalizing landscape, combine to overthrow the strict and sobering rule of the mind. (Kirkham 1969, 151)

However, "To Walk on Hills" is not simply an "emblem" but an embodiment of an experience which is central to Graves's poetic life. Long before he reconstructed the Goddess myth, hill-walking seems to have been part of his unconscious search for what Yeats called "a mythology that marries one to rock and hill." In his foreword to *The White Goddess,* Graves quotes the *Song of Amergin* as a brief summary of his poetic myth; two of its lines "I am a hill: *where poets walk*" and "I am the blaze: *on every hill*" seem to have had a special relevance for Graves. That there exists a sensual and sexual relationship between body and hill is suggested in "The Hills of May" (first published in 1920, and retained in *Collected Poems* [1975]). The poet identifies himself with the wind in amorous engagement with the "she who "walking with a virgin heart"—is "the green hills of May," and by symbolic extension, the Goddess of Spring. Like the

White Goddess whom she anticipates in Graves's mythic vision, she takes him as a lover, but is "too fine to stay":

> So she walked, the proud lady
> So danced or ran,
> So she loved with a whole heart,
> Neglecting man. . . .

In Graves's conception of the love relationship, it is the man who seeks integration in love, whereas the woman's wholeness remains unquestioned and her power regardlessly unpredictable.

In "To Walk on Hills," the heart is instinctively attracted to the unfamiliar sights and sounds which it encounters, but their novelty, leaves the head "glum":

> To walk on hills is to see sights
> And hear sounds unfamiliar.
> When in wind the pine-tree roars,
> When crags with bleatings echo,
> When water foams below the fall,
> Heart records that journey
> As memorable indeed;
> Head reserves opinion,
> Confused by the wind.

In the third passage the heart makes yet another attempt by pointing out a rarer and prismatic perspective of "three shires and the sea" (which is probably a reference to the view which Graves used to have from his parents' house in Harlech), and emphasizes that "Seldom so much at once appears / Of the coloured world." In the fourth passage, the cumulative physical weariness of legs under the direction of the heart brings the unmoved head to a "giddied" state. And although it has still "no word to utter," it has been "brought low," as the legs halt "To sprawl in a rock's shelter." The passage creates a trancelike state in which the head now stirred is resigned to the will of the heart. The rhythmic curve which turns downwards with

> *L*egs become weary, ha*l*ting
> To sp*r*aw*l* in a rock's she*l*ter,
> Whi*le* the sun drowsi*ly* b*l*inks
>
> [My italics.]

suddenly rises in "Oh head" before it drops abruptly with "brought low." This turn comes halfway in the poem, and the lines that follow commend the heart which does double duty, / As heart, and as head, / With portentous trifling. However, a heart that can do "double duty" cannot be an ordinary heart: it fills one with awe. Like the castle "on its crag perched" when seen from the hills behind Harlech, it unifies the sense of space and time. The heart has persuaded the head through physical therapy, as it were, to acquiesce into "quaint visions":

> Now a daisy pleases,
> Pleases and astounds, even,
> That on a garden lawn could blow
> All summer long with no esteem.
>
> And the buzzard's cruel poise,
> And the plover's misery,
> And the important beetle's
> Blue-green-shiny back. . . .
>
> To walk on hills is to employ legs
> To march away and lose the day.

The lines move, at the beginning of the poem, with labored effort and then gradually with a sense of assured effortlessness. The refrainlike propositional repetition—"To walk on hills is to employ legs," like "Trudge, Body" in a contemporaneous poem of the same title—acts both as a pull and an anchor. In the last passage, instead of the earlier sense of an attached weight there is rather a sense of release; because now "To walk on hills" is not simply "to employ legs as porters / Of the head and heart'" but "To march away and lose the day"; it is to be rewarded by "quaint visions" which are granted only to the "witless" shepherds Not . . . thus from solitude (Solitude sobers only) But from long hilltop striding. What is true of the persona is also true of the poem. The poem's "legs" are words which must move with a measure of casualness achieved under the direction of the heart that does double duty and not the head that ignores the heart and the senses. The poem's words as legs must not be like "the unstoppable / Legs" of a mechanical movement of the endless crowd, which move unnaturally "with never a stumble / Between step and step."

In the following passage from *The Telling* (Jackson [Riding] 1972, 12–13), Laura Riding uses a similar image of legs as porters of the poem:

> it was the uniform aspiration of the elder philosophers to use words well, to think to the mind's best, to employ the faculty of understanding, to

which words belong as legs to the walking creature, or wings to the bird in flight, with an athletic zest in the intellectual exercise of their humanness.

However, her emphasis on the intellectual rather than the intuitive truth seems to distinguish the dominant stresses in Graves's poetry from those one encounters in Laura Riding's. Her defining figure of words as legs of the walking creature or wings of the bird in flight would be relevant in Graves's case only with the significant modification that their athletic zest is in the human exercise of their intellect, not in the intellectual exercise of their humanness.

Related to the therapeutic value of walking, and its significance as a means of harnessing the body, is the image of compulsive walking or "compulsive tread" that recurs in Graves's treatment of the theme of enchantment and disenchantment in love. Unlike logic, which is "compulsive touch and tread / By a public voice dictated," the compulsive tread of poetry is always dictated by a private voice. Already in 1916, Graves had found an analogy for poetry in the process of walking. "Free Verse" emphasizes that his poems must not imitate the stiff march of soldiers on parade, but have a natural "run and ripple and shake." In *Steps*, he affirms that a "true" poem: "is moon-magical enough to walk off the page—if you know what I mean—and to keep on walking, and to get under people's skins and into their eyes and throats and hearts and marrows: that is more-than-coincidence at its most miraculous" (Graves 1958, 105). This transference of the energy of natural but compulsive walking to the life of a poem is not surprisingly similar to the analogy which Frost, one of the few contemporary poets for whom Graves had unqualified admiration, used: "The figure [a poem makes] is the same as for love. Like a piece of ice on a hot stove the poem must ride on its own melting."

At Charterhouse, Graves formed an enduring friendship with George Mallory, who took him climbing on Snowdon. Mallory published an article "The Mountaineer as Artist" in which he distinguished between two kinds of climber—"the arrogant sort" who "take a high line about climbing" and "those who take no particular line at all" and for whom it is "comparable with field sports." While both sorts are artists in so far as they view mountaineering as an emotional experience, there is, however, Mallory concluded, a serious difference which divides them.

> It seem[s] perfectly natural to compare a day in the Alps with a symphony; . . . but no sportsman could or would make the same claim for

cricket or hunting, or whatever his particular sport might be. He recognises the existence of the sublime in great Art, and knows, even if he cannot feel, that its manner of stirring the heart is altogether different and vaster. But mountaineers do not admit this difference in the emotional plane of mountaineering and Art. They claim that something sublime is the essence of mountaineering. (Mallory 1914, 40)

It is arguable that Graves's attraction for rock climbing and walking on hills was enhanced by his subconscious perception of the similarity between the challenges they pose and the processes of creating poetry. He writes, for instance, about the perseverance and intuitive sense of timing required in rock climbing, with a passionate seriousness which is strikingly similar to the way he writes about poetry. It is likely that Graves knew about Mallory's article. In *Goodbye to All That* he cites from his own essay on climbing, which he wrote at the time. Climbing is a "sport" that makes "all others seem trivial," and

With physical fitness, . . . a careful watch on the weather, proper overhauling of climbing apparatus, and with no hurry, anxiety or stunting, climbing is much safer than fox-hunting. . . . The climber trusts entirely to his own feet, legs, hands, shoulder, sense of balance, judgement of distance. (Graves 1929, 95)

In comparable manner, Poetry is a "truth" before which all other truths pale. The poet trusts entirely to his senses, his knowledge of the history of words, and finally his luck. Poetry is not a feverish adventure like fox hunting, involving the excitement of a group of participants, but an unhurried, groping struggle like rock climbing whose peculiar hazards require the will to "soldier on" in isolation. In fox hunting, the watchword is speed, while in rock climbing, the main requirements are coolness, patience, and balance. "There's a cool web of language winds us in / Retreat from too much joy or too much fear." And both "poise" and "balance" recur in Graves's poems suggesting controlled movement. With both the poet and the rock climber, rhythm is as compulsive as counting, touching things, arranging objects in his environment. And if sometimes the poet improvises, the improvisation derives from an intuitive sense of balance with which the rock climber sometimes improvises an imaginary foothold in the air.

Writing to Wilfred Owen in 1917, Graves uses the metaphor of climbing in order to emphasize the rigors of writing poetry,

It's the devil of a sweat for him [the poet] to get to know the value of his rhymes, rhythms or sentiments. But I have no doubt at all that if you turned seriously to writing, you could obtain Parnassus in no time while I'm still struggling on the knees of that stubborn peak. (Seymour Smith, [1982] 1995, [65] 61)

"Trudge, Body!" (Graves 1933) belongs to the Riding phase when Graves was grappling with uncertainties of various kinds on his road to achieving poetic certitude. One of these uncertainties was, as we now know from recent well-documented biographies, the nature of his relationship with Laura Riding. However, it was their shared commitment to poetry, a bond in which Graves was the disciple and Riding the teacher, that held it together. But to describe "Trudge, Body!" as a mere record of the mood of "pure despair" and trace this despair to sexual denial on the part of Riding, as Martin Seymour-Smith does in his biography ([1982] 1995, 238–239), is to miss not only the poem's concern with the harnessing of the body as therapy, but the more important metaphorical connection which Graves saw between this harnessing and the rigorous servitude of the Muse. In urging body through almost sensual provocation to continue its "trudge and climb" without, paradoxically, halting "*again* on any peak of time" (italics mine), in projecting an ascetic state of mind in pagan terms the poem suggests the possibility of reaching the timeless through time. "Pure despair, . . . in which the body has no hope, nor regret" but looks beyond despair seems analogous to the state of mind which Eliot struggles to arrive at in "Ash Wednesday": "Teach us to care and not to care / Teach us to sit still." However, Graves's sublimation is achieved not through creative stillness but creative drudgery.

> I'll cool you, body, with a hot sun, that draws the sweat,
> I'll warm you, body, with ice-water, that stings the blood,
> I'll enrage you, body, with idleness, to do
> And having done to sleep the long night through:
> Trudge, Body!
>
> But in such cooling, warming, doing or sleeping,
> No pause for satisfaction: henceforth you make address
> Beyond heat to the heat, beyond cold to the cold,
> Beyond enraged idleness to enraged idleness.
> With no more hours of hope, and none of regret,
> Before each sun may rise, you salute it for set:
> Trudge, body!

What makes poetry or rock climbing more than a just a mechanical skill, though mechanical skill is a prerequisite, is the intensity of love or of concentration with which the poet or the rock climber performs the act. Graves extends the analogy of walking, or balancing, as during rock climbing, to the process of being in love. To be in love implies the skill for a hazardous scaling of "the forward-tilted crag with no hand-holds" ("To be in Love"). And the "obstinacy of undefeat" that characterizes the rather untraditional portrait of the poet in "The Traditionalist" lies in that the poet's "feet [are] prepared for the conquest of crags / Or a week's march to the sea" with the alacrity with which he himself is ready to fall in love with "real women like you." That the connection between walking and being in love is not incidental and possibly owes its origin to Graves's mythic consciousness is suggested also by his discussion of feet, shoes, heels, lameness, and the hobble of the partridge in love in chapters 17 and 18 of *The White Goddess*.

The symbolic value of Graves's compulsive walking lies in a natural sense of life in contrast to mechanical movement. "Endless Pavement" is really about the experience of time or of love, not as walking on a well-leveled road but on such a passage of "pebbles, or rocks overgrown by grasses" that

> ... the man in love, as he turns to stare
> At the glazed eyes flickering past, will remain aware
> of his own, assured, meticulous, rustic tread—

The compulsive tread is, of course, not to be confused with the linear movement. "In No Direction" describes the eccentricity of neither following a direction blindly nor avoiding it altogether:

> To go in no direction
> Surely as carelessly,
> Walking on the hills alone,
> I never found easy.

The poem mythologizes what might have been a personal difficulty or habit into the desirable need to achieve a sense of balance along a line which is not absolutely linear. In his autobiography, Graves lists "finding it difficult to walk straight down a street" among many eccentric "habits of speech and movement" which he inherited from his father's side. By allowing himself to be distracted the poet follows a course which is neither consciously planned nor predictable:

> Either I sent leaf or stick
> Twirling in the air,

> Whose fall might be prophetic,
>   Pointing 'there,'
>
> Or in superstition
>   Edged somewhat away
> From a sure direction
>   Yet could not stray,
>
> Or undertook the climb
>   That I had avoided
> Directionless some other time,
>   Or had not avoided,
>
> Or called as companion
>   An eyeless ghost
> And held his no direction
>   Till my feet were lost.
>
>   (Graves 1938, 41)

Like the butterfly's crooked course, this intuitive rambling, this apparently directionless walk on hills implies a just sense of how not "to go in no direction."

That walking is also linked with the magic of poetry and opposed to pure philosophy and reason is suggested in two poems from *Mock Beggar Hall* (1924). It is significant because the whole tone of the book is philosophical involving a series of meditations on relativity and Time. As Kirkham points out, in "Attercop: The All-Wise Spider," "Graves's two previous poetic selves, Walter the romantic and James the philosopher, confront each other with their separate solutions to his plight, which is to be caught in the web of the 'All-wise, omnivorous / Attercop,' a 'capricious Beast' whose whims are the poet's destiny." The image of Walter and James "Like trapped and weakening flies / In toils of the same hoary net" expresses the poet's haunting sense of bloodshed, and the bloodthirsty, all-wise Spider who is controlling the poet's destiny "anticipates one aspect of the White Goddess." But it needs to be emphasized, I think, that despite the poet's conscious denial, Walter's "natural-magic charm" attributed to walking with careless feet on the grass at dawn evokes an alternative sense of life which is central to Graves's poetry:

> Go, cheerily stride at dawn
> With careless feet about the lawn
> Breaking the threads of gossamer;
> This, then, shall prove a token
> Of liberty, my sapient air,

> Attercop, whose proud name with hate be spoken
> His net too, shall be broken.

This striding strength linked with the "strength of the love affair" is evident in "Around the Mountain." Despite its beneficial effects, the lover's haunted "walk all night through summer rain . . . / To circle a mountain, and then limp home again," is terror ridden; but the blessing hoped for is ambiguous and the summer rain is really "Thin rain that shrouds a beneficent full moon." The intensity of the lover's devotion to the Muse "burns his feet," and "harries him out of doors in steady drizzle, / With neither jacket nor hat, and holds him there."

If the compulsive walk, then, can be seen as a reflection of the need for balance in opposing forces, integration with the self is suggested by Graves's use of the concept of the cowalker, the familiar ghost, or the lover's weird self. This is described in the following passage from Kirk's *Secret Commonwealth* (1691), which Graves uses as an epigraph to "General Bloodstock's Lament for England" (Graves 1951):

> This image (seemingly animated) walks with them in the fields in broad Day-light: and if they are employed in delving, harrowing Seed-sowing or any other Occupation, they are at the same time mimicked by the ghostly Visitant. Men of the Second Sight . . . call this reflex-man a Co-walker, every way like the Man, as his Twin-brother and Companion, haunting as his Shadow.

Or in *The White Goddess* (24) as "The weird, or rival, [who] often appears in nightmare . . . and takes countless . . . malevolent or diabolic or serpent-like forms."

"The Co-Walker," first published in *Poems 1968–1970* and revised under the title "My Ghost" for *The Green-Sailed Vessel* (1971), outlines the sense in which the poet's private struggle for self-integration is part of his integration with the public world:

> Pride brought its punishment: to be well haunted
> By a co-walker whom eventually
> All would-be friends and open enemies
> Came to identify and certify
> As me, distorting him in anecdotal
> Autobiographies.
>
> (Graves 1975, 502)

When the poet's weird "sits opposite you [the Muse] at a table" or when she meets "him in the newspapers, / In planes, in trains, or at

State banquets," the poet overtly seeks the Muse's aid "to disavow his clumsy capers: Silence him with a cold, unwinking stare." But this weird who haunts the poet-lover as his "cowalker" is not merely the bringer of conflict: for he is also the bringer of the second sight, which alone makes it possible for the poet to achieve a sense of integration with the Muse, a sense which is commensurate with "Walking in splendour through the plain / For all the world to see" (Graves 1975, 321). It is a dialectic which enables Graves to dramatize the moments when his sense of the public world finds an adequate and unobtrusive place.

In "The Undead," which is one of Graves's most impassioned attacks on the contemporary scientific pluto-democratic ethos, the image of the haunting ghost is transformed into that of the attendant splendor of love. The "Innumerable zombies / With glazed eyes shuffle around at their diurnal tasks," "keep the machines whirring" and "Speed along highways in conveyor-belt automobiles." As opposed to this movement of the dead, there are the "undead" whom the poet advises to wait to be surprised by the moment of miracle; which might come when they are walking in an unfamiliar side street:

> Accept it as your fate
> To live, to love, knowingly to cause true miracles,
> Nor ever to find your body possessed by a cold corpse.
> For one day, as you choose an unfamiliar side-street
> Keeping both eyes open, alert, not apprehensive,
> You shall suddenly (this is a promise) come to a brief halt;
> For striding towards you on the same sidewalk will appear
> A young man with halo of life around his head,
> Will catch you reassuringly by both hands, asseverating
> In phrases utterly unintelligible to a zombie
> That all is well:
>
> (Graves 1975, 294)

The power of walking is, then, related to the power of being in love; its compulsions are the compulsions of the Goddess. If the cowalker reflects the other side of the poet, the Muse provides for him an object of worship and adoration. A price that the poet-lover has to pay for the experience of love is the surrender of his social, male, or intellectual pride to the Muse who stands for life. His manner of approach is significant. Walking, especially walking barefooted, as opposed to walking on stilts or mounting a horse, is Graves's version of the ritualistic posture for paying homage to the Goddess. Graves's persona is not just a weak, dreamy lover, but one who has soldierly qualities: he is suppliant before the Muse. He has self-respect, not pride, feet, not stilts. In "Son Altesse," the image of walking in dust is suggestive of the Gravesian blend of honor and humility, of suffering and reward:

> Should I ride home, vainglorious after battle,
> With droves of prisoners and huge heaps of spoil,
> Make me dismount a half-mile from your door;
> To walk barefoot in dust, as a knight must.
>
> (Graves 1975, 308)

In "The Gorge," although her "queendom" and "my frontier" are divided almost inaccessibly by the howling "phantoms of the long dead," the concealed bridge which the lover has to cross "Swings and echoes under my strong tread / Because I have need of you" (Graves 1975, 329).

Reciprocally, the walk of the Muse is itself distinctive. In "Pygmalion to Galatea" (Graves 1927) her "fearless carriage" is also "graceful in going as well-armed in doing." Her "dancing gait" is original, though sometimes, as "In Trance at a Distance," some "demonesses who dare masquerade / As herself in your dreams" in time learn to "skillfully imitate" it. The lover can note even from the hill top that the stranger in the distance had "a sure and eager tread." The wind of inspiration is seen and felt as the visitation of the Muse whose "slender body seems a shaft of moonlight" and whose "tread like blossom [is] drifting from a bough" (Graves 1975, 204) In "Lyceia," which is Graves's version of Lycaon's story (Graves 1961b, 359), Lyceia is the divine she-wolf, the Moon-Goddess who "has a light foot / For a weaving walk." (Graves 1975, 201) In "The Home-Coming" the poet awaiting the arrival of his beloved in what are "potent lulls in love" or "her silence and her absence" is so fed on "hopes and fears and memory" that he does not recognize her when "she walked unheralded up through the dim light / Of the home lane." (Graves 1975, 366) In "Purification" the beloved, who wakes up from a nightmare of adulterous thoughts, is so haunted, despite the lover's reassurance that it was a bad dream, by the thought of having "murdered love even in dream" that in effort at purification

> (as the Great Queen yearly did at Paphos)
> Down to the sea she trod and in salt water
> Renewed virginity.
>
> (Graves 1975, 409)

"*Song:* The Promise," concerns the momentary lifting of doubts between the two lovers and the reality of a promise as real as

> the moon overhead,
> Or the firmness of your fingers,
> Or the print of your kisses,
> Or your lightness of tread
>
> (Graves 1975, 391)

In "Theseus and Ariadne," Theseus after deserting Ariadne is haunted by his "erroneous past," by

> "her set walk
> Down paths of oyster-shell bordered with flowers,
> Across the shadowy turf below the vines."

But now, Ariadne, the victorious queen,

> with a surer foot she goes than when
> Dread of his hate was thunder in the air,
> When the pines agonized with flaws of wind
> And flowers glared up at her with frantic eyes.
>
> (Graves 1975, 135)

In "The Portrait" we learn that "She can walk invisibly at noon / Along the high road" (Graves 1975, 172). The contrast is always between natural movement and an affected, counterfeit style of walking. The "private way" of the Muse that moves the poet in "Your Private Way" is her inimitable "walking-laughing way." "The Miracle" identifies "our habit of love" with the habit of "trudging perhaps across the moor / Or resting on a tree-stump, lost in thought," and then be "scorched by summer lightning" (Graves 1971, 16). The habit of love is certainly not walking through hell together, which "Records" makes clear. The joys of these records testify to "a past pilgrimage through . . . hell[s] boundless, without change of weather," which is the poet's alone, a walk not shared with the Muse.

Whether it is the poet-lover's, or the Muse's or the poem's movement—and all these are linked—the compulsive tread is variable and crooked, though not without a sense of direction. A new, visionary quality enters Graves's treatment of walking in poems in which there is a momentary, celebratory matching of the poet's tread with that of the Muse. There is even a sense of release, such as in "The Sweet-Shop Round the Corner," when the child, who loses his way because he had "matched his tread / with a strange woman's," experiences the horripilant fear of death (Graves 1975, 297). Or in "The Christmas Robin" (Graves 1975, 63–64), which first appeared in a slightly different version as "Wanderings of Christmas" in *Collected*

Poems 1938, the image of walking unites the two lovers with a luminous sense of a miracle:

> when, hand in hand, plodding
> Between the frozen ruts, we lovers paused
> And 'Christmas trees!' cried suddenly together,
> Christmas was there again, as in December.

The sense of effort here suggested by "plodding" points not only to the physical movement in heavy snow but also ominously to the later guttering of the "fantasy" of the second Christmas with which "we velveted our love." The poem speaks of the miraculous power of love as well as of the grim disenchantment that may be latent in it. In this poem the prophecy of the pain and death of love is symbolized by the image of

> the Christmas robin—
> The murderous robin with his breast aglow
> And legs apart, in a spade-handle perched
> who foretold "more snow, and worse than snow."

Iona and Peter Opie point out that "the mating of the robin with the Wren is in accordance with a centuries-old tradition." (1951, 130). Graves refers in *The White Goddess* (97) to Irish myths in which the Robin kills the Wren on St. Stephens's Day. This underlying sexual symbolism of the image of the murderous robin with his breast "aglow" probably made available to Graves the archetypal tale of love, betrayal, and death in terms of the inevitability of the seasonal cycle.

This sense of stained glory is echoed in "Cry Faugh!" where the beloved is urged to reject various concepts of love defined by philosophers, theologians, and scientists—all "antonyms of sacred and profane,"—and instead to come walking with him "in a golden rain." The way in which Graves presents a statement and dismisses it, as he moves through the gamut of the argument, suggests a kind of mental walk in which the lovers escape intellectual and philosophical snares.

In "The Oleaster," after stormy nights during which "crooked flashes of lightning animate us," and after the early morning munificent rain has fallen, the lovers awaken to the rain-drenched olives. With ritualistic compulsion,

> By mid-day we walk out, with naked feet,
> Through pools on the road, gazing at waterfalls

> Or a line of surf, but mostly at the trees
> Whose elegant branches rain has duly blackened
> And pressed their crowns to a sparkling silver.
>
> (Graves 1975, 273)

This passage clearly echoes the need at the end of "Attercop: The All-Wise Spider" from *Mock Beggar Hall* to walk on the lawn with naked and careless feet in order to break the gossamer-like threads of philosophy which I discussed earlier.

The most exquisite and the most complete articulation of the image of walking as an image of enchantment which carries at the same time Graves's characteristic sense of hazard is of course in "Sick Love." The poem has been amply commented upon, yet it seems to me that the most telling image in it is the image of walking. The sensuous joy of feeding on apples and feeling the sun is like the "royal array" needed for the effortless, smiling carriage "on the heavenly causeway." This, in the last lines, becomes a tightrope walk between two points of unfathomable dark:

> Take your delight in momentariness,
> Walk between dark and dark—a shining space
> With the grave's narrowness, though not its peace.
>
> (Graves 1975, 49)

What the poem really exhorts us to do is to accept joy not as a cushioned feeling but as a kind of entranced walk along a short tightrope with a dark beginning and an unknown end. Past and future are unknowable, and the present is the most worthy of rejoicing, but the rejoicing carries the strain and unease which comes from a sense of its essential limitation. The body is worthy of enjoyment, but this enjoyment is tainted not only by the fact that the body is subject to decay but also by the fact that the body itself may not always be willing (as poems such as "To Walk on Hills," and "Trudge, Body!" suggest). The fact that the title of the poem's first version in *Poems 1929* was "Between Dark and Dark" shows that the image of joy or love as a celebratory walk between two poles of mystery, which are both cramping and liberating, was dominant in Graves's mind when he wrote the poem.

We may also conclude that the power of walking is also related to the power of miracle. Trudging and plodding and wandering, and the sense of tension and conflict that they convey are but the necessary stage for the ease and effortlessness that can come only with miracle. "To Be in Love," "Fire-Walker," and "Acrobats" use the metaphor of walking to underline the ease that comes from an intuitive reckoning with hazard. In the former the lover is like a reckless boy who "Basket in hand, culling the red-gold blossom, slips through the furnace of love." To be in love is to experience the miraculous power which proves that "a leap of a thousand miles is nothing / And to walk invisibly needs no artifice" or

> To spring impetuously in air and remain
> Treading on air for three heart beats or four,
> Then to descend at leisure; or else to scale
> The forward-tilted crag with no hand-holds.

The richness and originality of the sexual symbolism here lies in its extension beyond itself to accommodate the labor and pleasure involved in the craft of poetry: "Teach me a measure of casualness / Though you stalk into my room like Venus naked" (Graves 1975, 277). Effortless walking in love presupposes a continual reckoning with its hazards and pitfalls; the measure of casualness that Graves achieves in his poetic style comes from a sense of stumbling between step and step.

WORKS CITED

Day, Douglas. 1963. *Swifter Than Reason: The Poetry and Criticism of Robert Graves.* Chapel Hill: University of North Carolina Press.

Fraser, G. S. 1959. *Vision and Rhetoric.* London: Faber and Faber.

Gilbert, Roger. 1991. *Walks in the World: Representation and Experience in Modern American Poetry.* Princeton.

Graves, Diana. *Womens Journal* (April 1973).

Graves, William. 1995. *Wild Olives: Life in Majorca with Robert Graves.* London: Pimlico.

Graves, Robert. 1916. *Over the Brazier.* London: Poetry Bookshop.

———. 1917. *Fairies and Fusiliers.* London: Heinemann.

———. 1916. *Goliath and David.* London: Chiswick Press.

———. 1920. *Country Sentiment.* London: Secker.

———. 1921. *The Pier-Glass.* London: Secker.

———. 1924. *Mock Beggar Hall.* London: Hogarth.

———. 1927. *Poems 1914–1926.* London: Heinemann.

———. 1929. *Good-bye to All That: An Autobiography.* London: Cape.

———. 1933. *Poems 1930–1933.* London: Barker.

———. 1938. *Collected Poems.* London: Cassell.

———. 1951. *Poems and Satires 1951.* London: Cassell.

———. 1958. *Steps: Stories, Talks, Essays, Poems, Studies in History.* London: Cassell.

———. 1961a. *More Poems 1961*. London: Cassell.

———. 1961b. *The White Goddess: A Historical Grammar of Poetic Myth*. London: Faber.

———. 1966. *Seventeen Poems Missing from Love Respelt*. London: Privately Printed. Bertram Rota.

———. 1970. *Poems 1968–1970*. London: Cassell.

———. 1971. *The Green-Sailed Vessel: Poems*. First Edition. London: Privately printed. Bertram Rota.

———. 1972. *Poems 1970–1972*. London: Cassell.

———. 1975. *Collected Poems 1975*. London: Cassell.

Hoffman, Daniel. 1967. *Barbarous Knowledge: Myth in the Poetry of Yeats, Graves, and Muir*. New York: Oxford University Press.

Jackson [Riding], Laura. 1972. *The Telling*. London.

Kirkham, Michael. 1969. *The Poetry of Robert Graves*. London: Athlone.

Mallory, E. 1914. "The Mountaineer as Artist." *The Climbers' Club Journal*. n.s., 3 (March): 40.

Opie, Iona, and Peter Opie, eds. 1951. *The Oxford Dictionary of Nursery Rhymes*. Oxford: Oxford University Press.

Seymour-Smith, Martin. 1956. *Robert Graves*. London: British Council and National Book League.

———. [1982] 1995. *Robert Graves: His Life and Work*. Revised edition. London: Bloomsbury.

Wallace, Anne. 1994. *Walking, Literature, and English Culture*. Oxford.

Graves and the Mythology of Desire

Simon Brittan

This brief essay discusses three poems which illustrate a general attitude toward women and toward sexuality, an attitude is displayed throughout Robert Graves's poetry, and one which is very much concerned with idealization. The essay examines what form that idealization takes and looks at the imagery it employs to achieve its effect.

The first of the three poems is "Love in Barrenness," and the second stanza in particular is relevant to the present theme:

> Below the ridge a raven flew
> And we heard the lost curlew
> Mourning out of sight below.
> Mountain tops were touched with snow;
> Even the long dividing plain
> Showed no wealth of sheep or grain,
> But fields of boulders lay like corn
> And raven's croak was shepherd's horn
> Where slow cloud-shadow strayed across
> A pasture of thin heath and moss.
>
> The North Wind rose; I saw him press
> With lusty force against your dress,
> Moulding your body's inward grace,
> And streaming off from your set face
> So now no longer flesh and blood,
> But poised in marble flight you stood;
> O wingless victory, loved of men,
> Who could withstand your beauty then?

After the bare, dreary scene set in the first, the shorter second stanza begins on an immediately more hopeful and expectant note, with "The North Wind rose; I saw him press." The image of the wind, personified and endowed with a character of its own by the capitalization, introduces a sense of watchfulness and upward movement into the almost static landscape set in the first stanza. The association is with coldness, but also with a sense of renewal and awakening. Further, the North Wind is Boreas or Ophion, mythologically associated with the Pelasgians, who claimed genesis from Ophion's teeth (Graves 1986, 27–28); also, in the Athene myth, the goddess banished the crow, recalled by the raven of the first stanza, from the Acropolis for bearing tidings of death, and introduced Boreas in the bird's place (100). The Pelasgians, in the widest sense of "all pre-Hellenic inhabitants of Greece," are associated with the custom of erotic orgies (28), and this sexual theme is introduced by the verb "rose" in the first line of the second stanza, and continued into the second line with "I saw him press / With lusty force against your dress." There is a sense here of the poet as outsider or voyeur, as he watches the wind pressing against the woman's dress and accentuating the curves of her body with erotic force. But Graves uses the verb "mould" rather than "accentuate"—"Moulding your body's inward grace" (l.13)—implying that her "body's inward grace" is to adopt a form not its own. Precisely this metamorphosis takes place, beginning in the following line, "And streaming off from your set face." Her face is "set" against the wind, but what has begun here is a process of petrifaction, a recurring image in classical mythology: "So now no longer flesh and blood / But poised in marble flight you stood" (2.15–16). If the purpose of classical (or of any) statues of the human form is to preserve a particular interpretation of beauty, the implications of the final two lines—indeed of the whole second stanza—are especially interesting and complex. The couplet "O wingless Victory, loved of men, / Who could withstand your beauty then?" suggests a helplessness, an inability to resist, which was not present when the woman was still "flesh and blood" (l.15), and this in turn implies an attitude to beauty, sexuality, and women in general which relies on a kind of idealization that demands stasis and immobility from its object rather than the "lusty force" demonstrated by the North Wind, or indeed than any manifestation of vivacity. Considered in this way, the "love" and "barrenness" of the poem's title take on meanings other than those first presented to the reader. The initial reaction to the title is likely to be its association with the poet's realization of love amid the barren physical landscape described in the first stanza. But, returning to that stanza, and to the line "But fields of boulders lay like corn" (l.7), we now have the knowledge to see the boulders as the rock from which statues are created, and which by being transformed in this way can come to life. Also, since they now contain the germ, still dormant in the first stanza, of what will become love, and thus a life force (after their encounter with the fertile North Wind) they bear closer resemblance to grains of corn than they first appeared to.

This points to a situation where "love" becomes possible only when its object has become distanced from the lover, or idolater, by taking on a form in which all the attributes of human love and all responses to it are impossible; and it is only in the two final lines of "Love in Barrenness," after the transformation of flesh and blood into marble, that any suggestion of love is made. The suggestion comes in the form, "O wingless Victory, loved of men, / Who could withstand your beauty then?" (2.17–18). By this time, the woman in the poem has become so distanced and impersonal as to be completely removed from human experience, and is now an idealized composite of those characteristics perceived by the poet as essential to a quality or idea in its highest possible form.

But this kind of idealization poses problems for the reader. The poem seems to claim that human love—for the poet at least—is an impossibility, since responses are awakened only after the woman's transformation. Furthermore, the final line, containing the idea of withstanding, suggests that the need to respond has been resisted and that the response now given is the result of helplessness. At the same time, however, there is no sense of real reluctance to submit to the power clearly exerted by this metamorphosed beauty: rather, the impression is of a willingness to succumb combined with a religious awe. But the real problem with this particular idealization is with the suggestion implicit in the penultimate line, "O wingless Victory, loved of men," that the vision of beauty perceived by the poet has universal rather than purely subjective validity.

The version of "Love in Barrenness" I have been discussing is the latest, found in the *Collected Poems* of 1938. The poem first appeared under the title "On the Ridge," in *Oxford Poetry* (1921); it appeared again in *Whipperginny* (1923) with the new title "The Ridge-Top." In the versions of 1921 and 1923, the two final couplets run as follows:

> So now no longer flesh and blood
> But poised in marble *thought* you stood.
> O wingless Victory, loved of men,
> Who could withstand your *triumph* then?

(My italics)

The substitution of "thought" for "flight" and of "triumph" for "beauty" gives an altogether different reading. For Hoffman, (quoted in Quinn 1994) these lines recall the "ancient goddess who rewards her idolater with the indifference of marble" while Quinn finds that "the transformation from living flesh to marble . . . is neither condemned nor romanticized, and that the answer to the question posed in the final couplet is that the woman's triumph is an empty triumph—a victory of barrenness over love consummated" (Quinn 1994, 96–97). What Hoffman seems to ignore, is that it is the poet himself who has brought about the transformation, that is to say, the statuesque qualities of the woman he is observing exist first and foremost in his own perception, so that it is not alone his idolatry, but this perception of her as of stone, that become the object of her "indifference." Viewing the two versions of the two final couplets together strengthens the idea of the equations: thought = triumph; flight = beauty. Both "thought" and "flight" have, in this context, a dehumanizing effect on the woman, and are offered as states of being directly opposed to that of being flesh and blood; the first word "But" of the line "But poised in marble thought/flight you stood" introduces a line which seeks to offer evidence of this dehumanization. But the two equations create very different effects. The coupling of "thought" with "triumph" creates an atmosphere of intellectual coolness and a distance which becomes unbridgeable, and it is "thought," with its suggestion of logic and of actions performed as the result of rational consideration, which triumphs over the poet as though the marble were symbolic of an irrefutable argument. Also, the idea of logical, rational thought processes may be set up to counter the traditional (romantic) cliché of the "poetic," so that (still in the terms of this cliché) the "triumph" becomes one of the intellectual over the passionate.

The later "flight" / "beauty" equation offers an immediately more accessible imagery and one very different from that of the "thought" / "triumph" version: beauty, associated with flight, is here that which cannot be withstood. The whole character of this imagery is, despite the marble, less static and less forbidding, and the nature of the poet's perception of the woman's indifference depends rather on the idea of a sensual, ecstatic soaring than on a more intellectual intimidation. The woman is still powerful, but in a way that conforms to traditionally "poetic" interpretations of unconcerned beauty, and the tone of this version is celebratory as well as implying the poet's feelings of awe.

The theme of the beloved statue occurs in book 10 of Ovid's *Metamorphoses*, in the story of Pygmalion and Galatea, which Graves used for two poems, "Galatea and Pygmalion" and "Pygmalion to Galatea." (The former was probably written after 1937: had it been composed before this date, Graves, who was in need of money, would have been likely to include the poem in *Epilogue* 1 (1935), 2 (1936), or 3 (1937); the latter was written in 1926 and appears in *Poems, 1914–1926*). In *Metamorphoses*, Pygmalion falls in love with an ivory statue he has carved for himself, representing his female ideal and created in response to what he perceived as the licentious nature of woman generally, and in particular to their willingness to prostitution in public. The women concerned are the Propoetides, who dared to deny the divinity of Aphrodite, for which they were punished by being turned to flint. During the Festival of Aphrodite, Pygmalion prays that he may have as his wife "one like the ivory maid"; Aphrodite understands the real meaning of his prayer and gives the statue, who becomes Galatea, the gift of life (*Ovid* 1955, 224–60). In *The Greek Myths,* Graves adopts a version of this myth which holds that Pygmalion carved the statue in the image of Aphrodite, with whom he had fallen in love but who refused to lie with him (211–12). There is no mention of this in Ovid, who states merely that Pygmalion's statue was so skillfully carved as to resemble "a real girl."

The woman we first encounter in "Pygmalion to Galatea" is a transient being between the statuesque and the human. Being able to reach Pygmalion must entail descent: she must step down physically from her pedestal, but there is also the implication of a debasement involved in accepting Pygmalion, who is, despite the moral rectitude he displays in Ovid, a human being and therefore imperfect. Before she steps down she listens to Pygmalion's song, which consists of a sequence of demands and conditions so stringent that they would be more suitably addressed to Galatea as statue than as human.

The first stanza of the song is concerned with Pygmalion's physical ideals:

> As you are woman, so be lovely:
> Fine hair afloat and eyes irradiate,
> Long crafty fingers, fearless carriage,
> And body lissome, neither small nor tall;
> So be lovely!
>
> (2.7–11)

There is an echo here, in "Fine hair afloat," of "Love in Barrenness": "poised in marble flight you stood" (1.16), but the emphasis is generally on perceptions of completeness and perfection: the power implied in "Long crafty fingers, fearless carriage" is balanced against the suppleness of "And body lissome" and the sense of proportion in "neither small nor tall." The final "So be lovely!" reads as a command, but with the stress on the initial "So"—"So be lovely," "Be lovely in this way"—there is an initial indication of Pygmalion's fear that he may be about to lose control over Galatea, and of his desire to create her as human being as he created her as statue.

The second stanza continues this theme of control:

> As you are lovely, so be merciful:
> Yet must your mercy abstain from pity:
> Prize your self-honour, leaving me with mine:
> Love if you will: or stay stone-frozen.
> So be merciful!
>
> (2.12–16)

The imperative, and its accompanying condition, in the fourth line of this stanza, "Love if you will: or stay stone-frozen," entail an acceptance of the three preceding conditions: loving must here be synonymous with being merciful and self-honoring, while not allowing mercy to be confused with or engendered by pity. The introduction of mercy and pity into Pygmalion's song implies the possibility of situations arising which might demand such responses from Galatea. This in turn indicates an acknowledgement on Pygmalion's part that his creation may be more powerful than him, and even morally superior. But being merciful also entails sexual acquiescence, granted in Galatea's reply to the song in lines 38–39: "Pygmalion, as you woke me from the stone, / So shall I you from bonds of sullen flesh."

The song's third stanza concerns Pygmalion's sexual jealousy and his desire that their love should retain a sense of mystery:

> As you are merciful, so be constant:
> I ask not that you should mask your comeliness,
> Yet keep our love aloof and strange,
> Keep it from gluttonous eyes, from stairway gossip,
> So be constant!
>
> (2.17–21)

Pygmalion's use of the word "gluttonous" carries an unintended irony, given that the only eyes likely to behold Galatea are his own; and the apparent concession made in line 18, "I ask not that you should mask your comeliness," is a hollow one and immediately negated by the two following lines, demanding that this love be "aloof and strange." The idea of mystery here can also be taken in a religious sense, with Galatea as goddess and Pygmalion as sole worthy priest. His jealousy continues throughout lines 22–26, which impose further rules to govern Galatea's behavior, and place her within the stifling confines of a private world inhabited by the two lovers only:

> As you are constant, so be various:
> Love comes to sloth without variety.

> Within the limits of our fair-paved garden
> Let fancy like a Proteus range and change.
> So be various!

"Let fancy like a Proteus range and change" probably refers to Proteus as described in the *Odyssey*, who has the ability to metamorphose; but it is tempting to consider the Proteus in *Metamorphoses*, mentioned in the context of his defeat by Perseus, who, by showing Proteus Medusa's head, turns him to stone (Ovid 1955, 111–15). Also interesting is the explanation Pygmalion gives for the necessity for variety: their love will perish without it. The effect of this, and of the whole song, is to create the impression of a Pygmalion who cannot or will not act: it is Galatea who must behave in this or that way and keep Pygmalion constantly entertained in order to sustain the intensity of his feelings towards her.

Lines 27–29 offer a summing-up of Pygmalion's womanly ideal:

> As you are constant, so be woman:
> Graceful in going as well-armed in doing.
> Be witty, kind, enduring, unsubjected.

It is difficult to reconcile "unsubjected" with the preceding twenty-eight lines; but a woman able to do so, to accomplish all the tasks set out for her in Pygmalion's song, while retaining her own freedom, would certainly correspond to the ideal of perfection the song expounds.

Pygmalion's final plea in line 35, "So be mine, as I yours for ever," may also be taken as a threat. He would feel justified in describing a Galatea who accepts all the conditions contained in the song as "mine," in the sense of "you exist solely and entirely as my own creation," and "So be mine," is as much as to say "Either be mine or be not at all," an echo of the "Love if you will: or stay stone-frozen" of line 15.

The final seven lines (37–43), constitute Galatea's reply at the moment of stepping down from her pedestal:

> Down stepped Galatea with a sigh.
> "Pygmalion, as you woke me from the stone,
> So shall I you from bonds of sullen flesh.
> Lovely I am, merciful I shall prove:
> Woman I am, constant as various,
> Not marble-hearted but your own true love.
> Give me an equal kiss, as I kiss you."

The ambiguity of Galatea's descending "with a sigh," with the suggestion of acceptance and regret rather than of eagerness and gratitude, is mirrored by the ambiguity of the final line, "Give me an equal kiss, as I kiss you." Her whole speech serves to point out the futility of Pygmalion's desire to create so unnatural a being as his ideal must ultimately be: since Pygmalion has made her perfect, he cannot ever equal her in any way, and his kiss is bound to be flawed. Able to meet all the demands of his song, she suddenly subverts their whole meaning by imposing a condition upon Pygmalion himself. The only release she can offer from this trap is release from the "bonds of his flesh," which in the light of what must be the nature of their relationship may well be "sullen"; so it becomes ominous that of all the conditions she vows to fulfil in her summary of lines 40–42 above, the idea of her mercy abstaining from pity, demanded in line 13, remains unmentioned.

The irony of "Pygmalion to Galatea" lies in the relation between desire, intention, and results. Pygmalion is moved, by women who of necessity fail to meet his overexalted ideals, to create an object he can see as worthy of his adulation, and this quite clearly must be a goddess-like statue. But he fails to see that the perfection of his creation will place him in precisely the same position as the "imperfect" women who first inspired him to create Galatea. In her statuesque form she is exactly as he wishes, and he can worship at ease, but in human form she can continually remind him of his foolhardy desire for her to be endowed with life, and the only thing she can offer him that as a statue she could not is the gratification of his sexual desire. As a statue she could, by her very silence, be merciful, without pity, beautiful, certainly constant, aloof and strange—all the conditions he must impose on a human Galatea are already fulfilled by her as a statue: by seeking to mate with a goddess, he has placed himself entirely at her mercy, and he himself, as much as Galatea, is a prisoner in their "fair-paved garden" (l.24).

Finally, Graves's poem "Galatea and Pygmalion" represents a complete dismantling of the relationship between idol and worshipper that has been constructed in "Love in Barrenness" and developed in "Pygmalion to Galatea":

> Galatea, whom his furious chisel
> From Parian stone had by greed enchanted,
> Fulfilled, they say, all Pygmalion's longings:
>   Stepped down from that pedestal on which she stood,
> Bare in his bed laid her down, lubricious,

>   With low responses to his drunken raptures,
>   Enroyalled his body with her demon blood.
>
> Yet young Pygmalion had so well plotted
> The art-perfection of his woman monster
> That schools of eager connoisseurs beset
>   Her famous person with perennial suit;
> Whom she (a judgement on the jealous artist)
> Admitted rankly to a comprehension
>   Of themes that crowned her own, not his repute.

It is as though Graves's concern here is to descend Plato's ladder, just as Galatea must step down from her pedestal, and to leave behind all the imagery of the divine and the universal, concentrating instead on the carnal and the individual. What occurs is a subversion of the idea of Galatea's purity, which must in turn entail a negation of her very self according to the reasoning that led to her creation. At the same time, Pygmalion takes on characteristics of the kind which, according to Ovid, he so much despised as to reject what he perceived as human passion in favor of the worship of a mute ideal. His desire to keep Galatea from the eyes of the world now reveals itself as nothing more than "greed" (1.2), his love as "drunken raptures" (1.6). What this poem is at pains to convey is a sense of irony—the use of the word "enroyalled" in line 7 is a good example—and it is stressed that it is Pygmalion's body, not his spirit, which undergoes this "ennobling" process—another anti-Platonic device. (The idea of the Academy is repeated in line 10, where "schools" of eager would-be lovers await their turn.) Furthermore, Galatea is now no longer either goddess or saint, but "demon" (1.7), so that the whole quasi-religious construct of the first two poems is finally undermined.

One key to this poem is the parenthetical justification of Galatea's actions as a "judgement on the jealous artist." Pygmalion's jealousy is clearly signified by his construction of a "fair-paved garden" in which to keep Galatea's beauty far from "gluttonous eyes." But his seclusion of Galatea denotes more than sexual jealousy. Galatea is Pygmalion's creation, quite literally a work of art, and if her admission of suitors to "a comprehension / Of themes that crowned her own" repute (2.13–14) is "a judgement on the jealous artist" (1.12) then there is an implication of a belief on Graves's part that to rarify art by seclusion is a morally reprehensible act: Pygmalion gets what he deserves. Given Graves' physical removal to Majorca, and his own artistic seclusion—his stubborn refusal to accept the poetics of modernism—this is an unusual belief for him to voice. This poem was written around the time of Auden's powerful advocacy of art as public property, and the animosity Graves bore Auden is well documented; but this is also the period when Laura Riding claims to have become a socialist, and it is likely that under her tuteledge Graves felt obliged to give Auden's ideas serious consideration, however reluctantly. There also remains the poem's statement on the nature of art: that any attempt to control it once it has been executed is doomed to failure—another interesting point in the light of Graves's constant revisions of his own work.

Works Cited

Graves, Robert. 1922. *Whipperginny*. London: Heinemann.
———. 1938. *Collected Poems*. New York: Random House.
———. 1959. *Collected Poems, 1959*. London: Cassell.
———. 1986. *The Greek Myths*. 2 vols. Harmondsworth: Penguin.
Ovid. 1955. *Metamorphoses*. Translated and edited by Mary M. Innes. Harmondsworth: Penguin.
Quinn, Patrick. 1994. *The Great War and the Missing Muse*. Selinsgrove: Susquehanna University Press.

The Breaking of the Spell: Graves's Dissatisfaction Poetry of 1937

PATRICK QUINN

IN EARLY 1937 ROBERT GRAVES AND LAURA RIDING WERE RENTING ACCOMMODATION in Lugano. Riding was interested in establishing some form of insiders' group to discuss the ways in which the world could be kept from falling victim to the irrationality of totalitarian regimes. This conviction was to lead eventually to the publication of *The World and Ourselves* and *The Covenant of Literal Morality* the following year, both of which documents sought to present political solutions to the European crisis, which was imminent in 1937.

Although Graves was sympathetic to Riding's loathing of fascism, he appears to have felt threatened by her defection from what he saw as the purely poetical nature of their vocation. By way of protest, he wrote "The Fallen Tower of Siloam," which can be read on one level as a pointed rebuke at Riding's backsliding into the public world of politics but, on another, as a celebration of the poet's aloofness and satisfaction in self-containment. The poem could even be said to augur the devastation of the corrupt world to which Graves believed he had said good-bye in 1929, but which still polluted his personal and poetic life. Symbolically, when the Tower of Siloam collapses, true poets such as Graves and Riding will recollect

> how grim it stood,
> . . . and what great fissures ran
> Up the west wall, how rotten the under-pinning
> At the south-eastern angle.

Until the corrupt world collapses and powders "the air with chalk," the poets must "be silent in Siloam, to fortell / No visible calamity." In other words, true poets should not write about the temporal nature of political events. This gentle rebuke to his mentor and Muse-figure marks the beginning of a series of literary and philosophical fissures which were to place strain on what had hitherto been an exceedingly productive poetic partnership between Graves and Riding.

Three particular poems written by Graves in 1937 illustrate how he was beginning to distance himself from Riding's unquestioning domination and beginning to oppose the poetic and political philosophies that she espoused, and that he had marginally embraced previously. In "The Laureate," "Galatea to Pygmalion," and "Leda," Graves not only criticises Riding's shift of opinion about the role of poetry for political ends, but he also confronts her demands that celibacy be a precondition for poetic inspiration.

"The Laureate" was written between 30 April and 4 May against the backdrop of the Guernica massacre and fears of war breaking out in Czechoslovakia. These developments troubled both Graves and Riding; yet, instead of writing at this time about the impending threat of war or about his unease brought on by the political situation in Spain, Graves was busy crafting a poem which was to reflect in part his feelings about those writers who had allied their artistic integrity with a political cause.

The poem is most likely addressed to W. H. Auden, who had written on 29 April 1937 to Riding requesting a number of poems for inclusion in a Random House anthology. Graves, who had little respect for Auden or for his poetry, had been in contact with him some ten years previously to complain that he (Auden) had borrowed significantly and without permission from Riding's poem "Love as Love, Death as Death." The "detestation" of Auden which R. P. Graves claims existed might be rather overstated (304), but the ill-feeling which Graves bore toward his contemporary was evident and must have arisen to some extent from his conviction that Auden represented an antipoetic influence. In Graves's words, he was "a synthetic poet, plagiarising in a curiously wholesale way. He gets hold of some good piece of work by someone which is not too well known, and vulgarises it. Homosexual and parlour communist" (O'Prey 1982, 263). According to Seymour-Smith, Graves's own justification for the poem is that it might be a description of any written-out poet like John Masefield (289), but the question of to whom the poem was addressed is not as important as the disturbing philosophical implications imbedded in the poem.

"The Laureate" centers upon a poet whose previous work has been inspired from within, from the poetic soul, but in this poem he is transformed metaphorically into a lizard, a cold-blooded creature which draws its heat from the sun: in other words, from external sources. He keeps his place in the sun by serving his adoring public, whose whims he follows just as the head of a sunflower follows the course of the sun across the sky. "The Laureate" provides an unequivocal assertion of Graves's belief that yoking poetic inclination to the pursuit of popular fame is tantamount to committing artistic suicide:

> Once long ago here was a poet; who died.
> See how remorse twitching his mouth proclaims
> It was no natural death, but suicide.

Graves feared that Laura Riding's interest in poetry was on the wane, that her energy was being channeled wastefully into the various political causes she had adopted. In *Epilogue 3,* Riding had shown that she was concerned about international politics, women's rights, and public morality, with the result that—as Graves perceived it—she was slowly drifting away from the poetic credos that she espoused in the 1920s and early 1930s. It is not at all unlikely that Graves was reconsidering his and Riding's cowritten essay "Politics and Poetry," which had appeared in *Epilogue 3* just days earlier, and wondering how Riding's conception of the poet's role had undergone such a significant alteration in such a short period. A brief passage of the *Epilogue* piece illustrates the point:

> The peculiar attraction which the political cause has for poets is to be explained by their rooted conviction that they are good. The goodness of poets and poetry is unquestionable, but it is not a goodness to be piously exemplified in a partisanship of humanitarian causes. . . . Goody-goody humanitarian causes draw them easily into membership by making them wince at the notion of all the injustices prevalent in the world of physical consciousness. Let it be declared as clearly as possible that the goodness of poetry is not moral goodness, the goodness of temporal action, but the goodness of thought, the loving exercise of the will in the pursuit of truth. Moral definitions may be invented for historical emergencies, but when a historical emergency passes, the moral definition passes with it. . . . The poet is concerned with truth which is not a historical product but which is always there of itself because it *is* reality: he is concerned with final truth only. (Graves 1949, 283–84)

At the time of writing "The Laureate" (with its obvious pun in the title), Graves must have been questioning why Riding was deviating from these sentiments; but the dynamics of their personal relationship prohibited him from broaching the subject directly without fear of recrimination. He therefore turned to poetry to deliver his message: to illustrate what might result if he were to abandon his true poetic vocation in favor of Riding's new enthusiasms:

> Like a lizard in the sun, though not scuttling
> When men approach, this wretch, this thing of rage,
> Scowls and sits rhyming in his horny age.
>
> Arrogant, lean, unvenerable, he
> Still turns for comfort to the western flames
> That glitter a cold span above the sea.

Here we have the husk of the embittered poet, sitting lizardlike, writing meaningless rhymes. Having abandoned his art, he is left unloved and unhappy, glimpsing the "flames" of his potential in the rainbow that bridges the "cold span above the sea."

As far as Graves was concerned, to subordinate one's craft to a political agenda (as Auden and Spender were to do in the 1930s) could result only in failure. His anxiety about Riding's drift towards politics, rather than poetics, was growing but at the same time he was beset by another difficulty which had emanated from their relationship. In "The Laureate" Graves makes allusion, either consciously or unconsciously, to the problem of sexuality, which seems to have dogged him throughout the 1930s. The reference to "horny age" in the above stanza is telling, for it subverts the expectation that the adjective should read "hoary"; indeed, Graves turns the phrase on its head by his use of a term which even in 1937 had connotations of lechery. This projection of the poet as an unfulfilled lover is sounded as a leitmotif through several poems written in 1937.

One of the cornerstones of Riding's philosophy, that "bodies have had their day," had forced Graves to pledge himself—ideologically at least—to a celibate lifestyle. Admittedly, a lapse in Graves's commitment to this ideology occurred in 1931 with a young German woman, Elfriede Faust, later Norman Cameron's wife. R. P. Graves quotes a letter to the artist John Aldridge from Riding explaining that she had granted a dispensation in Elfriede's case because Elfriede's body could be seen as an extension of that which she herself denied to Robert (162). The subsequent emotional complications of Elfriede's unexpected pregnancy may have distracted Robert from the notion of sex for several years, but the struggle between sexuality and the celibate life became an increasingly complex issue for him. The denial of his natural urges were evident in his poetry as early as 1933, as the witty "Down, Wanton, Down" illustrates. With his forced repatriation to London in August, 1936, Graves found himself back in the social circles which he had abandoned, and his diary entries suggest that he was not immune at that time to the sexual vivacity of new friends such as Robin Hale and old friends such as Mary Ellidge.

The intervening six celibate years between Graves's affair with Elfriede and his questioning of Riding's philosophy engendered a poem which he drafted while recovering from a colon operation. R. P. Graves points out that during his recuperation he was emotionally dependent on Riding, yet guilty at the same time on account of his lustful reflections and doubts about her dedication to the craft of poetry (272). At first glance "Leda" would appear to be a poem confirming Graves's faith in his lover's celibate decrees. But is such an interpretation overly simplistic? The short three stanza poem, "Leda," needs to be read in its entirety for an answer:

> Heart, with what lonely fears you ached,
>   How lecherously mused upon
> That horror with which Leda quaked
>   Under the spread wings of the swan.
>
> Then soon your mad religious smile
>   Made taut the belly, arched the breast,
> And there beneath your god awhile
>   You strained and gulped your beastliest.
>
> Pregnant you are, as Leda was,
>   Of bawdry, murder and deceit;
> Perpetuating night because
>   Stale after-languors hang so sweet.

In mythology, Leda was the wife of Tyndareus, king of Sparta. She bore four children to Zeus, who, having visited her in the shape of a swan, impregnated her, with the result that four offspring were born from two eggs. From one sprang Pollux and Helen, from the other Castor and Clytemnestra—representations of love and death (as some commentators have pointed out). In the myth there is little made of the rape itself, but the scene clearly made an impact on Yeats, who produced from the theme his poem of 1923, "Leda and the Swan." In his poem, Yeats tells the story of the swan's violation of Leda, but for her pains she is at least permitted a glimpse into the future. Graves's version of the tale has no such redeeming feature for the victim; the raping of his innocent heart by the wanton swan appears at first reading to offer nothing but horror.

The second stanza of Graves's "Leda" describes how, when Leda's sexuality is awakened and she realizes with whom she is having sex, she smiles at the anticipation of physical pleasure: her stomach is tightened and her back is arched to ensure that she may enjoy the deepest and fullest penetration. In the dance of sex, Leda strains and becomes one with the swan in her beastly enjoyment, her mind becoming subordinate to her senses. Herein is the homage to Laura Riding, for Graves suggests that by surrendering to sensual pleasure, the human is reduced to the status of a dumb beast, reminiscent of the Circe myth perhaps.

Nicholas Carter, in his study *Robert Graves: The Lasting Poetic Achievement*, goes so far as to say that the poem is flagellatory in a medieval sense. For Carter, the poem provides not only justification for the asceticism that Graves had been forced to practice, but also an admonition against masturbation (74); it also gives clear indication, according to Carter's erring interpretation, of the obeisance that Graves paid to Riding, who had made him slavishly servile to her demands of chastity, and whose domination anticipated the advent of the White Goddess a decade later.

But what are we to make of the last two lines, "Perpetuating night because / Stale after-langours hang so sweet."? Richard Hoffpauir is the only critic who offers a plausible answer to this puzzle when he suggests that Shakespeare's Sonnet 129 ("The expense of spirit in a waste of shame") might be useful in an interpretation of Graves's meaning (Sonnet 129 being the same poem which Riding and Graves dissected in their *Modernist Poetry* to demonstrate the way in which editors make significant changes to the meanings of poems by modifying spelling and punctuation as they see fit). The octet of Shakespeare's sonnet is reminiscent of "Leda":

> Th' expense of Spirit in a waste of shame
> Is lust in action, and till action, lust
> Is periurd, murdrous, blouddy full of blame,
> Sauage, extreame, rude, cruell, not to trust,
> Inioyd no sooner but dispised straight,
> Past reason hunted, and no sooner had
> Past reason hated as a swollowed bayt,
> On purpose layd to make the taker mad.

Graves's interpretation of the sonnet, as he explains it in *Modernist Poetry*, is germane to the understanding of "Leda." He clarifies the conflict between lust and pleasure thus:

The character and the moral of lust the whole world well knows, but no one knows the character and the moral really well unless he disregards the moral warning and engages in lust; no one knows lust well enough to shun it because, though he knows it is both heavenly and hellish, lust can never be recognized until it has proved itself lust by turning heaven into hell. (Graves 1949, 91)

With this clarification in mind, the final two lines of Leda become less problematic. Despite the admonishments of Riding, Graves recognizes the sweetness in the "stale after-langours." The enlightened choice of the word "languors," with its double entendre of mental suffering coupled with fatigue of the body is particularly apt. Lust, for the poet, is a disease, but it is also a source of energy from which life is experienced and poetry is created. To deny this duality is to deny a dimension of the poet's existence. (Coincidentally, Graves's first meeting with his future wife, Beryl Pritchard, took place while he was correcting proofs of "Leda," and this meeting—for those who believe romantically in love at first sight—might have exacerbated the sexual tensions that Riding's enforced chastity engendered.)

By 10 July Graves was recovering comfortably from his successful operation and was revising a poem which he had written in 1925, "Pygmalion to Galatea." While making revisions, Graves felt inclined to formulate a variation on the theme and wrote "Galatea to Pygmalion." According to Ovid, the women of Cyprus refused to venerate the goddess Venus; for revenge she cast a spell to make them sexually insatiable. Pygmalion, a young sculptor, was so outraged by his local women's licentious behavior that he lived alone and fashioned his own woman out of ivory. In love with his own creation, Pygmalion prayed to Venus that his art would be made flesh, and Galatea was magically created from the ivory by the goddess herself.

The first seven lines of Graves's poem recount the moment when Galatea steps off her pedestal; the last read as follows:

> Bare in his bed laid her down, lubricious,
> With low responses to his drunken raptures,
> Enroyalled his body with her demon blood.

The use of "lubricious," suggesting the smoothness of Galatea's marble body turned flesh, is chosen carefully to jar with its secondary meaning of lewdness or wantonness. The suggestion is that once freed from her marmoreal state of rigidity, from the fixedness of her artistic state, she responds in a lascivious manner, which catches her creator off guard. Her "low responses" to his drunken raptures somehow "enroyal his body" with "her demon blood." But why "demon" blood? And why, in the ninth line, does Pygmalion's creation become a "woman monster"? The answer is his dream woman, the creation of his own imagination, has made him a victim of her own whims and played on his jealousy. By the final stanza she is so much in demand that "schools of eager connoisseurs beset / Her single person with perennial suit"; Pygmalion is left bereft of her attention and love.

The correspondences between Graves's relationship with Riding and Pygmalion's with Galatea as they are articulated in this poem appear obvious enough; and on one level the poem is an allegory of a fading relationship. When they first met in 1926, Riding was, according to Miranda Seymour, "a woman [who] . . . fit . . . [Graves's] idea of a goddess, an omnipotent being" (131). By 1927, R. P. Graves informs us, "there . . . [was] no doubt that to be loved and directed by someone of Riding's evident brilliance and authority . . . was restoring Robert's integrity and calming his nerves" (55). Despite the complications of his broken marriage and the difficulties with repatriation to Majorca with Laura, Graves was more than willing to sacrifice his personal liberty in Riding's service in exchange for the betterment of his poetic consciousness. But by 1937 Riding's increasing engagement with political issues and public concerns was in conflict with the ideas she had encouraged Graves to accept incontestably: that the role of the poet was an exclusive one, and that historical time had effectively come to an end. Graves was troubled by this apostasy; and the last three lines of "Galatea and Pygmalion" air that betrayal:

> she [Galatea] (a judgement on the jealous artist)
> Admitted rankly to a comprehension
> Of themes that crowned her own, not his repute.

Riding's call for a collectivist effort of right-minded people to stop the patriarchal madness which was condemning humanity to destruction was problematic for Graves. The thought of sharing Riding with other people and external causes had very little appeal for him; moreover, he feared that success in the political realm would further alienate her from what he considered to be her true vocation: the writing of poetry. His fears later proved to be valid.

Throughout the remainder of 1937, Riding distanced herself from their joint poetic endeavors and grew more and more preoccupied with the writing of a dictionary and with political activism. She became so encumbered with these concerns that she reinvented herself in almost every way. It is perhaps fitting that the last poem in her *Collected Poems (1938)* is aptly entitled "Christmas 1937," marking the renunciation of her poetic career and the celebration of her nativity as a seeker after what Barbara Adams calls "purifying diction" for the achievement of truth (95).

102   PART TWO: POETRY

The despondency felt by Graves as he watched Riding drift further away from him is reflected in the number and kinds of revisions which he made to "Galatea to Pygmalion" between the conception of the poem in July and its final form in late October 1937. In the earlier drafts (written when Graves was recovering from his hospitalization) Galatea steps down from the pedestal and Pygmalion

> Bare in his bed laid her down obedient
> To lilt responses to his lively raptures,
> Enroyal his body with her beating blood.

There is no suggestion here of the bitterness that was to emerge in later versions. There is no suggestion of the lowness of Galatea's sexual responses, and here her rhythmic gyrations "enroyal" his body with "her beating blood." The image of Galatea as a "woman monster" in line 9 of the final draft is nowhere to be found; she is described simply as a being of "Greek perfection." Admittedly, all the drafts conclude with the offering of Galatea's favors to lesser men in order to aggravate Pygmalion's jealousy, but the growing rancour of tone through the drafting process suggests that Graves was certainly feeling intensely the lacerations of Riding's artistic and philosophical betrayal by the end of 1937.

Possibly, the early drafts have some biographical reference to Graves's troubled emotional condition as he helplessly observed Riding's overt flirtations with the young poet Harry Kemp during their collaboration on the political essay "The Left Heresy." By the end of the year, Graves's mood had grown sullen, and his faith in Riding had worn thin. And if Nicholas Carter's informed assumption that "No More Ghosts" is a love poem written to Beryl is accurate (Carter 1989, 64), perhaps then the scepter of that domination under which Graves had labored so faithfully for many years was soon to be broken by a more powerful spell: that of a kinder and more balanced love.

> We are restored to simple days, are free
> From cramps of dark necessity.
> And one another recognize
> By an immediate love that signals at our eyes.
>
> No new ghost can appear. Their poor cause
> Was that time freezes, and time thaws;

But here only such loves can last
As do not ride upon the weathers of the past.

WORKS CITED

Adams, Barbara. 1990. *The Enemy Self: Poetry and Criticism of Laura Riding.* Ann Arbor: UMI Research Press.

Carter, D. N. G. 1989. *Robert Graves: The Lasting Poetic Achievement.* Totowa, N. J.: Barnes and Noble.

Graves, Richard Perceval. 1990. *Robert Graves: The Years With Laura, 1926–1940.* London: Viking.

Graves, Robert. 1949. *The Common Asphodel: Collected Essays on Poetry 1922–1949.* London: Hamish Hamilton.

———. 1997. *Robert Graves: The Complete Poems.* Vol. 2. Manchester: Carcanet Press.

Hoffpauir, Richard. 1988. "The Love Poetry of Robert Graves." *University of Toronto Quarterly* 57:422–38.

O'Prey, Paul, ed. 1982. *In Broken Images: Selected Letters of Robert Graves, 1914–1946.* London: Hutchinson.

Seymour, Miranda. 1995. *Robert Graves: Life on the Edge.* London: Doubleday.

Seymour-Smith, Martin. 1982. *Robert Graves: His Life and Works.* London: Hutchinson.

Part III
Fiction

"Epics Are Out of Fashion": Graves's Short Story as a Model for His Longer Fiction's Narrative Techniques

IAN FIRLA

THE PAUCITY OF RESEARCH INTO THE SUBJECT OF GRAVES' FICTIONAL TECHniques, recent work by John Presley (Presley 1997) not withstanding, has left a gap in Gravesian scholarship that needs to be redressed. The short story "Epics Are Out of Fashion," besides being witty and offering an insight into some of Graves's personal likes and dislikes among the Latin poets of Nero's court, reveals a narrative technique which is apparently simple, but which contains intricacies and subtleties that, upon close examination, expose the structure of some of Graves's best known historical novels.

The proverbial "narrative hook" of "Epics Are Out of Fashion" is organized around a tension between "amazing event" and blasé reaction similar to that established by Graves in his critically acclaimed short story *The Shout*. *The Shout* was the first major piece of short fiction published by Graves. It appeared in the same year as *Goodbye to All That,* but according to Martin Seymour-Smith it was written in 1924 (117),[1] which predates even *My Head! My Head!* and, very significantly, the writing and publication of *A Survey of Modernist Poetry*. The dating of the original writing of *The Shout* is important. Graves, like most writers, varied his beliefs and allegiances over his career. When he first wrote the story, his opinions (later, mostly negative) of his modernist peers had not yet been formulated fully.

At first glance, the two stories, *The Shout* and "Epics Are Out of Fashion," could not seem more different. The narrative of *The Shout* is nonlinear, the notion of "self" in the story is shown to be fragile and easily fragmented, and the story is permeated with a particular psychological unease manifest in the polyphonous narrative confluence within the story: a combination of features that can be considered hallmarks of almost any modernist writer.

---

[1] R. P. Graves insists that the story was not completed until 1927 (Graves 1990, 25).

"Epics Are Out of Fashion," on the other hand, reads distinctly like the sort of traditionalist, conservative effort that is most commonly associated with Graves's name. There will be no attempt here to associate the Graves writing in the 1950s with a lingering modernist tradition nor to propose that, even in spirit, Graves maintained some kind of subconscious affinity with the movement that he so often derided; however, it will be argued that the differences between stories like *The Shout* and "Epics Are Out of Fashion" are predominantly stylistic and, by extension, that one can find distinctive features in both stories that can be associated with his historical fiction.

All three of Graves's biographers note Graves's claim that the protagonist of *The Shout*, Richard, was a surrogate for himself (e.g., Seymour-Smith, 117). The "deepest meaning" of the story, according to Seymour-Smith, is that the magician's shout can be paralleled with the practice of poetry in which Graves recognized "destructiveness" and something which he cagily refers to as "overtones even more sinister" (118) than the self-destructiveness of the poet through his craft. But Seymour-Smith does not offer an explanation of what these sinister overtones might be. He does claim, in an effort to extend the connection between the story and practice of poetry, that the shout "is not delivered by one of the right sex" (118). Presumably then, Seymour-Smith believes that the shout can be read as a metaphor for the sirenlike calling of the Muse to the poet.

The call of a Muse though, seems to impose, on Graves, an aspect of his work which may not yet be due the attention Seymour-Smith gives to it at such an early stage of Graves's career. Rather, the "shout" can be considered as a reflection of Graves's particular attraction/revulsion to the psychoanalytic methods of W. H. R. Rivers. In this formula, rather than the call of a Muse, the "shout" should be read as a metaphor for Rivers's prescription of purgative writing of poetry to vent the psychological traumas of a neurasthenic patient.

Both Patrick Quinn and Michael Kirkham identify the importance of Graves's study *The Meaning of Dreams* to the poetry he was in the early twenties. Quinn, for example, writes that "Graves was afraid that psychoanalysis would dry up his inspiration as it cured his neurasthenia" (Quinn 1994, 85). What has not been commented upon though, is that *The Shout* can be read as a story whose principle concern is exactly that which is identified by Graves in *The Meaning of Dreams* and which is recognized in his poetry. Crossley's psychological traumas can be paralleled easily with Graves's own, while the frustration of the cuckolded Richard can be recognized for the other, nonpoetic aspect of Graves's character. Where Crossley represents magic and experience, Graves, the neurasthenic soldier-poet in the story-as-autobiography can be clearly detected, while Richard can be read as the suppressed (or superseded) Graves of the middle-class, public-schoolboy upbringing. The narrator of the story then, is a third Graves: the one who hears Crossley's fantastic story (as Graves might interpret his own dreams) and then realizes the horrifying reality from the resultant fantasy:

> I put my fingers to my ears and ran out of the scoring box. I had run perhaps twenty yards, when an indescribable pang of fire spun me about and left me dazed and numbed. I escaped death somehow; I suppose that I am lucky, like the Richard of the story. But the lightening struck Crossley and the doctor dead. (21)

Not only does Graves blend traditional author/implied-author boundaries in this story, he also transgresses conventional narrative limitations by giving each story embedded within the principal narrative a part in the tragic conflation of coincidence in the conclusion. Though the story is narrated without the usual modernist stylistic innovations, its metafictive construct charges the tale with extratextual meaning.

Ultimately, the horrifying reality realized in *The Shout* lies in the recognition that, metaphorically, the poet-in-Graves might die. Quinn observes in Graves's self-analysis of his poem "The Gnat" that the magical aspect of the Gravesian trinity, the magician/poet, is threatened. And the possibility for the loss of magic (where magic is associated with the practice of writing poetry) is the horror of the story. When the narrator encounters Richard and Rachel after the events at the asylum, he receives the following soulless response:

> Richard looked blank; Rachel said: "Crossley? I think that was the man who called himself the Australian Illusionist and gave that wonderful conjuring show the other day. He had practically no apparatus but a black silk handkerchief. I liked his face so much. Oh, and Richard didn't like it at all."
> "No, I couldn't stand the way he looked at you all the time," Richard said. (22)

Richard and Rachel's blasé reaction to the recounted events of the story discredits the vivacity with which the narrator has recounted his incredible tale and reflects the tension Graves felt between himself (as a war veteran, poet, and writer) and English society. In effect, Richard and Rachel can be seen to represent the bourgeois and commonsensical element of British society to whom Graves was forced, as a result of their indifference to his neurasthenic traumas and literary aspirations, to say "good-bye."

Paul Fussell, in *The Great War and Modern Memory*, describes the division between society and himself that Graves felt so acutely:

> Everyone who remembers a war first-hand knows that is images remain in the memory with special vividness. The very enormity of the proceedings, their absurd remove from the usages of the normal world, will guarantee that a structure of irony sufficient for ready narrative recall will attach to them. And the irony need not be Gravesian and extravagant. (326)

But for Graves it was necessarily extravagant. Gravesian irony is predominantly situational and, furthermore, frustrating because it was Graves himself who was, unhappily, the central device for what must have begun to seem a self-fulfilling prophecy: the more distant the war became in collective societal memory expressed in media such as noncombatant popular fiction, then it was more than likely that his memoir would be read as a "kind of fiction" (Fussell 1977, 310). In Graves's case the longer his neurasthenia persisted, then all the more the events that Graves lived through began to be ascribed with an unreal and mythic quality by those who encountered Graves and his suffering. But Graves's mental suffering was too real—a reality closely felt which produced a paradoxical state, expressable only through writings with multiple degrees of irony, that can only have exacerbated Graves's condition.

Graves's frustration can be recognized in the resigned tone of the conclusion of *The Shout*. Just as the "myth" (which Crossley described and which was confirmed by the events that concluded the cricket match) had its significance for the narrator abruptly denied by Richard and Rachel, so too must Graves have begun to question the validity of his own experiences—a validity he desperately appealed for in *Good-Bye to All That*, but which he ultimately denies in the dedicatory epilogue by descrediting them as "anecdotal."

Why does he descredit his own story? The influence of Riding on Graves at this time cannot be underestimated. Graves begins the dedicatory epilogue to *Good-Bye to All That* by explaining why he chose not to include Riding in the body of his autobiography. He claims that "by mentioning you [Riding] as a character in my autobiography I would seem to be denying you in your true quality of one living invisibly, against kind, as dead, beyond event" (321). In other words, by appearing in the autobiography, Riding, as a person who was, at the time, very much a part of Graves's life, would have her past cast unmutably as a textual present. She would forever remain known, at least to Graves's readers, in the way he describes her rather than as a living, breathing, and *changing* individual. Clearly, while Graves was determined to say "Good-bye to you and to you and to you and to me and to all that" (5), Riding was not to be included in that breezy catalog. Riding then, can be seen to be the catalyst for Graves's expurgation of his former self. Through dedicating himself to her way of life and her approach to being-in-the-world, Graves is running from his unhappy past to what he hopes will be an idylic future.

The running away from troubles is the central theme of "Epics Are Out of Fashion" as well. The story describes, from the point of view of its narrator, the demise of Lucan and Petronius in Nero's court. Lucan, foolishly according to Petronius, is in the process of writing his epic on the Civil Wars. Nero, at the same time, is endeavoring to complete a similar project. The danger to Lucan in the story is clear: an arrogant and egotistical Nero would be unable to acknowledge that his underling, Lucan, was a better poet. Had Nero's epic been declaimed contemporaneously with Lucan's, the public would have seen the lesser quality of Nero's verses (for as Petronius tells us, "nobody denies that you're the greatest poet in the world" [Graves 1995, *Complete* 119]). Nero, naturally, had to dispatch with Lucan (or at the very least his epic) before his public humiliation were allowed to occur.

Graves has Petronius strongly, yet tactfully, recommends that Lucan cease writing by claiming that "epics are ridiculously out of fashion!" (117). Lucan becomes infuriated with what he recognizes as censure by Nero, declaims his work at a public banquet, is ordered not to write verse by Nero, becomes enraged with this infringement on what he perceives to be his artistic right, and begins plotting to assassinate Nero. Nero discovers the plot and orders Lucan to open his wrists in a warm bath. Before dispatching himself, Lucan condemns Petronius to Nero by explaining the subversive image of Nero that Petronius has sketched as a part of his "Trimalchio portrait." A panicky Nero decides that it is time that the court be "cleansed," and so Seneca and others are ordered to "the baths." A general sense of panic takes over the court which is the moment that the narrator chooses to flee Rome for Greece. From the relative safety of Greece, the narrator writes his account of the events.

A feature that emerges from this story that might almost be described as characteristic of Graves's fiction is the narrator's representation of himself to his audience. In "Epics Are Out of Fashion" the narrator presents himself as a dullard who is, by familial connections, intimately associated with the figures around whom the story takes place—figures about whom the reader is, by the narrator's stated intentions, intended to hold an interest more significant than for that of himself. But it is the speaker who, ultimately, attracts the most attention by subtle and suggestive narrative turns: it is as a result of the narrator's actions that Petronius is first allowed to tell Lucan of Nero's scandalous proclamation, and it is the narrator whom Petronious implores to appeal to Lucan in order to prevent him from antagonising Nero further (an appeal the narrator never makes to Lucan).

Graves's *Good-Bye to All That* is a very good example of a "story"—an "autobiography"—which is fascinating in itself but a story whose substance is overshadowed by the narrator's presence. Graves begins *Good-Bye to All That* by summarily accounting for the "stock" events of his life in a very matter-of-fact tone: "As a proof of my readiness to accept autobiographical convention, let me at once record my two earliest memories" (9). As the self-deprecatory tone of this and many other passages indicates, the speaker is not the person whom the reader is *supposed* to have his or her interest held by. Rather, the story of the autobiographer's life rather than the autobiographer himself is what is *supposed* to be gripping. In other words, Graves organizes the retelling of his life story such that he seems more an observer than a participant in the events; or, at least, that his participation is negligible and certainly uninteresting relative to the "chaps" about whom he has written: much like the narrator of "Epics Are Out of Fashion."

In the case of *Good-Bye to All That*, the story of a young man's war experiences and his subsequent realization that his country has betrayed him and thousands of others like him is what is "supposed" to interest the reader. But the speaker is telling a well-known tale and we, the readers, find ourselves drawn toward him, his idiosyncrasies, and his personality more than a story which, as has been demonstrated by a number of his peers (namely Edmund Blunden and Siegfried Sassoon), is flawed by inaccuracies in fundamental details. Graves, clearly, was not very interested in getting "facts" right.

Graves's use of "untruths," or at the very least transmitting events which were merely colloquial tales in the mess halls of the infantry as personal experience,[2] confuses conventional critical receptions

---

[2] Blunden and Sassoon marked up a copy of a *Good-Bye to All That* demonstrating the moments where Graves's facts were wrong. The "mistakes" identified by the two soldier-poets are refered to by R. P. Graves in an appendix to his 1995 edited version of the 1929 edition of *Good-Bye to All That*.

of autobiography. Indeed, traditional structuralist-critical techniques are beguiled by an author who shows autobiographical convention so little respect. Graves, clearly, was more interested in an oral storytelling tradition—a storytelling which is more concerned with moral guidance for the audience than with journalistically faithful reportage of fact. While the fictions of the mess hall may or may not have actually been experienced by any one soldier, they amount to a story of the collective myth of the soldiering experience—a collective myth grounded in truth because *someone,* if not the narrator, then someone else, experienced the events and, therefore, the experience is meaningful.

Wallace Martin describes this complication to structuralist analysis in his work *Recent Theories of Narrative:*

> In almost every respect, the questions the anthropologist must try to answer are the opposite of those posed by the literary critic: not "why is this story unique"? but "how and why is it so similar to others"?; not "what did this (identifiable) author mean"? but "what function does this (anonymous) collective myth serve when it is repeated on certain occasions"? For the critic, a single work is the locus of meaning; the anthropologist seldom treats less than several versions of a tale. (23–24)

Graves engages an anthropologist's perspective toward his autobiographical writing practices. Where convention (highlighted by Blunden and Sassoon's reaction) demands accuracy, Graves's method insists on an accuracy for the spirit or mood of the experiential moment.

In "Epics Are Out of Fashion" the narrator is endowed with the ability to make intuitive and insightful observations, but while so doing he is made to seem oblivious to the profound implications of his own words. In distancing himself from his implied author's voice and actions, Graves is working from a tradition of narrative as "personal history" or fictional autobiography which stretches back through the history of the novel. The story is recounted by a naive narrator who appears to be a proverbial "straw-man" set up by Graves to be knocked down in the tradition of the "everyman" of parables and fables for the betterment of the reader. Argentarius's story is a collection of hearsays and supposedly personal recollections—just like Graves's autobiography and just like Crossley's story in *The Shout*. The question of the annecdotal event's authenticity is not an issue in the story: the narrator's belief in them is.

Entering the text as readers with a willingly suspended disbelief, we are drawn into moral culpability with a narrator who, like so many others in Graves's fiction, (such as Graves's Claudius, whose apparent ineptitude saves him from certain destruction during Caligula's reign in *I, Claudius*), casts a naive aura in order to justify the preservation of his life. The narrator of "Epics Are Out of Fashion," is no exception. Despite the attempts on the part of Petronius to engage him in a futile attempt to prevent Lucan's rash actions, our narrator flees from the "cleansing" of the courts by his tyrannical emperor—long enough, anyway, to have penned his story for posterity. In this case, a record of his existence seems to be the sole purpose for his writing.

Argentarius, the fictional author and survivor of the debacles that make up the plot of "Epics Are Out of Fashion," closes his tale with a self-deprecatory gesture: "Thank goodness I was stupid at school, and never felt any literary ambitions whatsoever! But nobody in Rome could touch me as a long-distance man . . ." (119). Graves's dexterity in handling his subject comes through very clearly in this passage. The last two sentences of the story create a clever "inconclusion" by employing the ellipses as the closing punctuation. The dangling ending begs for an explanation for what remains unsaid by Argentarius: Why is Argentarius in such a hurry? Has he said too much? Is he about to move on? Or has he met his end at the hands of one of Nero's agents and so been prevented from finishing his story?

The latter seems unlikely. Argentarius's character as a resourceful manipulator of situations remains sound to the end of the tale and, one suspects, beyond. His words read "true" to an audience who have suspended their disbelief. Lucan and Petronius are dead, Argentarius, lives on—unashamedly. However, one can also read the ellipses as an "opening" to a new, unwritten, narrative—a punctuation which wryly hints at the implied author's awareness of his own ironical position in relation to the "truth" of the story he has just told.

In a letter held in the St. John's College Robert Graves Trust archive, Graves writes to Karl Gay on the subject of his translation of Lucan's *Pharsalia:*

> If Lucan were any *better* [Graves's emphasis] I should not continue; but he is so gloriously bad that I shall with a forward reassure uneducated readers that they miss nothing by not having the original before them. It is a sort of object lesson in how not to write poetry, and gives a wonderful insight into the mind of a typical awful Roman of the 1st Century.

While working on the translation of *Pharsalia*, Graves wrote "Epics Are Out of Fashion" for *Punch*. If Graves considered Lucan a "typical awful Roman," then his implied author's ironic position becomes abundantly clear: there was nothing much to save in the infighting at Nero's court other than himself.

The 1957 edition of *Good-Bye to All That* (1960) ends with a similar tone:

> Yet I do not seem to have changed much, mentally or physically, since I came to live here [Majorca], though I can no longer read a newspaper without glasses, or run upstairs three steps at a time, and have to watch my weight. And if condemned to relive those lost years I should probably behave again in very much the same way; a conditioning in the Protestant morality of the English governing classes, though qualified by mixed blood, a rebellious nature, and an overriding poetic obsession, is not easily outgrown. (281)

Yet, the prologue to the same work offers a Puck-like apology: "If any passage still gives offence after all those years, I hope to be forgiven." The counterpointal effect of these two apologies demonstrates Graves's sensitivity for the subject matter—after all, the subject is his own life. But while mistakes made can be regretted, the reassurance for the reader is to hear the author's affirmation that he would, upon reflection, "behave again in very much the same way." Like Argentarius, Graves abandoned a cleansing court in 1929 (former friends and colleagues such as Sassoon and Blunden publicly criticizing Graves's work as discussed above might constitute an environment in the literary world which Graves considered unwholesomely Romor) and in the prologue and epilogue written for the 1957 edition, Graves clearly shows no regret for having done so.

But is there something more which Graves wants to tell with Argentarius's story beyond offering an alternative reading of the assassination plot on Nero's life? Is Argentarius, like Graves, hinting that he too would live life the same way again? A trace of the subtext that Graves's narrator is unwittingly constructing can be discovered through an examination of Argentarius's character.

Argentarius does not judge his or others' actions on a bourgeois moral or ethical scale. The measure of the moral is left by Graves for the reader. Argentarius, who ends his story with the structurally convenient ellipses, proves himself to be of a questionable moral fiber. He describes how he has run straight from Lucan's banquet with "all the gold [he] could cram into a satchel." He has no shame in being a coward or expressing with near glee that "Petronius was in for it too!" (119). How are we to judge this man then?

A moment's reflection can potentially justify Argentarius's sense of relief in learning that Petronius "was in for it"; after all, it was Petronius who informed Argentarius of Lucan's foolish plan to write an epic on the Civil Wars. Since Argentarius had done nothing to curtail Lucan's epistolary pursuit, he, too, could have been connected with "the crime." With Petronius, the only person who remained alive who could demonstrate Argentarius's complicity in the affair, finding himself "in for it too," Argentarius was not as likely to be implicated. Read in this manner, Argentarius was saving his own skin at the expense of the lives of those around him.

Clearly, one must dig to find anything that is "likeable" about Argentarius; however, he would not have been around to write the story had he indulged in the time to pause and reflect on the impending fate of his family and friends and certainly would not be telling us this story had he taken the time to offer them his assistance. The use of the first person, in this sense, reduces the drama of the tale. Argentarius had to be alive to tell his story and so, obviously, survived the events of the narrative. What remains unclear is if Graves wants us to see Argentarius as someone attempting to "dupe" his readers into a complicity with him and his apparent innocence or, if Argentarius has, in fact, determined to be amoral in a world without scruples as a means by which to forestall an inevitable end orchestrated by Nero's court.

If we consider the latter, we might have an explanation for Argentarius's defensive posture. For example, he informs his audience that he was "stupid in school, and never felt any literary ambitions whatsoever." This self-depreciation can be considered analogous to Graves's frequent statements on the inconsequence of his own fictional works—on their being nothing more than "pot-boilers."

Most studies of Graves's *Claudius* books will, at some point, make mention of the similarities between Graves's persona and his protagonist. Clearly, a habit that has lingered from Graves early connection with himself to the central figure of *The Shout*. Martin Seymour-Smith, for example, observed that "[Graves'] misunderstood central character was an oblique caricature (but by no means a portrait) of himself—more particularly of his situation" (231). "His situation," according to Seymour-Smith and R. P. Graves, was an awkward struggle with his burgeoning popularity as the author of *I, Claudius* and Laura Riding's reticence to admit the "validity" of historical novels on the whole and her outrage at the recognition Graves was receiving for them (Graves 1990, 224). Ironically, by 1935 Riding was working on a historical novel of her own, *A Trojan Ending*, for which, according to Graves's diary of that same year, he was doing a substantial portion of the historical research.

Two poems that Graves wrote shortly after the publication of *I, Claudius* are exemplary of his struggle with the intellectual impasse he and Riding had reached—an intellectual impasse very similar to the one prophesied in *The Shout* and which was supposed to have been bid "good-bye" in *Good-Bye to All That*. "The Devils Advice to Story-Tellers" and "To Bring the Dead to Life" are both rather didactic works which clearly outline Graves's process as well the "Argentarian" posture he was forced to take by Riding with respect to his works.

In "The Devil's Advice to Story-Tellers," Graves pits "conventional" wisdom against "devilish" advice to would-be writers. Conventional wisdom says that, "Lest men suspect your tale to be untrue, / Keep probability—some say—in view." In other words, he is advising writers that no matter how incredible their stories might seem, they should make sure the tales remain credible in order to keep them believable. However, the "devilish" advice in the poem is to:

> Weigh out no gross of probabilities,
> Nor yet make diligent transcriptions of
> Known instances of virtue, crime or love.
> To forge a picture that will pass for true,
> Do conscientiously what liars do—
> Born liars, not the lesser sort that raid
> The mouths of others for their stock-in-trade:
> Assemble, first, all casual bits and scraps
> That may shake down into a world perhaps;
> People this world, by chance created so,
> With random persons whom you do not know—
> The teashop sort, or travellers in a train
> Seen once, guessed idly at, not seen again;
> Let the erratic course they steer surprise
> Their own and your own and your readers' eyes;
> Sigh then, or frown, but leave (as in despair)
> Motive and end and moral in the air;
> Nice contradiction between fact and fact
> Will make the whole read human and exact.

While the third and fourth lines from the end of the poem, "Sigh then, or frown, but leave (as in despair) / Motive and end and moral in the air"; seem to describe the conclusion of "Epics Are Out of Fashion," the dedicatory epilogue from *Good-Bye*, and *The Shout*, almost exactly. In each case, motive, moral, all manner of closure is avoided. Deceptively simple moralistic tales are in fact slippery and evasive with pluralistic conclusions. Graves's narrators are so ambiguous and their manner of retelling stories is so firmly a part of the story itself, that the "exactness" the narrators profer to be presenting, is in fact merely human exactness; in other words, not very exact at all.

This method is in part revealed through the story of Graves's "discovery" of the White Goddess myth while researching the Argonaut legend for his novel *The Golden Fleece*. The introduction to *The Golden Fleece* is dominated by critical commentary (in the exegetical style of *The Greek Myths* and *The Hebrew Myths*) on the sources for his rewriting of the myths as well as an explanation of the importance of the Goddess to the Argo's voyage. The level of critical commentary demonstrates that Graves did not take his facts lightly. Before reinterpreting what had been "conventionally" known, Graves took great pains to establish his facts. However, unlike his exegetical introductions or his scholarly studies, these longer fictional works similarily evade a simple form of closure.

Furthermore, biographical studies show us that Graves found it was important to "know" the persons and the places that he wrote about. To that end, as Seymour-Smith writes, Graves soaked himself in the atmosphere of ancient of Rome (229). His attention to detail was such that, as R. P. Graves notes, Eirlys Roberts, who had been asked to proofread *I, Claudius* for historical accuracy, was only able to detect one error: "the wrong colour to the hem of the prostitutes' gowns" (207). Graves may have been intererested in reinterpreting history, but it is abundantly clear that he was not willing to sacrifice historical authenticity in his period fiction for a self-serving thematic end.

The devilish advice of the poem can be, at least in part, considered an analysis of Graves's own method. For example, in "Epics Are Out of Fashion," Graves's attention to detail, cannot be as precise as it is in *I, Claudius* due to the brevity of the tale; however, the figures hardly seem created by "chance." Lucan and Petronius, not to mention Nero, are, obviously, very real historical figures. But historical accounts do not agree with Graves's view that Lucan was at the center of a plot to assassinate Nero "in the name of artistic freedom" (135). For this "tidy" end, Graves is indeed making use of "Nice contradiction between fact and fact [that] / Will make the whole read human and exact." Truth to the randomness and erraticity of human nature produces narratives that are less likely to mimic the realism of nineteenth-century literature and are more likely to correspond with the modernist concern with a reassessment of history in a world that bore an increasing alienation from a consoling Romantic relationship with landscape or a Victorian hope for social harmony.

The short story that follows the rules on the other side of Graves's "devilish advice" is "The Tenement: A Vision of Imperial Rome."

Here, Graves casts known historical figures into the background and instead gives us a meticulously detailed study of a day in the life of an historically annonymous rent collector and his tragic end in the collapse of a tenement building.

The almost obsessive attention to detail exhibited in the story allows Graves to showoff an intimate knowledge of Roman life. For example, rising from bed, Egnatius, the narrator, describes how he is dressed by his slave:

> He drapes one toga-end over my left shoulder, letting it fall to the thigh; next, winds the straight edge round the back of my neck and under the right arm, then grabs the mass of material low down and throws the other toga-end past the first, so that it hangs behind me. Finally, he fixes the "naval boss" at my midriff. That leaves me warmly swathed, except for the right shoulder, and provides a capacious pocket at chest level. (137)

The almost mundane personal details about the rent collecter that Graves presents to us raises the rent collector above a character who is, according to the devilish advisor and/or Riding's historical method, "guessed idly at" to one who is known intimately.

Again, "The Tenement" is told from the first-person narrative perspective. How though, does this narrator come to write his story if it ends with his death in the crumbling of the tenement? The answer to this apparent paradox is in a stunning self-reflexive narrative construction. Graves provides us with a direct reference to the relationship between himself and his implied author. In this case, the narrator is reborn as Graves. The story ends:

> Did any of us survive? I doubt it. My next distinct memory is of being a child once more. Martial music sounds. Mother lifts me up to watch, through a well-glazed English nursery window, the decorated carriages and red-coated soldiers of Queen Victoria's Diamond Jubilee procession. (279)

The slippage from implied to actual narrator employed by Graves challenges the very convention of autobiography. If Graves feels that he can represent himself *actually* as an historical personage without "resorting" to conventional rhetorical framing devices, then what effect does this transgression have on the "truth" and validity of his historical revisions? The sceptical response would clearly have to be "harmful."

Analeptic "research" can hardly be taken seriously by a scholar; however, this query does raise a vital issue. How serious was Graves about the mental "time travels" he made in his analeptic researching techniques? According to those scholars with whom Graves worked, not very. Raphael Patai, coauthor (with Graves) of *The Hebrew Myths,* claims throughout the memoir of his collaboration with Graves that Graves's historical reading and research was intensive. Patai does describe some of Graves's errant conclusions in his reworking of biblical myths as "pure Gravesian conjectures" (31) thereby implying that the conjectures occurred with some frequency; however, he also admits that Graves was ready to seek scholarly support for his ideas:

> Graves found numerous individual rites he claimed were re-enacted at the coronation of Jesus. So, as he later told me in the course of one of our long conversations in his home in Deya, it was my "Hebrew Installation Rites" that gave the solid foundation to what he had only suspected years before when he wrote his *King Jesus.* (33)

One, it should be admitted, can assume that Graves was, to a certain degree, playing to an "adoring" audience. A writer who conducts his research by traveling backward through time strikes a more interesting pose than one who spends days and weeks with his nose buried in books. Graves, it can be concluded, was perhaps not the soundest of scholars when it came to researching historical material, but neither was he simply a charlatan who "guessed idly at" moments of the past.

Just how profound and central this struggle is to Graves's consciousness can be registered by refering to the two editions of *Good-Bye to All That.* The "Queen's Jubilee procession," to which the narrator of "The Tenement" refers as his "waking" memory, is also the earliest memory cited by Graves in both editions of *Good-Bye* as "proof of [his] readiness to accept autobiographical convention." The 1957 edition has this recollection shunted to the very start of the autobiography from its former location, two pages in, in the 1929 edition. Evidently, Graves was playing with the notion of autbiography in both the story and *Good-Bye;* however, more significant is the clear reference he has made through the story to his supposed "analeptic" method of researching the past.

So why then create these association with pseudo-mysticism which I feel, quite frankly, can lead to questions about the author's intellectual integrity? In discussing *I, Claudius* R. P. Graves makes a very astute observation on what makes that novel so effective:

> Graves's use of the first person, usually a great risk for a novelist because of the considerable restrictions which it imposes upon him, succeeds brilliantly as an effective contrast to the horrors with which the novel is filled. Graves,—as Claudius—writes that he wishes his "eventual readers

of a hundred generations ahead, or more" to feel themselves "directly spoken to, as if by a contemporary"; and he adopts the same cool, laconic, matter-of-fact, almost conversational approach which had helped to make *Good-Bye to All That* such a success. (189)

While the conclusion of Graves's "Tenement" story can be read as somewhat tongue-in-cheek, Graves does, nevertheless, offer himself to be a little bit "Roman"; at least in mind. Interestingly, the two short stories discussed above were written about twenty-five years after the publication of *I, Claudius*. Whatever compelled Graves to produced this latter "potboiler" was still lingering within him. Stylistically, not much can be seen to have changed between the three works, and the associations between Graves and his narrators remains passionately strong.

In his poem "To Bring the Dead to Life," Graves explains the process of "assuming" an ancient character's identity for writerly purposes:

> To bring the dead to life
> Is no great magic.
> Few are wholly dead:
> Blow on a dead man's embers
> And a live flame will start.
>
> Let his forgotten griefs be now,
> And now his withered hopes;
> Subdue your pen to his handwriting
> Until it prove as natural
> To sign his name as yours.
>
> Limp as he limped,
> Swear by the oaths he swore;
> If he wore black, affect the same;
> If he had gouty fingers,
> Be yours gouty too.
>
> Assemble tokens intimate of him—
> A seal, a cloak, a pen:
> Around these elements then build
> A home familiar to
> The greedy revenant.
>
> So grant him life, but reckon
> That the grave which housed him
> May not be empty now:

> You in his spotted garments
> Shall yourself lie wrapped.

The last stanza of this poem has an ominous tone. In these closing lines Graves has decided that the revenant is greedy; that the past of the raised may become the present of the necromancer; that the writer may be forced to take the revenant's place in his spotted garments and take responsibility for his "spotted" past. This bleak vision is tempered, somewhat, by the qualifier "may" in that Graves seems to be saying that one only "may" suffer this fate—that the fate is not *accompli;* however, the mood created by the character's "forgotten griefs," "withered hopes," "gouty fingers," "limp," "greed," and "spotted garments" as having the potential to haunt if one dares try to raise him, is unmistakable. According to this poem, Graves most certainly regrets having breathed life into Claudius's embers.

Riding's dissatisfaction with Graves's successes may be one source for his personal regrets (and this poem was also not seen by Riding until it had received several revisions); however, there may be something more to it than that. What was Graves's purpose in distorting the history of Nero's assassination attempt in "Epics Are Out of Fashion"? Graves was not known to mistake historical details of this sort unless there was some intention to his "oversight." One moral which comes out of the story is a "warning" against trying to tackle the courts of a self-appointed literary giant. According to Seutonius, Nero is said to have uttered upon his death, "Dead! And so great an artist!" (243). Graves despised this sort of pomposity among his contemporaries, yet often, especially in his later years, stood accused of it himself. By writing a parable based loosely on the history of Nero's bloody purge of his court after his suspicions of a plot against his life had been raised, Graves may have found an opportunity to take a "poke" at some his less-than-favorite peers and also at himself by drawing an analogy between his own time and the famous corrupt Roman emperor and the "typical awful Romans" of his court.

There is a clear parallel between Argentarius's relationship with Lucan and the others and Graves's own antagonistic relationship with his contemporary literary community. Just as we can trace the shifts in attitude toward those falling in and out of Graves's favor through the expurgations and "corrections" made between the 1929 and 1957 editions of *Good-Bye to All That* and find a potential justification, or at least an understanding, for Argentarius's ambiguous relationship with morality.

Almost any one of Graves's Oxford lectures can serve as an example here; however, "Some Instances of Poetic Vulgarity" is the most obvious choice for the purposes of this paper. In it, Graves makes his connection between poets and Nero's court. In this example we can see where the subtext of "Epics Are Out of Fashion" becomes primary subject matter. He writes, "I pair Byron and Nero as the two most dangerous bounders of all time" (Graves 1995, *Collected* 361). Byron, according to Graves, "adored no Muse, but acted as male Muse to scores of infatuated women" (361). In other words, he was, by Graves's terms, a false poet. Other poets considered "false" by Graves among his contemporaries included Auden (who "is as synthetic as Milton . . . developed his real talent for producing light verse" [235]); Pound (whom he unabashedly mocks in a paper entitled "Dr. Syntax and Mr. Pound" [117]); and even Eliot (of whom he was greatly sceptical as a poet but with whom he maintained a "neutral" friendship). The list could go on at great length and, in any case, other critics (see especially Patrick McGuinness' paper in this volume) have engaged the subject in more detail. That the majority of poets derided by Graves had affinities with the modernist movement is a clear indication that Graves, post-Riding, post–*A Survey of Modernist Poetry*, was not a huge fan of the movement.

The parallels are clear, the poets named above can readily be subsituted for the classical poets of Nero's court while Graves and his attitudes toward those poets can replace Argentarius's. The allusions from one story to the next, from one poem to the next, from essay to essay or essay to story and poem and so forth never seem to stop. Besides his passion for "the goddess" Graves had one other story to tell and that was of his cantankerous relationship with the world. He told the story well, though in some cases he retold it too often and it began to wear. By the 1960s most serious critics had begun to tire of antics which at one time must have seemed refreshingly iconclastic but which were rapidly becoming routinely establishmentarian.

In his paper on Blake, "Tyger, Tyger," Graves criticizes James Joyce for having "the same illusion of superior power as Blake, . . . the same reckless impiety and the same sense of persecution" (Graves 1995, *Collected* 535) but for also being schizophrenic (Graves's tone indicates that he considered this mental condition as necessarily degrading one's abilities as a writer.) He goes on to critique *Finnegans Wake* for being more "memorable for its schematic patterns . . . than for any clear message that [it] conveys," (535). If we accept

Joyce as being exemplar of the modernists, we can begin to see the trouble that Graves was having in relating to his peers.

The modernist's intentional obscurity, or as Stephen Spender put it in his work *The Struggle of the Modern*, their

> all-inclusive works, mansions themselves containing many mansions, but without foundations. Foundations were not planned, partly because a modern house should be made of materials that need no foundations, but more significantly because the attempt to build foundations meant inevitably reverting to beliefs or philosophies which were fragmented, partisan, not capable of dealing with the modern experience as a whole, and for that reason reverting to the past. (257)

Graves's historical novels have very firm historical, philosophical, and structural foundations. But Graves's tenement had once crumbled, too—in Graves's case, the crash came in the form of psychological trauma resulting from his time in the trenches and persisted through his years of struggle as a neurasthenic. Dennis Brown, in *The Modernist Self*, holds Graves's poetry of the 1920s as a model "in literary-historical terms" and considers that "it is worth noting how innovatory this writing is in its awareness of modern psychological insights and terms, and how 'Modernist,' in fact, it feels at times" (58).

In *Good-Bye to All That*, Graves asserted that "A conditioning in the Protestant morality of the English governing classes ... is not easily outgrown" (1960, 20–21). What then, became Graves's newspaper issues? And were these issues ever able to escape the confines of his "Englishness"? I believe it can be fruitful to examine thematic connections between the one work which explicitly deals with Graves's newspaper issues, *Good-Bye to All That*, and some of the historical novels, which explore similar "affective" issues but in a more discrete manner.

Briefly, turning to his longer fiction, we can see the same sort of patterns emerging. The thematic connections between *Count Belisarius* and *Good-Bye to All That*, for example, can be, on a basic level, obvious—both works are about soldiers—however, Graves's manipulation of a large number of historical sources allowed him to cull selected passages from the disparate historical accounts. The differences between the recorded histories gave Graves authorial licence to manipulate historical "evidence" in order to suit his thematic purposes. An apparent irony in Graves's technique emerges in the closing pages of *Count Belisarius* when Graves reveals the process of his own novel by explaining what his narrator perceived to be Procopius's bitterness: "Sometimes [Procopius] told the truth, sometimes he distorted the facts, sometimes he lied—according to his vindictive purposes" (546). The process with which Graves parallels himself is the one he observes Procopius to have used. Procopius is portrayed in the novel as a calculated manipulator with "vindictive purpose." However, Graves contrasts this "vindictive purposefulness" with his narrator's voice, which is portrayed as an honest one. The implied alignment with Procopius is in structure and method only. Graves's fictional narrator was a tool through which Graves could address the problem with Procopius and his contemporaries and how they have (mis)represented the fate of Belisarius for whom it is quite clear that Graves felt a soldierly sympathy—a misrepresentation that Graves wanted to see corrected.

On one level, Graves's *Belisarius* novel bears on the reader's sympathy through the narrator's sincerity. As a character in Graves's novel, Eugenius does not stand to gain from being "untruthful." Such parallels between Eugenius in *Count Belisarius* and the other narrators discussed here are unmistakable. In presenting himself to the reader, the narrator describes himself as, "a person of little importance, a mere domestic" (3). The narrator's criticism of Procopius amplifies Belisarius's tragedy since, according to Eugenius, Belisarius was not only treated cruelly in life, but also in remembrance. Through this subtle subtext, Graves continues his attack on the society that he shows to have been "turn-coatish" in *Good-Bye to All That*. On another level, the representation of Belisarius, stripped of rank and status, blinded and left to beg for coppers with St. Bartimaeus's wooden bowl in front of the monastery dedicated to "Job the Prophet" (557–59) draws the reader's empathy at a most primary and sentimental level. Similarly, Graves depicts soldiers like Sassoon in *Good-Bye to All That* as valiant warriors who were, in turn, exploited by profiteers and vote-scrounging politicians who saw only the "horrors" of the front while on gentrified "Cook's Tours" (1960, 205).

On the other hand, while Eugenius is infinitely likeable and Argentarius's ethics are questionable, both narrators are supremely honest. At least Graves constructs them to appear to be honest. They are, in the first instance, just like Graves: endearingly self-depreciating. We are also drawn to them for their wit. Argentarius's opening lines of "Epics Are Out of Fashion," for example, immediately allies the reader to him through humor: "Petronius did his best. He wasn't a bad fellow at heart, though he had the foulest mind in Rome and drank like a camel" (131). While he may slip in our estimation as a result of his apparent cowardice and treachery, we do not have any reason to believe his story any less than we do the accuracy of the witty observations that do not bear the same significance as a revisionist historical argument.

When we take into consideration Graves's passion for rewriting and reassessing myths and histories, the responsibility of the narrator who is representing Graves's findings becomes critical. The narrator is Graves's principal rhetorical tool. Our disbelief may be suspended when we enter the story, but Graves makes sure we know where it has been hung. In this sense, Graves holds our hands through his works. The stories are to be enjoyed, but he makes sure we read them as more than simply pleasant "tales." Graves was too outspoken a critic and too voluminous a writer to ignore the self-referential intertextuality of his broad subject areas.

Graves's own criticism of his greatly ignored historical novels as "potboilers" must be taken with a grain of salt. Graves shows so much zeal in reattacking the targets he had set his sites on in the 1920s in the short stories written so many years later that we must consider that either Graves had a masochistic streak for suffering a past raised from "the dead," or that he felt comfortable and secure in assuming an identity (much like Argentarius does when he flees to Greece) and writing about issues from a politically safe distance—but writing about issues none the less.

Each of the historical novels and each of the stories examined in this essay are based on very similar structures. Naturally, when it comes to style, stories such as *The Shout* and "Epics Are Out of Fashion" read as though they have been written by two different authors—or at least a writer in two distinct phases of a career. Nevertheless, a nearly modernist tale such as *The Shout* is not substantially different to a classically tailored story such as "Epics": thanks to—or, perhaps, because—Graves's method and subject are always substantially the same.

WORKS CITED

Booth, Wayne C. 1983. *The Rhetoric of Fiction*. London: The University of Chicago Press.

Brown, Dennis. 1989. *The Modernist Self*. Hong Kong: MacMillan.

Fussell, Paul. 1977. *The Great War and Modern Memory*. New York: Oxford University Press.

Graves, Richard P. 1990. *The Years with Laura*. Toronto: Viking.

Graves, Robert. 1955. Letter to Karl Gay, 20 January. Robert Graves Trust Archive, St. John's College, Oxford.

———. 1960. *Good-Bye to All That*. Toronto: Penguin.

———. 1977. *I, Claudius*. Harmondsworth: Penguin.

———. 1983. *Count Belisarius.* New York: Farrar Straus & Giroux.
———. 1995. *Collected Writing on Poetry.* Edited by Paul O'Prey. Manchester: Carcanet.
1997. *Robert Graves: The Complete Poems. Vol. 2.* Manchester: Carcanet Press.
1995. *Complete Short Stories.* Edited by Lucia Groves. Manchester: Carcanet.
1995. *Good-Bye to All That.* Edited by R. P. Graves. Oxford: Berghahn Books.
Kirkham, Michael. 1969. *The Poetry of Robert Graves.* London: Athlone.
Martin, Wallace. 1994. *Recent Theories of Narrative.* London: Cornell University Press.
Patai, Raphael. 1992. *Robert Graves and The Hebrew Myths.* Detroit: Wayne State University Press.
Presley, John, 1997. "Narrative Structure in Graves's Historical Fiction." *Gravesiana: The Journal of the Robert Graves Society* I/3:292–304.
Quinn, Patrick. 1994. *The Great War and the Missing Muse.* London: Associated University Press.
Seymour-Smith, Martin. 1982. *Robert Graves: His Life and Works.* London: Hutchinson.
Spender, Stephen. 1963. *The Struggle of the Modern.* London: Hamish.
Suetonius. 1989. *The Twelve Caesars.* Edited by Michael Grant. London: Penguin.

Robert Graves and the Historical Novel in the 1930s

CHRIS HOPKINS

FAMOUSLY, ROBERT GRAVES CLAIMED THAT HE WROTE *I, CLAUDIUS* AS A "BESTseller" because he needed the money. However, it, together with the sequel, has remained his most popular work, though it is hardly a "potboiler." Critics such as Martin Seymour-Smith have pointed out what most readers would assert: that it is a completely engaged and engaging novel. What I would like to do in this essay is to introduce some of the contexts for the historical novel in the 1930s and then to suggest similarities and differences between Graves's novels and other novels of the same type in the period.

No one has so far remarked even upon the fact that the Claudius novels resemble a specific 1930s subgenre of the novel. But this does seem to be the case, and it provides a fruitful if indirect approach to the novels. The subgenre in question, the historical novel, has an interesting but largely forgotten history, in terms of the 1930s. Graves might be thought mainly to have chosen this genre because of its popularity, but his novels also resemble other historical novels of the period where popularity was not the only issue. For the historical novel became during the 1930s a particularly political subgenre, often used to reflect on contemporary events, particularly economic crisis, the rise of fascism, and the possibilities of communism. As these topics suggest, it was, in fact, often a leftist subgenre, particularly when it dealt with a sense of crisis and radical change. Though there were more popular historical novels, in some ways those of Robert Graves are more like these leftist versions.

For left-wing writers, the attractions of the historical novel were several. Firstly, its essential focus on history gave an immediate affinity to Marxism with its stress on the centrality of history. Secondly, the relatively traditional novelistic traditions that the historical novel tended to use were close to some of the realist tendencies encouraged by left-literary critics. Thirdly, it could be used for pointing towards historical parallels with a modern sense of crisis. This sense of crisis is a particularly important similarity between Graves's and leftist uses of the historical novel, as some comments by Graves in a letter to T. E. Lawrence suggest:

> I chose Claudius for a number of reasons : the first was that he was a historian before he was anything else and because he lived in an age in which every moral safeguard of a religious or patriotic or social sort had gone West—things were just disintegrating. He realised this and found it impossible to reintegrate them. The best he could do was to be a historian & keep historian's faith. (Seymour-Smith, 256)

I will return to this vision of the historian's role later.

This interest in the historical novel in the period has not been much noticed, and views of left writing during the decade are more usually focused through discussion of the contemporary proletarian novel and notions of socialist realism. Left interest in the historical novel may, in the light of this usual critical approach, seem rather surprising. However, it is well attested by the number of leftist novels of this type. Examples include works by Phyllis Bentley, Jack Lindsay, Leslie Mitchell (Grassic Gibbon), Naomi Mitchison, and Sylvia Townsend Warner. Not all of these predate *I, Claudius* (and even Jack Lindsay's novels, which are among the earliest examples, are more or less contemporary with it). And anyway Graves showed few signs of much interest in modern novels. I do not therefore so much wish to argue that Graves is directly influenced by this tradition as that his version of the historical novel picks up some similar possibilities and then does very different but not wholly unrecognizable things with them.

Historical novels were written about many different periods of history, but ancient Rome was particularly popular. Jack Lindsay wrote *Rome For Sale* (1934) and *Caesar Is Dead* (1934), Phyllis Bentley wrote *Freedom Farewell (1936),* Leslie Mitchell wrote *Spartacus* (1937), and Naomi Mitchison wrote *The Blood of the Martyrs* (1939). The popularity of Rome may have been influenced by Mussolini and his Italian Fascism, with its Roman stage properties, in connection with a sense that the Roman Empire was a particularly good place for exploring tyranny. (Evelyn Waugh tried to give this neo-Roman identity a positive resonance when he wrote about the achievements of the Italians in building new roads in conquered Abyssinia.) In addition, Rome provided a model of a political culture with democratic elements which had been subverted and overthrown by tyrants. The epigraph to Bentley's *Freedom Farewell* quotes historian

Theodor Mommsen to make this point about the applicability of Roman history to modern crisis:

> The history of past centuries ought to be the instructress of the present, though not in the vulgar sense, as if one could simply by turning the leaves discover the conjunctures of the present in the records of the past; it is instructive because the observation of earlier forms of culture reveals the organic conditions of civilisation generally—the fundamental forces everywhere alike, and the manner of their combination so different. . . . In this sense the history of Caesar and of Roman Imperialism is in truth a more bitter censure of modern autocracy than could be written by the hand of man.

It also may have seemed a particularly modern and familiar seeming culture, with an emphasis on commerce and urban life, and a sense of a traditional set of values displaced by new values. Its imperial role also provided an analogy for Britain, as did the notion of its decline. Above all, a sense of a cultural crisis on which world civilization and progress depended could be focused on Rome.

The question of parallels between past history and the present is, of course, a vital one for the historical novel, and one which can be handled in a variety of ways. Some novels unashamedly use the past as an unreal place where there is more color, where things happen with more vividness. Others attempt to give some sense of a past which is genuinely different from the present, rather than an exciting and fantastic setting. A third possibility is to suggest illuminating parallels with the present. There are no absolute distinctions between these approaches, and although the first approach is sometimes dismissed as historical romance, it seems likely that there is always some element of the past which can be seen to possess a drama lacking in the present. Equally, it seems unlikely that the other two approaches can be entirely separated. The novel form suggests the possibility of communicating a shareable experience, and to write an historical novel suggests that this different past can at least speak to the present. An historical novel may show parallels with the present, but it would never want to present the past as identical with the present, because the grounds of the comparison and its ability to reveal would then collapse.

Most left historical novels do not try to erase differences between past and present, but point to resemblances. In *The Historical Novel* (1937), Lukács specifically worries about the use of the historical novel as a parable form for the political present, saying (of some German examples), "the direct and conceptual relationship with the present which prevails today reveals an immanent tendency to turn the past into a parable of the present, to wrest directly from history a *fabula docet*, and this conflicts with the real historical concreteness of the content" (408). His anxiety is that forcing the past into the shape of the present modernizes history and hence falsifies the kind of understanding of the dialectical process of history, which is the particular value of the true historical novel. His sense of the history and the novel is shared by some English critics of the period (for instance Ralph Fox and Philip Henderson), and by some leftist novelists themselves. Jack Lindsay's *1649*, for example, shows a number of characters who under the Commonwealth oscillate between joining in with the egalitarian and or revolutionary Leveler and Digger movements and joining in new commercial and industrial ventures. Such an oscillation seems bizarre, but it comes, I think, from Lindsay's sense that his novel refers both to the present and the past. In reference to the present, capitalism is decaying and coming to an end, to be replaced by the supremacy of the proletariat. But in reference to the past, the emergence of a new mercantile and industrial bourgeoisie and a rejection of feudal monarchy is a positive move forward in the dialectic of the class struggle. Lindsay partly motivates these shifts as struggles of consciousness for his characters, but they are also partly about his own uses of the historical novel to understand both the seventeenth century and the twentieth century.

The insights into history and the present which the historical novel thus envisaged can provide include a sense of a dialectic not only between different social forces, but also between individual human consciousnesses and external events and relationships. This is something which classic realism can explore, since it assumes a world made up of private but not self-contained consciousness and an external world which has some real and shareable substance. For leftist historical novelists, the genre had an inbuilt sense of objectivity (it could explain stages in history) together with an ability to explore the interaction of the external social world with internal consciousness.

Graves too was attracted to objectivity. As is well known, he claimed to be influenced by his great-uncle Leopold von Ranke, the founder of modern "objective" historiography. I think that in some of the discussions in the Claudius novels about the nature of historical writing, one can hear Rankean ideas being expressed. For example, there is the debate between Pollio, Livy, and the young Claudius. Livy says, "If I come across two versions of the same episode I choose the one nearest my theme, and you won't find me grubbing around Etruscan cemeteries in search of any third account which may flatly contradict both—what good would that do?" (109). Pollio, on the other hand, tells Claudius after Livy's angry departure that he knows that Livy has never even been to the Public Record Office to check a single brass tablet for factual accuracy. Ranke's historical method precisely stressed the proper and critical study of sources and the need to evaluate and interpret different sources of evidence. Claudius distinguishes between Livy and Pollio by saying that, "there are two different ways of writing history: one is to persuade men to virtue and the other is to compel men to truth. The first is Livy's way and the other is yours: and perhaps they are not irreconcilable" (109). However, as many historiographers have pointed out, the establishing of objectivity is always from a certain viewpoint, is always interpretative. Indeed, like historical novels, history does have to locate the past partly for the needs of the present. History as both a quest for, in Ranke's phrase, "what actually happened" and an interpretation of an inherently disputable truth is signaled by the quotation from Tacitus in the epigraph of *I, Claudius*:

> A story that was the subject of every variety of misrepresentation, not only by those who then lived but likewise in succeeding times: so true is it that all transactions of pre-eminent importance are wrapt in doubt and obscurity; while some hold for certain facts the most precarious hearsays, others turn facts into falsehood; and both are exaggerated by posterity.

The past has to be explained in ways which make it intelligible for the time at which the history is being written. So one question to ask about Graves's novels in comparison with the kind of leftist novels of crisis discussed above is what kind of objectivity and truth each seeks and with what end.

There are resemblances in the uses of history in both cases. There are, for example, some references in the Claudius novels to economic and political matters which very much suggest resemblances to the present in the leftist tradition. A good example is the discussion in *Claudius the God* of how competition is a bad thing, and how state controlled monopolies would benefit the people. Messalina argues that the free market does not benefit the people:

> The trouble with merchants is that they won't stick to a single task or let their rivals stick to one. None of them is interested in serving the community, but merely in finding the easiest way to make money. A merchant may start with an inherited business as a wine-importer . . . and then suddenly break into the oil-business, underselling some old-established firm in his neighbourhood; perhaps he will force this firm out of business or buy it up, and then perhaps dabble in the fig-trade or slave-trade and

either crush competitors or get crushed himself. Trade is constant fighting, and the mass of the population suffers from it, just like noncombatants in a war. (205)

Though this is imaginable as a Roman concern, it also seems to suggest an analogy with the present. (Interestingly, Messalina uses a leftish argument about competition though in a context which makes it clear that it is the personal rather than the social advantages that really interest her.) However, such moments of resemblance, though noticeable, are comparatively few, and especially so in the case of political analogies.

Often in such novels the restoration of the Republic serves as an analogy for attempts to throw off dictatorial forms of government and provides a parallel between the politics of Rome and those of a modern state. For example, in Bentley's *Freedom Farewell,* there is a great deal of attention paid to political meetings and different political groups. Thus Caesar is involved with the Popular Party: "At last he had something serious to do. He hurried about indefatigably all day . . . 'a small group . . . those who find the present constitution unworkable . . . dining with Brutus tonight . . . men only . . . plebeian dress'" (62). And Cicero is shown to love the trappings of constitutional government:

> He loved the feeling of the debate, how opinion swayed this way and that. . . . [H]e loved summing up the various resolutions, disentangling them, putting them to the vote in logical sequence, so that the stupidest patrician . . . was in no doubt as to what he was voting for and what the result of his job would be. . . . [H]e beamed with happiness, when his name was written at the bottom of an important bill. (131)

The sense in both these passages that it is not only Roman politics which are referred to is strong. Modern subversive groups are evoked by Caesar's recruiting activities, and accusations of modern parliamentary complacency by the description of what Cicero loves about the Senate.

Claudius's republican sympathies might appear to be an analogously political topos, and up to a point I think they are. However, in the end, there seems to be little interest in the novels in the republic as a political system, and all of Claudius's attempts to inculcate republican virtues fail as soon as attempted. I think this is because in Graves's novel there is a strong assumption that such liberty is already lost, and that politics is inherently corrupted. The focus shifts from the possibilities of politics to the possibilities of an individual retaining some kind of integrity. In fact, Claudius is a heroic figure for Graves not because of his actions but because of his recording of the truth.

This indeed is an immediately striking peculiarity of Graves's Claudius novels. Where in other examples of the period there is a stress on action and on the ways in which action comes from individual engagements with social and political movements, Graves is much more interested in the possibility of maintaining distance from the lunacies of the world while also being a truthful witness to them. Thus, though he does focus the novels on a figure who plays an important part in the world of Roman politics, much of the pleasure of the novels, and of Claudius himself, comes from a sense of withdrawal. Even when Claudius is present at events, the retrospective account he will give to posterity is more important than what actually happens. While other novels—such as those of Bentley and Lindsay—stress the immediacy of Roman politics, their applicability to the modern scene and their complexity, Graves stresses rather the function of Claudius as writer.

Indeed, Claudius himself often points to writing as his essential function. Many things beyond his control happen to him, but writing a truthful record is something over which he has control. At the beginning of *I, Claudius,* Claudius draws attention to the part of him in which he invests most, his true history:

> This is not by any means my first book: in fact literature, and especially the writing of history . . . was until the change came, my sole profession and interest for more than thirty-five years. . . . In the present work, I swear by the Gods, I am my own mere secretary, and my own official annalist: I am writing with my own hand, and what favour can I hope to win from myself by flattery? (9)

This is the most important sense in which Claudius can hope to be objective and to tell the truth to the present. On the one hand to be his "own mere secretary" is a fairly minimal claim, but it is also the most truthful kind of witness that anyone can attempt. To write of himself in a way which goes beyond the demands of his age, but also is useful to a future present which will really be able to appreciate that truth is the kind of simultaneously personal and objective truth which he claims. A paragraph later Claudius writes of his account—and indeed of himself—as being a "confidential history": "This is a confidential history. But who, it may be asked, are my confidants? My answer is: it is addressed to posterity. . . . Yet my hope is that you, my eventual readers of a hundred generations ahead or more, will feel yourselves directly spoken to, as if by a contemporary"

(11). The ambiguity of a "confidential history" is an important one. It speaks both secretly to one's self and to one other: the confidant or reader. It is an account both completely private and completely public. This is like the objectivity to which other historical novels of the 1930s aspire, in that it can represent the formation of an individual consciousness and something which transcends individuality. This takes us back to Graves's letter to T. E. Lawrence, where Graves himself sounds somewhat like the Claudius who addresses the reader and himself at the beginning of the novel:

> What you're really saying is "This is not an idealistic, hopeful book and it isn't even a portrait of a heroic 'minority' character resisting tyranny bravely: Claudius is no Brutus." No indeed he wasn't. . . . I wrote the most popular book I could write while keeping within the limits of personal integrity: that is, Claudius is an old story but I identify myself with him as much as any historical character I know. (Seymour Smith, 256)

Brutus is, indeed, a prominent figure in several of the 1930s historical novels with which I have compared Graves's *I, Claudius*. As always, Graves says *Good-Bye to All That*, without cutting himself off from familiar forms of expression, or refraining from comment, but without really entering into a social and political world in which he he has no faith.

WORKS CITED

Bentley, Phyllis.1936 *Freedom Farewell*. Harmondsworth: Penguin.
Crofts, Andy. 1990. *Red Letter Days: British Fiction in the Thirties*. London: Lawrence.
Garrat, G. T. 1938. *Mussolini's Roman Empire*. Harmondsworth: Penguin.
Graves, Robert. 1939a. *I, Claudius*. Harmondsworth: Penguin.
———. 1939b. *Claudius the God*. Harmondsworth: Penguin.
Hopkins, Chris. 1995. "Syliva Townsend Warner and the Marxist Historical Novel." *Literature and History* 4/1:50–64.
Lindsay, Jack. 1934a. *Rome for Sale*. London : Ivor Nicholson and Watson.
———. 1934b. *Caesar is Dead*. London: Ivor Nicholson and Watson.
———. 1938. *1649: A Novel of a Year*. London: Methuen.
Lukács, Georg. 1981. *The Historical Novel*. Harmondsworth: Pelican.
Mitchison, Naomi. 1939. *The Blood of the Martyrs*. London: Constable.
Montefiore, Jan. 1996. *Men and Women Writers of the 1930s—The Dangerous Flood of History*. London: Routledge.
Seymour-Smith, Martin. 1982. *Robert Graves: His Life and Works*. London: Hutchinson.
Waugh, Evelyn. 1936. *Waugh in Abyssinia*. London: Longmans.

Graves's Milton

Ian McCormick

This essay opens with a brief archaeology of seventeenth-century reason. This is largely presented in a partisan manner, for the layers excavated are idiosyncratically those which Graves wished to explore in writing *Wife to Mr. Milton*. In the period covered by the text, Graves proposes that Milton was shackled by his subjection to reason, rhetoric, and polemic; the true poetic spirit slept. At one level, the sublimation of the poetic is worked through in terms of the Puritan's suppression of the folkloric, the Catholic, and the ritualistic. For the purposes of this essay, I hope to demonstrate that Graves developed an argumentative opposition between the folkloric and the rational. At the same time, I contend that these are not as obviously oppositional as they first appear. Both Graves and Milton were fascinated on the one hand by the latent logic of the folk, as well as by the irrationality of reason. Reason constructs taxonomies, systematic classifications, but it must also accommodate or suppress the anomalous, the hybrid, the monstrous. Milton, I argue, seeks to totalize as a means of control, but he is also outside, beyond categorization: he is a she-man, Tiresias, hermaphrodite, a fossil, No-man, a phoenix. The metaphoric and metamorphic play on Graves's part serves his satirical demolition of Milton. This demolition works through metaphors of sexuality, identity, size (or stature), and the lifeless and will be explored in the course of the essay. More broadly, the opposition between the rational and the folkloric, I contend, serves to reveal Graves's deep suspicion of Milton's poetry. I will conclude that Graves's resistance to Milton helps to elucidate the conception of poetic thought that was to be developed in *The White Goddess*.

My archaeology of Miltonic reason, following Graves closely, is rather a literal one. I begin with the discussion of fossils in chapter 11 of *Wife to Mr. Milton*. Milton's confidently delivered pronouncements serve to exhibit his seemingly exclusive adherence to the faculty of reason. This early section of the text is also the vehicle for resonant themes concerned with the nature of Nature and the fecundity of

Creation. Milton holds that the fossils (mainly sea shells of various kinds, found inland) are not the debris of the flood of Noah's time. Rather, they are self-generated, "naturally moulded by an extraordinary plastic virtue latent in the earth of those quarries wherein they are discovered, in conscious imitation of the living creatures directly created by the hand of God" (133). Milton's belief is ridiculed: "the power to give secret birth to a second or mock-Creation" is "incredible and well-nigh blasphemous" (134). The forms appear to contradict the infinite prudence of nature, which tends "to design everything to a determinate end, and by no way or means that contradicts or runs counter to human ratiocination." It appears, that such "curious figures, adornments and contrivances" have been "elaborated . . . with no more reasonable end than to make a vain exhibition of pattern and form." According to Milton, "the wisdom of the Supreme Nature . . . commands not only the production of commodious and useful things, to maintain men's health, but also that of beautiful and curious things to instruct his eye and cheer his soul" (136–37). One recalls the marvelous, teeming fecundity of nature speculated upon by Milton in *Comus,*

> Wherefore did Nature pour her bounties forth
> With such a full and unwithdrawing hand,
> Covering the earth with odours, fruits and flocks,
> Thronging the seas with spawn innumerable.
>   709–12

Yet the rational faculty that has produced these speculations is here at its closest to the poetic faculty, harmoniously combining Mother Nature and paternal reason. To use Milton's terms, *Naturans* still orders the *Natura Naturata.* The rational and the whimsical combine in a state of virtuoso reverie. The gendering of this topic is rendered all the more corporeal, however, at the parodic limit of the discussion, perhaps as Graves recalls his design satirically to entrap Milton. As the conversation proceeds, the fossils lose their lofty artistry and are clothed in flesh, as certain of the stones perfectly resemble "the secret parts of a man's body." One of the speakers (Uncle Jones) recalls seeing "flint stones strangely like human paps, having not only the *mamma* but the *papilla,* too, surrounded by an *aureola* and studded with small protuberances" (137). Milton objects that these are partial objects, and that to link them with Nature is therefore a kind of blasphemy. It is as though Milton fears the fossilized fragmentation of caricature that these stones signify. There is a deeper fear, of course, in Puritan terms, of the flesh, which is neatly linked here in the limited posterity of becoming merely a fossilized object. It is as though Milton himself has become a species of fossil. Such stones were collected by seventeenth-century virtuosi along with other curious phenomena such as monstrous births, as instances of the sport or the play of nature, *lusus naturae*.[1] Nature as female was prone to such local waywardness and indirection, a larger theme, not just of the theology of the time, but also of Graves's text. But there are problems here, to which I shall return, concerning the relative limits, and the gendering of reason, nature, and creativity.

For the moment, Milton appears to be beyond Nature's accommodation, and indeed, a major burden of the text is precisely judged to convey such an impression. The discussion proceeds to gigantic bones, a topic which Milton finds curiously (and obsessively) congenial, "Mr Milton continued to speak of giants, comparing their heights, and the trustworthiness of the authors who measured them, for near an hour longer" (139). Yet this self-aggrandizement is the product of the fragmentary. It is not a giant, but merely the bone of a giant, picked clean and wasted away by time. By identification with Milton, the passage as a whole seems to be suggesting two things which will be reinforced subsequently. On the one hand, Milton's redundant decoration of his poetry is merely a cold parody of nature's fecundity; on the other, Milton's posterity is a fleshless survival from the past. Through the metaphor of the bone, we find Milton proudly, but ironically, lusting after gigantic origins; he will piece together bits of history to create that modern giant, the epic poet. And yet, as the narrator reminds us, we are to note that Milton's stature "was not above the middling; yet he hopes, by taking religious thought, to add four or five cubits to it and straddle across any hall or court like a Colossus of Rhodes" (158). Taking Marie's point of view, and Graves's reconstruction of Milton, the reader is encouraged to accept a monstrously reductive caricature of the epic poet. The passage dealing with fossils and Nature serves the general tendency of the text to strip off the accumulated layers of poetic glory heaped upon Milton by subsequent generations. We are left merely to dig up fleshless remains.

Milton's role in the text is strictly delimited. As a result, we tend to encounter him subsequent to prior sympathetic identifications

---

[1] These anomalous objects were collected with a view to incorporating them within a more encompassing and more intricately regular system of nature. As Francis Bacon had suggested, they should enable us to discover more profound regularities by a greater understanding of nature's seemingly secret and irregular processes.

with his wife. Milton is an anonymous and distant figure, symptomatically unnamed on his first appearance.[2] He then appears under the pseudonym of Tiresias. In her journal, in contrast, Milton's wife, Marie, recomposes her own identity, as it were, against and rising above dusty layers of history. In contrast to Marie, Milton refuses to own his productions; he refuses to permit his name to appear anywhere between the covers of a pamphlet (39); he introduces himself as a nonidentity ". . . I have no name; for by profession I am a poet" (37). Marie's identity is shifting, accommodating, fluid. She can dress herself up in borrowed robes without losing her true self. (Milton's borrowings only beget a loss of self.) This theme emerges early in the Misrule ceremonies, which often, as in masquerade, indulged the playful substitution of identities in a harmless metamorphic game. This is particularly interesting in Marie's case as she notes "As for myself, I dared that night to assume man's clothing" (7).[3] Nonetheless, the playful gender reassignment of Marie as a man, valuably prepares us for the satirical unmanning of Milton. Satirically, the epic becomes mock-epic; Milton's martial tones, marshaling reason, lose their manly authenticity. At this stage, we only know Milton by his presentation of himself as Tiresias. Subsequently, he provides an explanation for this entitlement, stating that he was shaved during youth because of the plague. He notes,

> until my hair had grown again to its full natural length, I was feeble and womanish, with headaches, megrims, and ill vapours ascending from the stomach to the brain, and also I conceived strange amatory fancies for persons of my own sex. Indeed to one friend, who was of Italian blood and died long ago, I was in my affections more like a solicitous wife than a trusty comrade. I can yet remember how a woman's heart longs for a man, but because of a sense of decency, common to us both, I was never catamite to this friend, and therefore my remembrance is void of shame. . . . Doubtless the poet Tiresias who, as the Greeks allege, killed a sacred serpent, and so became for a while a woman in body

---

[2] He recalls perhaps the figure of "nobody":

> Until this nobody shall consent to die
> Under his curse must every man lie-
> The curse of his jealousy, of his grief and fright,
> Of sudden rape and murder screamed in the night.

See "Nobody" in *The Centenary Selected Poems,* ed. Patrick Quinn, pp. 79–80.

[3] Later, in the Puritan reverend Proctor's words, she will be called "a harlot . . . like the Turkish knight in the mummering play, . . . a frantic termagant and a Babylonian witch" (98).

was, when at last he was restored to masculinity, the better poet for his long unmanning; for the power to put apt speeches in the mouths of women is necessary for the complete poet. I am assured that the Greeks in this legend made reference not to the serpent slain, but to serpentine locks unluckily shorn off. For in the man's hair resides the holy masculine virtue of man. (152)

The notion of endangered manhood, as well as a deeper question of patriarchal power and values that Milton seeks to enforce in his relationship recurs in the comically uncanny scene in which Milton suspects that his wife is about to cut his hair while he is asleep. Clearly, Milton saw himself as a version of Samson. Marie takes pocket scissors to trim her nails; he accuses her of being Delilah. She replies, "Did you fear that I was come to cut off your heartbreakers [a man's long side locks] and so annul your holy masculine virtue? God forbid that I should ever lie in one bed with a lisping she-man!" (317). Milton, it appears, is closer to his sublimated female self than to his female partner. Milton explains that ancient bards "would not suffer their locks to be shorn, and thereby kept their prophetic power unimpaired" (153). These taunts have to be read in the context of Milton's belief that in order to compose a great epic or dramatic poem "a man must first achieve the satisfaction of his natural flesh" (152). I feel that there is Satanic side here; Milton exhibits Satan's "bad eminence," and we may take "bad" in the sense that Graves used it in his discussion of monsters. He points out that an etymology of "bad" is the Old English 'baeddel,' or 'hermaphrodite'—"something that *boded* ill; from which the word *bad* comes" (Graves 1969, 15). Elsewhere, Graves noted of Milton that "diabolic ambition impelled him to renounce the true Muse and bloat himself up" (Graves 1995b, 91).

Milton's self-aggrandizement serves paradoxically to extinguish any living selfhood. In contrast, Marie's lively paintings serve to reclaim aspects of lived experience that the Puritans appeared to suppress. From the outset Marie is identified with the folkloric, the carnivalesque, the mysterious, and the unexplained. Marie's lively imagination is stressed, and it is pointed out that she was born "under the capering sign of Capricorn, and on Twelfth Night too." The identification of Marie with local customs serves to open the journal and to guarantee folk authenticity. In a deeper sense, Marie's journal serves as a communal folk imaginary whose expulsion by Puritan dogma is imminent. The journal commences with a Twelfth

Night party.[4] It should be noted that such cases of Misrule were nonetheless subject to "ancient law" (5); the episode is for instance, clearly defined in temporal terms: "The merrymaking continued after this manner until midnight, when Christmas certainly ended. Then the Lord of Misrule rapped on the floor with his rod, and commanded us to pull down the holly and ivy from the walls (12)." The passage proceeds to foretell a puritanical future with "the pleasant company scattered, the house no longer in our possession, even the Christmas feast abolished by order of Parliament" (13). Marie's world is clearly closer than Milton's to the myth-making, festive imaginary that was in important respects foundational in *The White Goddess*, where Graves noted that,

> English social life was based on agriculture, grazing, and hunting, not on industry, and the Theme was still everywhere implicit in the popular celebration of the festivals known as Candlemas, Lady Day, May Day, Midsummer Day, Lammas, Michaelmas, All-Hollowe'en, and Christmas. . . . [I]t was also secretly preserved as religious doctrine in the covens of the anti-Christian witch-cult. Thus the English, though with no traditional respect for the poet, have a traditional awareness of the theme. (24)

The text supplies a whole range of other examples of the strange and the marvelous.[5] It is worth looking, for instance, at the description of Henry I's Royal Park, which was

> enclosed with a wall to be a harbourage for all manner of wild beasts procured from other princes, to run at large; he had camels, and lynxes,

---

[4] "They came masked and dressed in very rich clothes, or in such grotesque disguises as the skins of wild-beasts, or the foreign garbs of Turks or Jews or Chinamen; or they assumed the characters of rufflers or fools or antics or astrologers or county sluts, disguising not only their persons only but also their voices. The Lord of Misrule who controlled the festivity, that otherwise might have run out of hand, was my brother Richard, the eldest of us all, whose profession was the law" (5).

[5] There follows another spectacle at Enstone, which also partakes of a marvelous quality. These are the grotto waterworks "wonderfully contrived by nature herself." Yet they have also been deemed "worthy of all imaginable advancement by the arts of the engineer" (37). Art and nature are in the kind of pleasurable unity that has already been noted in the case of the carnivalesque Misrule ceremonies. The licence for such activities is socially accommodating, for it combines both the dignity of the royal visit with the antics of the king's fool who "goes down on all fours and barks like a water dog and shakes his ears, the bells of his cap jangling, and comes barking through the fall of water." He is a monster in the sense of something to be

and leopards, and lions, but they remained there not long, for they preyed on one another and did not procreate their kind. At last was left only a porpentine, a beast like a hedge-hog who (they say) rattles his quills and shoots them out at the hunting dogs. (33)

In a sense the passage serves as a metaphor of England approaching civil war, with Cromwell foreshadowed in the beastly porpentine. But Milton, like Henry I, is identified in his own kind of way with the exotic, as the systematic collector of dead cultural products. As will emerge in the discussion of his poetry, Milton is a collector, but he deadens by random assembly. As deadly propagandist, his precursor also appears as the porcupine rattling its quills. Again Milton is a species of exotic other, he is not quite the British hedgehog. The sense of Milton's alienation form the vernacular also appears in the passage dealing with an echo (33). An unlearned coachman has the first attempt, and the words "Hobbledy Gobbledy, Gibble, Gabble—ALE" and "Hobbledy, Gobbledy, Glibber, Globber—BEER" are returned (34). This operates as a contrast to Milton's more eloquent performance. Milton complains that the coachman does not know how to address the Nymphs: "your coachman stood not at the true *centrum phonicum*, or speaker's place" (35). Although Milton's words are returned by the echo, they have to be translated from Latin. The coachman's words, for all their alliterative nonsense, culminate at least in the decently intoxicating vernacular of ale and beer. As the coachman notes, "S'neaks, Echo mocks at honest English, but to Paris French she answers pat! A pox on this stale creature" (36). Milton's muse, it appears, is a lofty and exclusive one, a sweet confection of the foreign and exotic, rather like the zoological disaster of Henry I's Royal Park.[6]

Before proceeding to the next section of this essay, I would like to note the importance of sound in the text. I have already shown the contrasted uses Graves made of the echo. Graves comes back to the relation between sound and poetry, noting Marie's response to Milton's masque, which she finds "exceeding fine poetry." She notes that "the verses fascinated my mind with their serpentine mazes of sound," but her next comment, "and the argument bit in deep" (78)

---

shown and exhibited, like the "dogs at St. Gile's Fair at Oxford [which] leap through paper-hoops" (43).

[6] Echoes are heard later in the text with the discussion of the bombus or sympathetic echo; and the antipathetical bombus. The metaphors bespeak the notion of oneness with oneself and with a wider community (86), especially in the extended, folkloric notion of magical sympathy and antipathy between objects and living beings.

suggests the unwanted intrusion of reason in the midst of sensual and sensuous pleasures. Her brother, James, notes that the poem "appeared a compost or mosaic of many other poems" (78). He concludes,

> The man who wrote this, though I dare call him a very skilful poet, yet seems uncomfortable in the imaginations of his heart and unhappy in the acuteness of his mind . . . It is a poem rather to admire than to love; and here is another paradox, for how can a man truly admire what he does not love. (79)

The double sense of a lack of sincerity and a mere assembly of poetic bits and pieces is developed in the subsequent imagery of Milton's "pluming." James outlines that this might be understood

> as furnishing his naked wings with borrowed plumage. For he has plucked out the feathers from other poets' wings to make himself a great immortal Phoenix . . . [h]e has stolen the laborious honey from the hives of his fellow poets, to spread it thick upon his own white roll . . . I think I can read his secret: he is more passionately set on literate fame than in love with poetry itself. (79)

James's analysis turns out to be close to the mark, for Milton later confirms the view that the poet must "seek out and gather up for his use a huge store of various learnings, with all the arts and sciences linked together philosophically in a commodious and comprehensive system" (132). In the text, Milton emerges as a hardworking reworker, not the source of anything genuinely original and refreshing: "he was industrious in reviving or refurbishing certain old notions that had been long put aside or forgotten, and made them seem novel by the cracking vehemence of his oratory" (237).

It is also noted that Milton writes, "as though he were perfecting himself in martial exercises" (132). Milton, indeed, is very dexterous as finding lofty military analogies for himself. Thus, just after his marriage, upon experiencing the custom of the ride to rough music, the "skimmington," Milton, "when the rout had gone by, began to discourse learnedly upon it, . . . observing that a flouting sort of antimasque of a sordid nature had customarily followed Roman generals when they rode through their city in god-like triumph, which was a reminder to them of their mortality" (163). It is worth noting precisely here how the episode deploys a sense of power, and of superiority, to the low, the local, and the ritualistic. The observer, meanwhile, looks on from his bad eminence. Despite his "arduous professional training," it could be argued that Milton is (in Graves's words) a kind of *Joculator*, "or entertainer, not a priest: a mere client of the military oligarchs." The term comes from *The White Goddess*, and I think the following sentence is comically apposite in its de-sublimation of the "low": "He would often make a variety turn of his performance, with mime and tumbling" (22).

Before I conclude it would be sensible to contrast the criticism of Milton as man and as poet, with Graves's own sense of what creates and drives the process of creative thinking. In *The White Goddess*, he stated that

> poetry is rooted in love, and love in desire, and desire in hope of continued existence. However, to think with perfect clarity in a poetic sense one must first rid oneself of a great deal of intellectual encumbrance, including all dogmatical doctrinal prepossessions: membership of any political party or religious sect or literary school deforms the poetic sense. (409)

Graves proceeded to note that the poet must "learn to think mythically as well as rationally" (Graves 1961, 409). According to Graves, Milton's "austerities were not a gauge of his virtue: they were founded on a mystical belief in the magical power of chastity as a means to immortality" (Graves 1995b, 88). Higher morality is "the morality of love" ; "without love he cannot be a poet in the final sense" (Graves 1995b, 91). *Paradise Lost* is overpowering, "But is it the function of poetry to overpower?" (Graves 1995b, 91). Milton is "depressing and therefore evil" elsewhere his "vulgarity and classical vapidity are characteristic of the passages which intervene between the high flights, the communicated diabolisms" (Graves 1995b, 92).

I noted earlier the accumulated layers of poetic glory heaped upon Milton by subsequent generations. Excavating the tercentenary of the outbreak of the Civil War, at a time of world war, Milton appears (in Graves's words) to have endorsed an "undisguised Fascism" (vii). Wordsworth's lines—"Milton, thou should'st be living at this hour / England hath need of thee"—are, for Graves, a monstrously incorrect depiction of Milton. For his part, I contend, Graves excavated not a giant but a fossilized bone. The satiric reduction is a necessary one, for it appears to be part of a larger uneasiness in the text concerning the self-aggrandizement of the reasoning subject that might result in the straitjacket of the purely systematic or, at worst, the totalitarian ideologies of the modern period. Graves's own poetic projects such as *The White Goddess* rarely succumbed to these tendencies; rather, they worked through primitive resemblances, intuitive patterns, and a scholarly *bricolage* which was rigorous without being rigid.

One might begin to understand Graves's work less in terms of Jungian archetypes than through the appealing celebration of folk myth, custom, ritual, and carnival to be found in the work of Mikhail Bakhtin. Graves's organization of the cultural and the mythic, less systematic, more sportive, and playfully open, was in the future. Distancing himself from Milton as an unmanned patriarchal Muse, Graves was to make his own detour through the epic in his playfully inspired prose-poem of cultural metamorphosis, *The White Goddess*.

WORKS CITED

Graves, Robert. 1943. *Wife to Mr. Milton*. London: Cassell.

———. 1961. *The White Goddess*. London: Faber.

———. 1969. *The Crane Bag and Other Disputed Subjects*. London: Cassell.

———. 1995a. *The Centenary Selected Poems*. Edited by Patrick Quinn. Manchester: Carcanet.

———. 1995b. *The Collected Writings on Poetry*. Edited by Paul O'Prey. Manchester: Carcanet.

Part IV
The White Goddess

"The Nature of the Goddess": Ted Hughes and Robert Graves

NICK GAMMAGE

TRACING THE EXTENT OF ONE WRITER'S INFLUENCE ON ANOTHER IS INEVITABLY problematic, and the conclusions can be at best provisional. This is how Ted Hughes described the problem, responding to a question about how much he had been influenced by his reading of D. H. Lawrence:

> Inevitably a writer like Lawrence, who brought to consciousness and formulated so much that was coming to life in the country as a whole, is blended into the cultural air we breathe. It is not easy to know what is our own, and what came through him—it is probably impossible, since so many of his ideas were not original with him either. (Letter to the author, 1 May 1980)

This is particularly relevant here, since much of what Hughes says about Lawrence is equally true of Graves. I want to look at what Hughes has said about his reading of *The White Goddess*, and its influence on the development of his thinking. I also want to look at how he deals imaginatively with that element of Nature that is of central interest to both Graves and Hughes: the vigourous creative impulse that Hughes identifies as the feminine aspect of Nature, and which Graves dramatizes as the White Goddess.

Hughes was given his copy of *The White Goddess* by his English teacher in autumn 1951 shortly before entering Cambridge, where the book remained close by him throughout his three years. He says much of what he found of interest to Graves in that book was already of great interest to him. It has often been assumed that Hughes's early poem "Song" was written as a sort of hymn to the Muse goddess that Graves evokes in that book. Clearly the female addressed in "Song" does share genetic characteristics with the mythic deity at the heart of the White Goddess. But Hughes says that "Song" was written more than two years before he read the book, in June 1949, when he was eighteen. The poem, he says, came "literally out of the air" (Letter to the author, 15 Dec 1992). The White Goddess was the first thing by Graves he had read.

Although much of the detailed material in *The White Goddess* such as the tree alphabet was new to Hughes, he was already familiar with the outlines of the Middle Eastern, Egyptian, Welsh, and Irish mythology it contains and knew some of the detail. This is how he describes his first reaction to the book:

> I recall my slight resentment to find him taking possession of what I considered to be my secret patch. . . . I regarded all that as my speciality. And in particular, I suppose, what really interested me were those supernatural women. Especially the underworld women. (Letter to the author, 7 April 1995)

He goes on to describe the book's "big effect" on him: "I suppose through Graves I began to see the whole thing had roots in biology—rather than in the fantasies of different or related nations. I began to see it more as a language in itself" (Letter to the author, 7 April 1995).

By the time Hughes came to Graves he had an intimate, firsthand knowledge of the landscapes of the west and south Yorkshire of his boyhood, with their violent extremes of weather. His fascination extended beyond the physical nature of that world, to its inner pulse. His brother, ten years older, had large hunting territories which passed to Hughes. His early years, he says, were lived in a "kind of dream of being a Palaeolithic hunter" (Letter to the author, 15 December 1992). He had experienced the births and deaths of that landscape, and the rhythm of its natural cycle. By 1951, too, he also had an intimate knowledge of Jung's *Psychological Types* and, as he put it, "read Graves through Jung" (Letter to the author, 7 April 1995). The biology of the White Goddess can be located in Graves's exploration of the vigorous, irrational but supremely pure raw energy of both the external and internal world, which primitive man used mythic systems and their rituals to dramatize and control. What Graves dramatizes in the image of the White Goddess is the tension between two principal aspects of that life impulse—both the creative and destructive potential. These are the two key possibilities of human behavior and are functions of the organism's most fundamental drives: to survive and to reproduce.

This finds its most natural expression in the annual cycle of nature. Hughes is concerned with the forces driving this cycle, showing life at its most extreme, often just clinging on under almost unbearable pressure, battling against the odds in a harsh landscape. Like Graves he identifies this intuitive impulse, the creative element of the drive to survive and reproduce, as feminine. The energy is essentially sexual energy. In the story behind his Crow sequence, for example, he imagines the divine source behind the bungling, bemused male god as a creatress, not a creator. His landscapes are mythic landscapes, full of mythic possibilities.

Although Hughes's and Graves's focus is the same, there are fundamental differences in the way they evoke and describe the energy, and the nature of this difference illustrates the tension between the male impulse to control and rationalize, and the female, irrepressible intuitiveness. For all the excitement of the chase, there is something distancing and detached in Graves's evocation of the goddess. Take, for example, the first line of the dedicatory poem with which the book opens: "All saints revile her and all sober men." This is measured, cool, and polished, and virtually lacks any pulse at all. It is as if this control of the verse and the emotion behind it was part of Graves's defence mechanism—a means of controlling the threat of the energy. This may be what Hughes has in mind when he writes of Graves's poetry operating at "some kind of witty dry distance," while accepting that Graves's best poems can be "perfect" and "irreducible" (Letter to the author, 7 April 1995). Graves is reverential, but cautious. There is of course another voice operating throughout *The White Goddess* which is the exuberant, breathlessness of his brilliant exploration of the development and migration of mythological systems. It can be heard in his acutely observed and sensitively realized account of the historical and religious context in which, in England, the spontaneous energy represented by the mythic goddess was gradually repressed by Teutonic, Puritan rationalism, until the neurosis exploded in the Civil War. This is one of the most rigorous and consistently successful things in the book.

It is tempting to put this tendency to try and control the energy, sometimes through a display of assertive virility, down to a personality body armor. However it may also have developed as a means of coping with another aspect of the dangerous irrational: the almost unimaginable horror of trench warfare. That is clearly one way of reading *Good-Bye to All That*. And it is possible to see one obvious source for both Graves's and Hughes's interest in protecting the vigorous life of the spirit, in their horrified obsession with the way the spirit of a generation—indeed of a nation—was killed by the mechanised slaughter of World War I. Hughes grew up preoccupied by what his father, and his father's generation, had been through in that war and the way in which it had left the English psyche in a state of traumatized shock. For Hughes the war became a key mythology through which he was able to explore the creative and destructive elements of Nature. Graves, of course had firsthand experience of that mythology. But there was also another shared experience which may have influenced both writers even more. Both had immediate, firsthand experience of the repressive tendencies of puritanical religion. Nonconformism may have been in decline by the early part of the century, with its membership falling dramatically in the years after the war, but both Graves and Hughes knew and understood its capacity to shackle the spirit. For Hughes the black Pennine chapels were a potent image of that. Refracted through that lens, their work can be seen, to a significant degree, as an attempt to help the spirit fight back.

Hughes's poetry, like the imaginations behind ancient cave paintings, tends to explore all of this through myth. He celebrates the fundamental life impulse behind the shark's bite, the thrush's stab as a pure manifestation of the spirit. As with Graves, his most natural mode for celebrating it is through the voice of the storyteller. His poetry is an imaginative recreation of that energy, and he gives an illuminating insight into its nature when he writes of the drive which gives his mythic creation Crow his never-say-die resilience. Crow, he explains, is like the mythic Trickster figure:

> Trickster, demon of phallic energy, bearing the spirit of the sperm, is repetitive and indestructible. No matter what fatal mistakes he makes, and what tragic flaws he indulges, he refuses to let sufferings or death detain him, but always circumvents them, and never despairs. Too full of opportunistic ideas for sexual samhardi, too unevolved for spiritual ecstasy, too deathless for tragic joy, he rattles along on biological glee (Turner).

In his passages on twinhood in *The White Goddess,* Graves identifies the core conflict in human nature between this voracious life-giving energy and the rationalizing element. The issue is how successfully the two key elements can be accommodated without the energy being destroyed. Both Graves and Hughes know the best chance of achieving this is through mythic or religious ritual.[1] But their writing sets about it in different ways. Hughes's poetry is itself an emanation of the energy, as if his own biological apparatus is attuned to it.

The energy surges throughout his work, whether it is in his descriptions of fierce weather, the resilience of the snowdrop, the swoop of

---

[1] "If you accept the energy, it destroys you. What is the alternative? To accept the energy and find methods of turning it to good, or keeping it under control—rituals, the machinary of religion. The old method is the only one" (Hughes 1971a).

a tern, or the grittiness of a farmer working through a downpour. It is re-created most persuasively in his collections *Moortown* and *River,* and most theatrically in his Crow poems.

In this characteristic moment from *Moortown,* in which Hughes the farmer delivers a ewe of her dead lamb, the mimetic rhythms work both to evoke and control the energy, and the expression of tenderness:

> and as I pushed
> She pushed. She pushed crying and I pushed gasping.
> And the strength
> Of the birth push and the push of my thumb
> Against that wobbly vertebrae were deadlock.
> A to-fro-futility
>
> ("February 17").

Like Graves, Hughes recognizes this natural life impulse as a fundamentally sexual drive. As examples of this, to demonstrate the natural life cycle, Graves mentions that an aspect of the sacred hawthorn tree was "its strong scent of female sexuality," and he recounts how much of the mythic sanctity of the hare could be traced to it being "prolific" and "mating openly without embarrassment." Hughes recreates this imaginatively. The sexual nature of the energy is there in many of his early poems, such as "Macaw and Little Miss" and "Esther's Tomcat." And in *Gaudete* he describes one of the village women celebrating the rediscovery of her sexuality by anointing her face with the "spermy stems of bluebells," imagining her lover rearing inside her like an uncontrollable horse. The forces working to control this energy are imagined as masculine.

He describes what is needed to establish a balance between the two in an interview which coincided with publication of *The Iron Woman,* a book primarily concerned with the need to reestablish that balance.

> Men are the perpetrators of the crime but not necessarily destructive. The male is destructive once he's lost touch with the biological reproductive powers of woman. That's a break which has historically happened and is now trying to repair itself. That is what feminism is about.... But equally woman needs a little logical element to turn her energies to creative social use. She needs a male component if anything is to be born at all. Men and women are two parts of one system, not two separate systems. I wanted to reach that balance (in *The Iron Woman*) and make sure nobody was blamed for things going wrong. (Hughes 1993)

The ideas here are reminiscent of Blake's prophetic books and Jung's notion of the feminine aspects of the male. They echo, too, the conflict which Graves charts in the concluding chapters of *The White Goddess*. It is a short step from here to what both Graves and Hughes have to say about Keats and Coleridge coming face-to-face with the Goddess and recognising something in themselves.

When Hughes comes to explore this tension, his landscapes are mythic, almost dreamlike. Indeed some of his poems, radio plays, and short stories are almost direct accounts of dreams which—as with his verse diary entries in *Moortown*—Hughes tried to get down as quickly and accurately as he could. One of these dreams, charting the damage caused by opposition between male and female elements, became the 1962 radio play "The Wound."

Written at the same time that Sylvia Plath was writing *The Bell Jar* (although Hughes says he did not know that at the time), "The Wound" conjures up a nightmare world in which a queen and her attendants, damaged in some way by their experiences at male hands, literally tear apart the male ego. It recalls the lineage of god-destroying creatresses from Tiamat to Astarte to Venus. Crucially, the act of destruction is seen as offering the male the chance of rebirth into something fuller, more whole, just as *The White Goddess* offers life through the death of Puritan rationalism.

The attempt to heal and restore the damaged female is a recurrent motif in Hughes's work. Behind the bungling God in *Crow* is a feminine creative spirit whom Crow manages to glimpse in her agony of being destroyed by male logic, reason, and repression.

His quest to find and heal her reaches a successful climax and consummation in the sexual union described in "Bride and Groom Lie Hidden For Three Days"—a Crow poem not collected until *Cave Birds*. Again in *Gaudete*, the drama revolves around a Protestant minister's attempts to repair a damaged female deity in a mythic underworld. Graves's images for the cause of this damage—mythically through the murder of Tiamat by her son Marduk and historically through the suppression of Mary worship, are given—as Hughes gives them to us—as images of an internal conflict within the male. This is how Graves puts it:

> It will be objected that man has as valid a claim to divinity as women. This is true only in a sense: he is divine not in his single person, but only in his twinhood. As Osiris, the spirit of the Waxing Year, he is always jealous of his weird Set, the spirit of the Waning Year. (Graves 1979, 110)

The sexual nature of the irrational energy helps account for the attractiveness of its manifestation in myth, poetry, and drama—Lady

Macbeth against Duncan, Set against Osiris, Edmund against Cordelia/Edgar. It also helps explain the sexual attractiveness to the village women of the animal like Reverend Lumb in *Gaudete*. And before the drama of Gaudete dramatizes the inner conflict between the two halves of the self—the rational and the irrational—it is signposted in one of the book's epigraphs from Parzival:

> Their battle had reached the point where I cannot refrain from speaking up. And I mourn for this, for they were the two sons of one man. One could say that "they" were fighting in this way if one wanted to speak of two. These two, however, were one. For "my brother and I" is one body, like good man and good wife. Contending here from loyalty of heart, one flesh, one blood, was doing itself much harm.

One of the aspects of this battle which Graves records in *The White Goddess* is what he calls the "love chase"—originally the chase and conquest of the resisting male by the fertility and sexual energy of the female. It is a fertility rite, and also an image for a spiritual journey into rebirth.

Hughes's writing is concerned with this conflict from very early on. It is central to the inspiration, for example, behind his short stories "The Rain Horse" and "The Harvesting," in which the mythic characteristics of horse, greyhound, and hare help to carry his meaning. The epigraph to "The Harvesting" is in fact a couplet from an old witches' song, which he may have found for the first time in *The White Goddess* where Graves restores it in full, as an example of the love chase: "And I shall go into a hare / With sorrow and sighs and mickle care" (Heaney 1982, 26). This couplet, recalling what Graves had to say about the promiscuity of the hare, makes clear the difficulty of making the transformation into a more complete, liberated state.

"The Rain Horse" and "The Harvesting" are set on the same south Yorkshire hillside (Letter to the author, 15 December 1992). In the first the narrator, out of place in the countryside. feels threatened by the animal presence of the horse. In the second, things go much further. Grooby, equally out of place on a hunting trip, becomes the hunted because he cannot cope with the heat and the sheer presence of the hare he is hunting, and with which he suddenly comes face-to-face. His discomfort is contrasted with the natural instinct of the local colliers' dogs. He cannot cope and loses consciousness.

Although Hughes came to his view of the conflict from sources wider than Graves, he says his reading of *The White Goddess* helped to bring the essential nature of the conflict, in England, into clearer focus and give it a clear historical and religious context:

> Gradually, after Graves plus Blake, I began to see the religious aspect of that Civil War division. Again, I had all that in my locker—because of my early experience of methodist puritanism in the Calder Valley.... So once the big picture was there, from Blake, Jung, Graves and my own experience of what the conflict cost me in modern England, everything else I read gradually filled in the detail.... In the end I began to see Shakespeare's work as the magnetic field where the whole disaster was given a wonderfully complete descriptive and prophetic pattern. (Letter to the author, 7 April 1995)

In *The White Goddess* Graves had recognized Shakespeare's acute awareness of the diabolic element of Nature. But in the long essaying accompanying his *Choice of Shakespeare's Verse* for Faber in 1971, Hughes took this notion much further. The taproot of Shakespeare's poetry, he explains, is "a sexual dilemma of a peculiarly black and ugly kind" (Hughes 1971b, 181). And Hughes argues that this dilemma in Shakespeare's own nature mirrored the crux of the religious dilemma of his times. Hughes took this even further in his intricately detailed study of Shakespeare's plays and long poems, *Shakespeare and the Goddess of Complete Being*, which he published to the same mixture of wonder, scepticism, and bafflement which had greeted *The White Goddess*. His argument is that the plays chart the progress of Shakespeare's exploration of that sexual dilemma within the broader religious context. The hero, rejecting the diabolic—which he repeatedly locates in female sexuality—is rejecting an essential part of his own nature, with dire consequences. At one of the points in the book at which Hughes summarizes his argument, he describes how this rejection of the diabolic—part of the goddess of total unconditional love—is actually the rejection of part of his own soul:

> The female, as Goddess of Divine Love, is identified, in occult fashion, with the hero's own soul: this is a fact which he both knows and does not know.... He apprehends the truth about the nature of the Goddess, which is that she is herself half (or strictly speaking one third) enigmatic, demonic animal, but intellectually he rejects that his soul is the same. His intellectual rejection of that unwanted half of himself (and of life) is the tragic error from which his (and her) tragic fate explodes. (Hughes 1992, 214)

The hero, Hughes argues, cannot separate the two aspects of the goddess—the creative and the destructive—and so ends up rejecting both, rejecting both Gertrude and Ophelia, Cordelia and her sisters. The plays are an attempt to heal the breach and bring the soul back to life.

This was the neurosis-inducing split that Graves had described, brought about by the suppression of Mary worship and tree lore by an increasingly repressive and fearful patriarchy. In a footnote to his section on *The Tempest*, Hughes acknowledges the accuracy with which Graves maps out the conflict and the context within which Shakespeare was writing. *The White Goddess*, he says, can be read as "a rich primer for the genetic tributaries that enrich the bloodstream of Shakespeare's Goddess and hero" (Hughes 1992, 458).

If Hughes detects the aspects of the goddess working acutely within Shakespeare, then within Hughes's own work the closest we probably get to this powerful Goddess-Muse is in the subject of those moving prayers to a damaged deity with which *Gaudete* closes. Yet we can find an even starker evocation of the goddess in his work for the theater. Given the immense energy the goddess generates, it is easy to focus on just two of her aspects—Hecate, goddess of the underworld, and the love goddess Venus. But as the divine source of all things, creatress and inspirer, the third aspect that Graves identifies—White Goddess as mother—is equally significant. Reading Graves through Jung, the importance of this third aspect would have made a considerable impact on Hughes. And, indeed, the mother figure has an important place within the work of both writers.

Not only is motherhood central to the creation myths that interest them, but giving birth and nursing is central to the flourishing of the natural world, which they observe so closely. Indeed, this is what gives many of those *Moortown* poems much of their tenderness. Given his interest in the mythic material behind Graves, Freud, and Jung, it is hardly surprising that Hughes pays very close attention in this context to the Oedipus myth.

And it is in his development of Jocasta, in his adaptation of Seneca's *Oedipus* for Peter Brook, that he gives us I think his most vibrant dramatisation of the Goddess in all her aspects—diabolic, tender, and motherly.[2] It is his most potent conjuring of the beauty within the creative impulse in Nature.

In Seneca's version of the story, Jocasta's urging of Oedipus not to run away from his dilemma takes just a few lines and could have been given to a third servant. But in Hughes's version, Jocasta's

---

[2] Ted Hughes's adaptation of Seneca's *Oedipus* opened at the Old Vic on 19 March 1968. It was directed by Peter Brook, with Sir John Gielgud as Oedipus and Irene Worth as Jocasta.

much longer speech as mother-wife is a searing, red hot, top-speed invocation of the life impulse in nature—resourceful, intuitive, determined and reproductive. But the speech was not in his adaption from the start. He wrote it as he watched the early rehearsals, and in particular as he watched Irene Worth developing the character of Jocasta. When he gave the speech to her, and when the rest of the cast heard it, they were stunned by its energy. What Irene Worth recalls most about the speech is that it expressed not a fear of that energy, but an intuitive love and celebration of it. This is Hughes's account of where the speech came from:

> Early on I developed the feeling that the play is really about Jocasta.... That may have been because Oedipus as Sir John (Gielgud) described himself had to be not exactly passive but Hamlet-like in the suffering, sensitive soul-searching vein. Olivier's Oedipus would obviously (as Sir John pointed out) have been far more aggressively monopolist of the feeling of the play.Irene, as it happened , did have a kind of aggressive, tigerish, elemental approach. She gripped my imagination. (Letter to the author, 28 July 1993)

What both Ted Hughes and Robert Graves give us, in a combined effort which amounts to one of the richest elements of this century's literature, is their celebration of that tigerish, elemental energy, and their account of how to accommodate and nurture it.

WORKS CITED

Graves, Robert. 1979. *The White Goddess.* London: Faber and Faber.
Heaney, Seamus, and Ted Hughes, eds. 1982. *The Rattle Bag.* London: Faber and Faber.
Hughes, Ted. 1971a. "Interview with Ekbert Fass." *The London Magazine.* January.
———. 1971b. *A Choice of Shakespeare's Verse.* London: Faber and Faber.
———. 1977. *Gaudete.* London: Faber and Faber.
———. 1979. *Moortown.* London: Faber and Faber.
———. 1992. *Shakespeare and the Goddess of Complete Being.* London: Faber and Faber.
———. 1993. "Man of Mettle: Interview with Blake Morrison." *Independent on Sunday.* 5 September.
Turner, Alberta, ed. 1985. *45 Contemporary Poems: The Creative Process.* London: Longmans.

Robert Graves, the Esoteric Tradition, and the New Religion

DIONYSIOUS PSILOPOULOS

THE INFLUENCE OF THE OCCULT HAS BEEN UNDERVALUED IN GRAVES'S PROSE AND poetry. This essay defines the nature of the occult tradition within which Graves operated. It identifies a particular tradition—the chthonic esoteric tradition—to which Graves subscribed and shows the ways in which that tradition is related to pre-Christian sources in a matriarchal religion which, through secret societies, consistently opposed the patriarchal god of the solar tradition that became established as Christian orthodoxy. Graves produced a manifesto, *The White Goddess* (1948), intended to explain the chthonic esoteric tradition, a manifesto written out of a deep study of the history of religion and mythology, but written in a state of mind in which Graves felt he was having the truth of the universe dictated to him from without. This manifesto is an apocalyptic work, written in expectation of a new age and a new divinity—that of the Great Goddess—which would transform civilization and initiate a new world order.

The origin of the esoteric-occult tradition is obscure and debatable. In *The Birth of Modernism: Ezra Pound, T. S. Eliot, W. B. Yeats and the Occult* (1993), Leon Surette asserts that "Occultism's claim to belong to a tradition much older than Christianity cannot be taken seriously" (49). In his study of the occult sources of Pound's *The Cantos, The Celestial Tradition* (1992), Demetres P. Tryphonopoulos agrees with Surette's assessment, adding accurately that "the intellectual content of the occult is almost all derived from the Hellenistic period" (25). However, if we accept that during the early Christian period the esoteric-occult tradition found expression in early Christianity, Gnosticism, Hermeticism, and Neoplatonism; and if we accept Gnosticism not as a Christian heresy, but as an offshoot of the esoteric-occult tradition, as scholars such as Richard Reitzenstein (1978), Edwin Hatch (1955), Gerald Massey (1883), G. R. S. Mead (1906), and Carl Jung (1993) have proven, then we must acknowledge the existence of an uninterrupted esoteric-occult tradition through the ages, and we must give credence to occultists' claim of an uninterrupted pre-Christian lineage.

Surette's main argument in *The Birth of Modernism* is that the roots of modernism lie deep in the occult, that is, in the esoteric tradition. In my endeavor to outline the history of the esoteric tradition in order to establish the impact that it had on Graves, I realized that its doctrines constituted a homogenous body in appearance only, while in reality they were disseminated mainly by two inimical factions. I use the term "chthonic esoteric tradition" to refer to the esoteric body of initiates who remained faithful to the fundamental body of the esoteric tradition as it was before the split in human consciousness, that is, to the philosophy and state of consciousness symbolized by the Mother Goddess. The chthonic esoteric tradition is mainly associated with the feminine principle. Because of the split in human consciousness, marked by the advent of the patriarchal religions, the main body of the esoteric tradition changed and acquired a solar character since it accepted the new principles and philosophy dictated by the patriarchal religions. Unlike the fiery, flexible, artistic disposition of the chthonic tradition, the spirit of the solar tradition is typified by rigidity, technocracy, and conformity to the rational, analytical powers of the human brain.

Moreover, apart from the existence of the solar and chthonic tradition, I realized that in the Western Christian world there existed Church mythologists who, having no access to the teachings of the esoteric tradition (either chthonic or solar), interpreted literally the metaphysical and mythological doctrines that constituted solar Christianity. Thus, in the Western Christian world, the esoteric tradition no longer forms a unified body and, most importantly, its teachings (both solar and chthonic) do not coincide with those of the external religion.

Graves's knowledge of the esoteric tradition is staggering, despite the fact that he was not a member of any secret society or occult group. An expert in Greek, Jewish, and Irish mythology, as well as a serious student of the history of religion, Graves shares Yeats and Pound's belief in the theme of secret history. After the suppression of the matriarchy by the patriarchal creeds, the chthonic esoteric tradition, that is, the tradition which remained faithful to the esoteric mysteries of the Goddess, survived through the centuries to reinstate the religion of the Goddess in the spiritual consciousness of people.

The struggle of the chthonic esoteric tradition against the patriarchal spirit is discernible in human history. According to Graves, in ancient Greece the patriarchal Olympian religion was not taken seriously. "[A]lmost everyone mocked at it in private" (1972a, 50) and even Homer, the national poet of the ancient Greeks, was "a member of a secret mystery religion which had survived from matriarchal times, with seats at Eleusis, at Corinth, on the island of Samothrace and elsewhere" (1972a, 50). Even after the powerful emergence of Christianity, the strongest of the patriarchal creeds, the chthonic esoteric tradition managed to survive under the guise of several secret societies. Graves believes that in the early Christian European world, the cult of the Goddess was disseminated from a Saracen Sufic society to the Order of the Knights Templars; the Templars then communicated the secret, heretical knowledge to the Albigenses and Troubadours, and were also responsible for the rise of Freemasonry.

Furthermore, Graves shares Pound's belief that early Christianity had access to the esoteric tradition of the mysteries of the Goddess, and that it had appropriated the rituals and esoteric beliefs of the original cult of the Mother Goddess, adapting them to the new solar principles. The ties, however, with the original esoteric source were cut by the Church mythologists, who suppressed the solar esoteric teachings of the early Church and inaugurated, according to Graves, the cult of Mammon. Graves's belief in the cult of Mammon corresponds to Pound's belief in the conspiracy of usura.

Familiar with the theory of eternal recurrence, Graves believed, like Yeats and Pound, that the dawn of a new age was at hand; that two thousand years of patriarchal, primary occupation were giving way to the fast approaching antithetical cycle that would bring back the cult of the Mother Goddess. For Graves, the religion of the Goddess is the only remedy to the anarchy of the present era or transitive period. If humanity insists on reacting against the rising antithetical spirit and clinging to old patriarchal values, then, Graves believed, the catastrophe of humanity would be imminent. The Muse poets, who for Graves are the natural heirs of the chthonic esoteric tradition, and who, in *The White Goddess*, he equates with priests and magicians, are those who will help the Goddess ascend to power.

In "The Uses of Superstition: A Talk at M.I.T., 1963" (1969a), Graves confesses that even though he was raised a devout Protestant, he abandoned his "faith in the Christian doctrine at the age of fifteen being no longer able to subscribe intellectually to the main tenets of the Apostle's Creed. [He] began to doubt that a Father God had created heaven and earth" (205). Graves did not see his rejection of Christianity as an irreligious act. Paradoxical as it might sound, Graves was a very religious man, yet his religious yearnings could not be satisfied by Christianity. His poetic intuition rebelled against the strict patriarchal morality, which he considered obsolete and insufficient for the spiritual needs of humanity. The Christian Bible, the mouthpiece of patriarchal morality, was for Graves an unacceptable and "dangerous book" (1972a, 62), "edited . . . by a monotheistic and misogynous Guild of prophets; they set themselves to delete all favorable reference to women who controlled men by their intuitive wisdom" (Graves 1965b, 49).

Unsatisfied with the morals of his age and armed with his poetic intuition, Graves undertook a lifelong study of the history of religion in order to discover the spiritual values that would satisfy his religious yearnings. In his pursuit of everlasting values, Graves followed closely the history of Christianity, and his conclusions about its origins coincide with those of the esoteric tradition. Specifically, he believed that Christianity was not an autonomous religion, but a continuation of the patriarchal creeds that spread throughout Europe after the fall of matriarchy.

In *Mammon and the Black Goddess,* Graves attributes the moral anarchy and mental confusion of the present era to the schism in human consciousness that took place when patriarchy superseded matriarchy, or when the balance between the masculine and feminine principle was disrupted by the rise of the patriarchal creeds (1965a, 145); this schism is also apparent in the esoteric tradition itself, which was subsequently divided into the chthonic and solar fractions. Like his contemporaries Yeats and Pound, Graves adheres to the chthonic esoteric tradition and is its harbinger. Like Pound, Graves was convinced that the cult of the Mother Goddess was the original European religion par excellence, that the "Great Triple Moon-Goddess [had] . . . mothered the Mediterranean races" (1946, 8), and that as a "goddess of life and death . . . [the Goddess] ruled Europe long before any male gods appeared" (Graves 1972b, 122). Relying basically on primary sources, that is, on "Welsh-Irish-Greek-Roman-Gallic religious traditions," on "early Christian literature (the Apocryphal Gospels and Acts and 'Sayings of Christ') and Egyptian and Talmudic tradition, and of Josephus, etc." (Graves 1982, 320), as well as on Frazer's *The Golden Bough* (1954), Graves traced the origins of Christianity to the esoteric patriarchal creeds that preceded Christianity, and that, after the fall of matriarchy, were differentiated from the original body of the chthonic esoteric tradition.

St. Paul was, according to Graves, responsible for the institution of Christianity. Graves hints that Paul was an Alexandrian Gnostic who had access to the esoteric tradition and held the key to the understanding of Christian myths and symbolism, which connected Christianity with the preceding patriarchal cults. In "The Bible in Europe," Graves states that "Paul was the chief architect of Christianity, though officially ranking below Peter. . . . Paul's claim to have once risen to the third of seven Heavens (II. Corinthians XII, 1–4) shows that he was acquainted with the pre-Christian Alexandrian Gnostics who invented this concept and whose influence on the 'Gospel according to St. John' is well known" (1972a, 43–44). Paul, an adherent to the solar esoteric tradition, formulated the new religion in accordance to the requisites of patriarchy and obliterated, therefore, any reference to the name of the Great Goddess. Paul, according to Graves, initiates "the third stage of cultural development—the purely patriarchal, in which there are no Goddesses at all" (1988, 389), and in which the Supreme Being is identified as a male entity, "credited with male thoughts and actions and served by male priests to whom women owe implicit obedience" (Graves 1972a, 46). Graves hypothesized that Jesus was an Essene initiate who took literally the occult eschatological belief that the end of the world was imminent and whose mission was to undermine the cult of the Mother Goddess. He believed that Christ never compared himself to God nor considered himself the savior of humanity by dying on the cross for its sins. In fact, according to Graves and his collaborator Joshua Podro, in the much disputed *The Nazarene Gospel Restored* (1953), Christ survived the cross and probably lived the life of an ordinary man (xii). Furthermore, Graves and Podro accuse the Church of deliberately suppressing the facts concerning the story of the historical Jesus, namely that Jesus "neither preached to the Gentiles, nor encouraged his apostles to do so, nor showed any concern for their fate, and that he hourly expected the literal fulfillment of eschatological prophecies. [Graves and Podro] hold also that he officially died on the cross; but afterwards when he recovered from his deathlike coma and found that the kingdom of Heaven had not come, it was gradually borne in upon him that his sacrifice had been premature" (1953, 633).

In a sense, however, Christ's sacrifice had not been premature since it triggered the genesis of Christianity, which Graves calls "a stubbornly patriarchal religion" (1972a, 27). Christianity, in accordance with the demands of its founder, declared war on the female and strove to eradicate any trace of the former cult of the Goddess in the religious consciousness of people. When formulating the new religion, St. Paul, a Gnostic initiate who had never met Christ in person, never meant to make divine the historical Jesus. In his Epistles he expresses his belief in the metaphysical concept of the Gnostic Christ or Son of Anthropos, that is, the Christ who exists within the human soul and is the symbol of the divine, transcendental nature of humanity. Paul's belief in the Gnostic Christ and not in the actual personality of Jesus made him an enemy of Christ's apostles, who agreed to support the literal rendering of the Christian myths. Graves, in "The Bible in Europe," commenting on Paul and James's troubled relations, probably resulting from Paul's heretical belief in the Gnostic Christ and not in the literal interpretation of the Christian myths by the Apostles, hints at Paul's Gnostic affiliations and states that "there seems to have been a complete breach between James and Paul at their second meeting in Jerusalem which took place some thirty years before the destruction of the Temple" (1972a, 46). When Paul died, some of his Gnostic ideas were suppressed and some tampered with, an act which probably explains what Graves calls the "confused sense" of "Paul's story . . . given in the Acts of the Apostles" (1972a, 43). Moreover, Graves and Podro, in *The Nazarene Gospel Restored,* claim that "the original Nazarene Gospel was terse, factually accurate and intellectually satisfying to those students of the law and the prophets for whom it was primarily intended. But Gentile heretics pivoted it, mistranslated it into pedestrian Greek, recast it, and then subjected it to a century long process of emendation and manipulation" (1953, xiii).

Graves, however, does not identify the Gentile heretics who emendated the original Gnostic gospel and suppressed the founder of Christianity who, for Graves, is the Gnostic and not the historic Christ. What is certain, though, is that these Church mythologists, according to Graves, have frozen the Christian myths "beyond the point where they can be unfrozen" (1969a, 27). Thus, Graves, versed in the esoteric tradition, believed, like Pound, that this conspiracy of the Church mythologists or the gentile heretics led to the suppression of not only the elements of the chthonic esoteric tradition or the single poetic Theme that Graves refers to in *The White Goddess,* but also of the solar esoteric tradition, which constitutes the foundation of Christianity. Once the roots of Christianity were cut off from its esoteric fountain and the esoteric symbolism of the myths forgotten, patriarchal Christianity gave birth to the pseudo-cult of Mammon. According to Graves, the vicious circle started with the "suppression of matriarchy by patriarchy, led to the suppression of patriarchy by democracy, of democracy by plutocracy, and of plutocracy by mechanarchy disguised as technology" (1972c, 117). Referring to the degeneration of Christianity into the cult of Mammon, Graves, in "What Has Gone Wrong," using an analogy from Greek mythology, asserts that the gods who usurped the place of Zeus or Jehovah, the patriarchal god, lack the power to satisfy the religious sentiment of people, while Zeus or the Christian God can no longer intervene and ask the assistance of his mother, the Goddess, since he has denied her in the first place (1972c, 116).

Graves's belief in the existence of the god of Mammon reflects Pound's belief in the conspiracy of usura. Mammon and usura represent the same concept, that is, the anti-poetic spirit which destroys religious sentiment and debases human nature to a mechanical level. Echoing Pound, Graves asserts in "What Has Gone Wrong?" that "Mammon . . . exploits the discoveries of science for the benefit of international financiers, enabling them to amass more and more money and it is hoped eventually to control all markets and governments everywhere" (1972c, 112). In other words, Graves insists that an existing conspiracy of international profiteers is responsible for persecuting the chthonic esoteric tradition as well as extinguishing the esoteric flame in patriarchal Christianity.

The conspiracy of Mammon has debased Christianity to such an extent that it can no longer be considered a religion, since its original myths, based on the chthonic and solar esoteric traditions, have been subverted and forgotten, so that its rituals can no longer satisfy the religious instincts of people. Graves, an adherent of the chthonic esoteric tradition, believed that after the official establishment of patriarchal Christianity in the Roman world, this tradition went underground on a mission to preserve the spirit of the Great Goddess in the world. In *The White Goddess,* Graves maintains that several attempts have been made by the adherents of the Goddess to intervene and heal the rift between Christianity and the cult of the Goddess: "various attempts at bridging it by the Clementines, Collyridians, Manichees and other early Christian heretics and by the Virgin-worshipping palmers and troubadours of Crusading times have left their mark on Church ritual and doctrine, but have always been succeeded by a strong puritanical reaction" (1988, 425).

After the suppression of the early chthonic Gnostic sects, the Knights Templar were responsible for the propagation of the antithetical knowledge in the Western world. Graves believed that the Templars, who "had been collaborationists with Islam during the Crusades" (1969b, 222), received their secret heretical knowledge from their affiliation with "mystical Saracen freemasonry" (1969b, 222). In his introduction to Idries Shah's *The Sufis* (1977), Graves maintains that the Templars "were accused of collaborating with Saracen Sufis" (xiv), who were part of an "ancient spiritual freemasonry whose origins have never been traced or dated" (viv). Sufism, which according to Mircea Eliade is "one of the most important traditions of Islamic esoterism" (1978, 3, 122), is analogous to Gnosticism; its affiliations lie with the chthonic esoteric tradition since Sufists insist, like the Gnostics, on Gnosis, that is, on the direct, initiatory mystical experience of the individual with the Supreme

Being. In *A History of Religious Ideas,* Eliade affirms that the Sufists "were staunchly antirationalists; for them true religious knowledge was obtained by a personal experience ending in a momentary union with God. . . . One can detect in Sufism the influences of Neoplatonism, Gnosticism, and Manicheanism" (1978, 3, 124). Graves remarks that after the dissemination of Sufism by the Templars in the European world, "Sufi thought continued to be a secret force running parallel to Orthodox Christianity" (1977, xix). In "The Anti-Poet: Oxford Chair of Poetry Lecture II," Graves argues that this secret heretical force inspired the Albigensian heresy and the Troubadour movement (1962, 67). Graves, in "The Bible in Europe," stressing the feminine antipatriarchal manner of the Troubadour movement, affirms that "women's gradual restoration to moral responsibility and freedom of choice in love—though the priesthood was still withheld from them—came with the romantic Troubadour movement, a product of the Arabo-Persian tradition" (1972a, 58). Furthermore, he believes that like the Troubadour movement and the Albigensian heresy, Freemasonry commenced as an offshoot of the Sufic branch of the chthonic esoteric tradition, disseminated by the Templars in the Western world (1977, xix–xx).

According to Graves, Sufism was also responsible for Mariolatry or the worship of the Black Virgin, that is, the worship of the Triple Moon Goddess in the figure of the Virgin Mary. In *The White Goddess,* Graves describes how the cult of Mary came to England from the Holy Land via Spain, and how the figure of Mary was another symbol for the Great Goddess, or Aphrodite. The Troubadours were for Graves enthusiastic devotees of the cult of Mary or, in other words, adherents of the chthonic esoteric tradition. Graves, in *The White Goddess,* maintains that "the lyre-plucking, red-stockinged troubadours, of whom King Richard Lion-Heart is the best remembered in Britain, ecstatically adopted the Marian cult" (1988, 396). Furthermore, he believes that the symbolism of the cult of the Black Virgin is pertinent to Gnosticism. Graves asserts in "The Bible in Europe" that the Black Virgin "represents Mary as wisdom—the use of 'black' for 'wise' having been borrowed by the Crusaders from Saracen usage, the two words in Arabic being almost identical" (1972a, 58). In Gnosticism, the Virgin Mary takes the place of the Christian male Holy Spirit and is identified with "Sophia, Wisdom; and Wisdom was female" (Graves 1988, 157). Furthermore, the Gnostics, who were the carriers of the esoteric tradition, were aware of Mary's association with the Great Goddess. In *The White Goddess,* Graves remarks that "in Gnostic theory . . . Jesus was conceived in the mind of God's Holy Spirit, who was female in Hebrew and, according to Genesis I,

2, 'moved on the face of the waters.' The Virgin Mary was the physical vessel in which this concept was incarnate and 'Mary' to the Gnostics meant 'Of the sea'" (1988, 157). Graves identifies Mary "Of the Sea" with the Great Goddess, or Aphrodite, the "'Wise One of the Sea' . . . the Minoan Dove-goddess who rose from the sea at Paphos in Cyprus every year with her virginity renewed" (1988, 157), and who during the yearly Eleusinian mysteries brought forth the Divine Child, who "was produced by mystagogues, dressed as shepherds, for the adoration of the celebrants" (1988, 157).

The myth of the Divine Child or Son of Adam, "celebrated at the Dionysian and Delphic mysteries ages before [the historical] Jesus was born" (1982, 341), is presented in Graves's historical novel *King Jesus*. In *King Jesus*, Jesus, who has declared war upon the female (1946, 342), becomes in the end, ironically, the Goddess's victim, the sacred king who has to be sacrificed annually for the welfare of his people. The impact of Frazer's *The Golden Bough* on Graves's *King Jesus* is apparent. According to Vickery, Graves's *King Jesus* is a "mythopoeic rendering of the cultural adaptability of the dying and reviving god figure" (1973, 148). Furthermore, Vickery, summarizing Frazer's basic argument of the *Golden Bough*, states that "to many primitive peoples . . . the priest-king is regarded as an incarnation of various divine beings, that is, he constitutes the connecting link between men and the gods. . . . As a result his life is considered to be sympathetically bound up with the prosperity and welfare of the country as a whole" (1973, 50). At the end of Graves's *King Jesus*, just before the ascension of Christ, the Apostles, who had followed their master, observe "near the summit three women [who] stood side by side on a knoll: Mary the mother of Jesus, Mary his queen, and a very tall woman whose face was veiled. These three beckoned to him as if with a single hand, and he went towards them, smiling. But before he reached them, a sudden mist enveloped the mountain and, when it cleared, Jesus and the three women were gone" (1946, 351). By presenting Jesus as the sacrificial victim of the Goddess, Graves expresses his conviction that the patriarchal spirit did not succeed in extinguishing the worship of the Goddess in the religious consciousness of people after all. Graves believes that the "Theme," that is the cult of the Goddess or the chthonic esoteric tradition, "reasserted itself popularly with the Virgin as the White Goddess, Jesus as the Waxing Sun, the Devil as the Waning Sun" (1988, 473).

In his introductory letter to "The Feather Bed," Graves expresses his dissatisfaction with the patriarchal god, whom he considers "violent, blundering, deceitful," and at the same time proclaims his sympathy for Lucifer, the morning star, whom he regards as "the hope of eventual adjustment between ancient habits and present needs" (Kirkham 1969, 7A). Graves is not a Satanist in the modern, Christian sense of the word, nor a "charlatan who imposes upon reality a world of private fantasies" (Steiner 1960, 340). Satan, or the Serpent or Devil, is for Graves one of the twin sons of the Great Goddess, specifically the son who represents the dark half of the Moon Goddess, the subconscious powers of the human psyche. In *The White Goddess,* Graves demonstrates that the Goddess "has a son who is also her lover and her victim, the Star-son, or Demon of the waxing year. He alternates in her favor with his tanist Python, the Serpent of Wisdom, the Demon of the Waning year, his darker self" (1988, 393). Lucifer is the son who brings forth the Light or Star-Son, that is, the Son of the Mother who precedes or gives way to the Son of Man or Star-Son, the waxing days of the Moon. In Christian mythology, interpreted in esoteric terms, Christ is the Son of Man or Star-Son, that is, the Son who dominates or represents the fourteen waxing days of the moon. But it is the second half of the moon, the fourteen waning days, or the Son of the Mother, who will give birth to the Star-Son or Son of Man. Thus, John the Baptist represents, in Christian mythology, the Son of the Mother, the twin brother of Jesus, and the *prodromos* or forerunner, who prepares the way or gives way to the Star-Son or Son of the Father.

In matriarchal times, when the symbolism of the twins and the Goddess was understood, there was harmony and unity in the religious consciousness of people, as the two sons of the Goddess, the son of the Mother and the son of man, alternated equally in her favor. After the Fall, however, when patriarchy superseded matriarchy and the original myths were suppressed and forgotten, the Devil or Lucifer was no longer considered one of the twin sons of the Goddess and brother to the Star-Son, but the embodiment of evil, equated in the consciousness of early Christians with the female, an association which inevitably promoted unresolved dualism. Graves, in *The White Goddess,* remarks that "the new God claimed to be dominant as Alpha and Omega, the Beginning and the End, pure Holiness, pure Logic, able to exist without the aid of woman; but it was natural to identify him with one of the original rivals of the Theme and to ally the woman and the other rival permanently against him. The outcome was philosophical dualism with all the tragi-comic woes attendant on spiritual dichotomy" (1988, 465).

This unresolved dualism, which patriarchal Christianity imposed on the Western world, constitutes, for Graves, the source of the spiritual anarchy, confusion, and degeneration that wracks Western civilization. In a sense, Graves becomes the advocate of the Devil or

Serpent, affirming in *The White Goddess* that "the goat is bleating in protest that the Goddess's head is turned away and insists that it is now his turn to be cosseted. In Christianity the sheep are permanently favored at the expense of the goats and the Theme is mutilated" (1988, 425). Since the Theme is mutilated, that is, since the chthonic esoteric tradition has been suppressed, the rituals of Christianity, devoid of their original meaning, can no longer satisfy the religious hunger of people, nor can they reenact the past and help humanity remember its prelapsarian state.

According to Eliade, contemporary Western society "is in quest of a new myth, which alone could enable it to draw upon fresh spiritual resources and renew its creative powers" (1960, 25). Graves felt intuitively the need for a new religion, and as a poet he felt responsible for reestablishing communication between humanity and its divine source. Cohen, in *Robert Graves,* argues that the remedy Graves proposes for the lack of spirituality in contemporary Western society "lies in the revival of goddess-worship, the reversion from patriarchal to matriarchal society, and the abandonment of cold intellectuality" (1960, 96). Even though Graves did not officially declare himself the prophet of the Great Goddess, his sympathy for and support of the Goddess are still overwhelming. He remarks that the times are not "propitious for reviving her worship, in a civilized world governed (or misgoverned) almost exclusively by the ambitious male intelligence" (1958, 95). And yet, Graves does not rule out the possibility that the Goddess will dominate the world's religious stage once again. In his Y.M.H.A. speech, Graves observes that since the Catholic Church recognizes the divinity of the Virgin Mary, it is only a matter of time before the cult of the Goddess reasserts itself. According to Graves, "the Catholic Church has given the Virgin Mary many of the attributes that belonged to the ancient Triple Moon-Goddess; and she can now legitimately be saluted as 'the Queen of Heaven.' [Consequently] . . . social changes may well follow: changes that will obviously be reflected in religious dogma (if this system collapses)" (1958, 99). Like Yeats's *A Vision* (1965) and Pound's *The Cantos* (1986), Graves's *The White Goddess,* is, in a sense, a manifesto declaring the rise of the Goddess in the religious consciousness of Western people. Graves, in *The White Goddess,* commenting on the future of religion in the West, recognizes the inability of Christianity to cope with the spiritual impasse that it has created, and affirms that a solution probably lies in the demythologizing of Christianity to uncover its essential truth. The unraveling of Christian myths would metamorphose Christianity into a mystery cult and would reveal that its essential truth is irrevocably linked with the cult of the Great Goddess. Moreover, for Graves, as for Yeats and Pound, the new divinity is Christ, not the patriarchal Christ or the Son of the Father, but Christ, the Son of the Mother: "A mystical Virgin-born Christ, detached from Jewish eschatology and unlocalized in first-century Palestine, might restore religion to contemporary self-respect" (1988, 481). However, a mystical, Virgin-born Christ, faithful to the Goddess, will also acknowledge his other half, his twin brother, and thus reestablish unity and bring forth a new state of consciousness, symbolized by the Black Goddess. The Black Goddess, who presupposes the assimilation of the opposites in the human psyche, that is, in mythical terms the harmonious alternation of the twins in the Goddess's favor,

> promises a new pacific bond between men and women, corresponding to a final reality of love, in which the patriarchal marriage bond will fade away. Unlike Vesta, the Black Goddess has experienced good and evil, love and hate, truth and falsehood in the person of her sister; but chooses what is good: rejecting serpent-love and corpse flesh. Faithful as Vesta, gay and adventurous as the White Goddess, she will lead man back to that sure instinct of love which he long ago forfeited by intellectual pride. (1965a, 164)

And yet, Graves, like Yeats, was not too optimistic about the progress of humanity and its conversion to the new religion. In *The White Goddess,* Graves predicts "no change for the better until everything gets far worse. Only after a period of complete political and religious disorganization can the suppressed desire of the Western races, which is for some practical form of Goddess-worship, with her love not limited to maternal benevolence and her after-world not deprived of a sea, find satisfaction at last" (1988, 484–85).

Works Cited

Cohen, J. M. 1960. *Robert Graves.* Edinburgh: Oliver and Boyd.

Eliade, Mircea. 1960. *Myths, Dreams, and Mysteries.* Translated by Philip Mairet. New York: Harper.

———. 1978. *A History of Religious Ideas.* Translated by Willard R. Trask. Vol. 3. Chicago: University of Chicago Press.

Frazer, James. 1954. *The Golden Bough.* London: Macmillan.

———. 1946. *King Jesus.* London: Cassell.

———. 1958. "The White Goddess: A Talk for the Y.M.H.A. Centre." In *Steps.* London: Cassell.

———. 1962. The "Anti-Poet: Oxford Chair of Poetry Lecture II." In *Oxford Addresses on Poetry.* London: Cassell.

———. 1965a. "Intimations of the Black Goddess." In *Mammon and the Black Goddess*. London: Cassell.

———. 1965b. "Mammon Annual Oration." In *Mammon and the Black Goddess*. London: Cassell.

———. 1969a. "Two Studies in Scientific Atheism." In *The Crane Bag and Other Disputed Subjects*. London: Cassell.

———. 1969b. "The Uses of Superstition: A Talk at M.I.T., 1963." In *The Crane Bag and Other Disputed Subjects*. London: Cassell.

———. 1972a. "The Bible in Europe." In *Difficult Questions, Easy Answers*. London: Cassell.

———. 1972b. "Speaking Freely." In *Difficult Questions, Easy Answers*. London: Cassell.

———. 1972c. "What Has Gone Wrong?" In *Difficult Questions, Easy Answers*. London: Cassell.

———. 1977. Introduction to *The Sufis*, by Indries Shah. London: Octagon.

———. 1982. *In Broken Images: Selected Letters of Robert Graves, 1914–1946*. Edited by Paul O'Prey. London: Hutchinson.

———. 1988. *The White Goddess*. New York: Farrar, Straus and Giroux. Reprint, London: Faber and Faber, 1948.

———, and Joshua Podro. 1953. *The Nazarene Gospel Restored*. London: Cassell.

Hatch, Edwin. 1955. *The Influence of Greek Ideas on Christianity*. New York: Harper and Row.

Jung, Carl and C. Kerenyi. 1993. *Essays on a Science of Mythology: The Myth of the Divine Child and the Mysteries of Eleusis*. Translated by R. F. C. Hull. 1949. Reprint, Princeton: Princeton University Press.

Kirkham, Michael. 1969. *The Poetry of Robert Graves*. London: The Athlone Press. Quoting Robert Graves, *The Feather Bed* (Richmond: Hogarth Press, 1923).

Massey, Gerald. 1883. *The Natural Genesis*. London: Williams and Norgate.

Mead, G. R. S. 1906. *Thrice-Greatest Hermes§ Studies in Hellenistic Theosophy and Gnosis*. 3 vols. London: The Theosophical Publishing Society.

Pound, Ezra. 1986. *The Cantos of Ezra Pound*. New York: New Directions.

Reizenstein, Richard. 1978. *Hellenistic Mystery Religions*. Translated by John E. Steeley. 1911. Reprint, Pittsburgh: Pickwick.

Steiner, George. 1960. "The Genius of Robert Graves." *The Kenyon* Review 22: 340–65.

Surette, Leon. 1993. *The Birth of Modernism: Ezra Pound, T. S. Eliot, W. B. Yeats and the Occult*. Montreal: McGill-Queen's University Press.

Tryphonopoulos, Demetres P. 1992. *The Celestial Tradition: A Study of Ezra Pound's The Cantos*. Ontario: Wilfrid Laurier University Press.

Vickery, John B. 1973. *The Literary Impact of the Golden Bough*. Princeton: Princeton University Press.

Yeats, William Butler. 1965. *A Vision*. New York: Collier. Reprint, New York: Macmillan, 1936.

Part V
Influence

Telling the Truth—Nearly: Robert Graves, Daniel Defoe, and *Good-bye to All That*

STEVEN TROUT

AT FIRST SIGHT, ROBERT GRAVES AND DANIEL DEFOE SEEM UNLIKELY SUBJECTS for comparative discussion. Certainly their careers, as well as their artistic sensibilities, could hardly have been more different. Graves became a published poet while scarcely in his twenties, and eventually pursued his art, with comparatively few distractions, outside his home country. Defoe, on the other hand, was inextricably tied to—and obviously in love with—the cutthroat politics of late-seventeenth- and early-eighteenth-century England. A resilient businessman (twice bankrupt), Whig pamphleteer, Tory journalist, and even, at one point, a double agent working for both political parties, Defoe began his career as a novelist late in life, while in his sixties. Pragmatic and brazenly opportunistic, he would hardly have sympathized with Graves's often slavish and impoverishing devotion to the Muse; nor would Graves have admired Defoe's endlessly vacillating service to political causes.

Thus, it is ironic that *Good-bye to All That*, a mosaic of interpolated documents and anecdotes, actually looks like a Defoe novel, especially *A Journal of the Plague Year* (1722). A work whose seamless blend of history, folklore, and outright fiction could only be called prophetically Gravesean, the *Journal*, like Defoe's more celebrated novels, employs a number of rhetorical techniques that appear two hundred years later in Graves's autobiography, including the ploy of establishing credibility through innumerable "quoted" documents and the straight-faced recitation of bizarre anecdotes, always carefully qualified, yet cunningly fixed in the reader's mind as actualities. So, despite their pronounced differences, Graves and Defoe both deserve the title applied by Paul Fussell to the author of *Good-bye to All That*: "manic illusionist" (Fussell 1975, 206). Both are experts in deception, in the presentation of myth through what we might call factual rhetoric, a rhetoric that *claims* direct referentiality and absolute exactness. The following analysis, then, examines this rhetoric in both writer's works, though obviously focusing on Graves's, and offers the following conclusion: that by mischievously applying Defoe's fictive strategies to a presumably nonfictional autobiography, Graves parodies and subverts the entire notion of factual representation and makes a radical departure from the expectations of his audience.

Ian Watt has credited Defoe with the development of "formal realism," a "set of narrative procedures" whereby the novel presents itself as "a full and authentic report of human experience" (Watt 1957, 32). Although subsequent critics (see for instance, Lennard J. Davis's chapter on Defoe in *Factual Fictions: The Origins of the English Novel*) have persuasively modified this view of Defoe's position in the history of English fiction, Watt's assertion may serve as a useful starting point for our consideration of Graves and Defoe's affinities. The key word in his definition of "formal realism" is "authentic." For Defoe, who addressed an audience presumably unaccustomed, perhaps even hostile, to fictionalizing conducted outside of clearly defined, traditional genres, establishing authenticity often meant such literal procedures as posing as the editor of his own work, or numbing the reader's awareness of invention with a barrage of statistics, inventories, bills, letters, journal entries, and the like. At the same time, however, Defoe tentatively established the novel's claim to an authenticity, or truth, that transcended mere facts by asserting, as one modern critic has put it, that "[t]he truth is not the record of what happened merely, but the believability of the mode of writing that conveys it, or something like it. The writing can be true and the events fiction" (Seidel 1991, 14). As we will see, *Goodbye to All That* expresses a similar duality: more than any other World War I writer, Graves sensed that his text offered myths (stories that, while not literally true, lend a sense of order to experience and arguably achieve a different kind of authenticity), rather than the reconstruction of historical reality; yet Graves's myths, like Defoe's, ingeniously mask themselves in rhetoric that constantly pressures the reader to accept the imaginary as the factual, the creative as the documentary.

Before considering the rhetorical kinship between these two writers in greater detail, however, we must first briefly examine Graves's literary milieu, especially the assumptions of critics who evaluated World War I narratives at the end of the first postwar decade. Thus, this essay is divided into two main sections, followed by a conclusion: the first section will examine the critical camp, a large one in the late 1920s, that judged the literature of the Great War as historical evidence, rather than artistic expression; the second, how Graves's autobiography responds to, and subverts, such expectations through rhetorical methods strongly reminiscent of Defoe's.

1. Recapturing the Real War

When *Good-bye to All That* appeared in 1929, concern over factual accuracy often dominated the critical discussion of war-related fiction and autobiography—even though Modernism had already raised serious questions about traditional notions of capturing reality in writing. Critics typically rated "war books," as novels and memoirs depicting combat experience came to be known, according to their perceived fidelity to historical "facts"—whether a writer had accurately related the details of a particular battle, for example, or whether he had presented a supposedly isolated incident, such as drunkenness among officers, as a common occurrence. Thus, what mattered to many critics was not how the Great War could be used as material for creative and imaginative writing, and translated into compelling myths, but how it could be *recorded* by presumably (and impossibly) noncreative and nonimaginative writing. For these critics, most of them veterans, the representational or "photographic" value of a war book was everything.

In the wake of poststructural theory, such assumptions seem dubious. Indeed, many late-twentieth-century theorists, especially Hayden White, have pointed out the impossibility of an exact correspondence between signifiers and signified events—between historical discourse and historical reality—just as many Modernist works of the 1920s mark, through the death of the omniscient narrator, the end of confidence in an uncomplicated, mimetic relationship between life and art. In other words, for a growing number of critics and artists in the twentieth century, there is no such thing as purely factual discourse. Yet one need only turn to book-length studies of World War I literature from the late 1920s and early 1930s for evidence of a preoccupation with supposedly factual representation, as opposed to symbolic or mythic truth. Jean Norton Cru's influential work of so-called historical criticism, *Temoins* (1929, revised, translated into English, and published under the title *War Books: A Study in Historical Criticism*), is a good example; not content with castigating fellow Frenchmen such as Henri Barbusse for specific inaccuracies and errors, Norton Cru goes so far as to measure the veracity of World War I narratives—memoirs and novels alike—by examining the service records of the authors. Thus, in Norton Cru's conception of truth, imagination and myth have no place; the literary record of the war is reserved for those veterans who have witnessed the most violence, and whose meritorious wartime performance "entitles" them to speak. Something like Hemingway's depiction in *A Farewell to Arms* (1929) of the Caporetto retreat, which he did not witness firsthand, will not do.

Norton Cru's counterpart in England was Cyril Falls, whose opinionated reference work, *War Books: An Annotated Bibliography of Books about the Great War* (1930), represented the most comprehensive study of World War I literature then available in English. Like Cru, Falls prefers to be given "just the facts," and his bibliography invariably belittles the more overtly artistic and interpretive literature. Hence his dismissal of *All Quiet on the Western Front* as "frank propaganda" or his acerbic reaction to Graves, "another example of the intellectual whose intelligence with regard to the War penetrates a much shorter distance than that of the plain man" (Falls 1930, 202). Perhaps the most revealing thing about *War Books* is its legalistic language: Falls treats novels and memoirs as "evidence" and "testimony," never as expressions of myth. Listen to his description of texts which supposedly distort war experience by ignoring its brighter side:

> Yet the falsest of false evidence is produced ... by closing up scenes and events which in themselves may be true. Every sector becomes a bad one, every working party is shot to pieces; if a man is killed or wounded his brains or entrails always protrude from his body; no one ever seems to have a rest. Hundreds of games of football were played every day on the Western Front ... but how often does one hear of a game in a 'War book?' (xvi–ii)

Falls deftly argues that works such as Erich Maria Remarque's *All Quiet on the Western Front* or Graves's *Good-bye to All That* falsify by dwelling on the violence and horror of the Great War at the expense of its more "positive" features. But his position is disturbing. Are writers truly obligated to recognize every facet of their war experience? Or, to put it another way, are "games of football" as important as the wounds inflicted by modern weapons or the virtual annihilation—not unheard of at the Somme—of entire battalions? Graves, I think, would say "no." Falls denies writers the freedom to respond creatively to their experience, and, in the process, forgets that the subjective manipulation of "evidence" is inherent in any interpretation of the Great War, including his own.

Although war-veteran critics such as Norton Cru and Falls did not speak for everyone, their critical standards were, at the very least, pervasive, especially during the so-called war-book boom of 1928 to

1930, when more World War I narratives appeared than ever before or since. During the spectacularly successful run of R. C. Sherriff's war play *Journey's End*, for example, which opened in London in December 1928, the *Times* was inundated with letters that judged the play not on its theatrical merits, but on its presentation of historical evidence. Again and again, one finds letters denouncing Sherriff's tortured, dipsomaniacal hero, Denis Stanhope, as an anomaly, a libelous distortion of the facts. Thus, even though Graves composed *Good-bye to All That* at a pell-mell pace (in order to take advantage of the war-book craze), and in the midst of a consuming personal crisis (the breakup of his household following Laura Riding's suicide attempt), he could hardly have been unaware of the way that many World War I accounts were received, or of the degree to which his own book either conformed to or violated the norm.

2. Rhetoric and Subversion

The remainder of this essay considers how Graves undermines this insistence on historical fidelity, as narrowly defined by critics like Falls, by exaggerating the claims to authority and literal accuracy often expected of war writers, while simultaneously shaping his material to fit the demands of myth. The rhetoric employed in this parody is, I will argue, essentially Defoe's, and Graves adapts it to his subversive purposes with characteristic brilliance, irreverence, and cunning. Two techniques shared by Defoe and Graves stand out: first, the weaving together of anecdotes, often carefully qualified or discounted as hearsay; second, the inclusion of supposed "documents." As we will see, both of these techniques contribute to the illusion of factual discourse in *Good-bye to All That* (especially for the uninitiated, first-time reader); at the same time, however, Graves uses them to destabilize this discourse, blurring the line between firsthand knowledge and rumor, as well as the boundary between actual documents and creative artifice.

Both Defoe's and Graves's anecdotes follow a simple formula: the more bizarre an event, the more detailed the description. Take, for instance, Defoe's implausible account, in *A Journal of the Plague Year*, of a man so overcome by grief that "his head [literally] sank into his body." Characteristically, Defoe devotes an entire paragraph to this weird tale, tracing the progress of the head, inch by inch, as it settles into the man's torso. Then comes the ending, which draws the reader in with its laconic, matter-of-fact tone: "The poor man . . . languished near a year in that condition, and died. Nor was he ever once seen to lift his eyes or look upon any particular object" (135). Elsewhere in the *Journal,* Defoe uses specific numbers to authenticate his stories: for instance, when a desperate family blows up a watchman, and then escapes quarantine, the narrator specifies that two victims of the plague are left behind, and that "[c]are was taken to give them nurses to look after them" (72). And finally, the innumerable geographical details in Defoe's anecdotes add to their aura of factual authenticity, as when the narrator overhears the screams of a bereaved woman while "[p]assing through Tokenhouse Yard, in Lothbury" (98). Like the obscure Dublin place names casually thrown out by Joyce in *Dubliners* or *Ulysses,* Defoe's geographical specificity seems, literally, to ground the text in a concrete reality.

No less impressive, as a similarly subtle piece of rhetoric, is the now notorious account in *Good-bye to All That* of machine gunners removing cartridges from their gunbelts in order to "rap out" a "daily exchange of courtesies" with the enemy. As Paul Fussell points out, such a procedure is impossible (1975, 207). Yet the important thing to note about passages like this—and the book is filled with them—is just how effectively Graves has masked this piece of trench folklore behind language that gives the *impression* of factual reportage. So, in this particular anecdote, Graves slips in a technical detail that momentarily suspends the reader's disbelief: the German reply, he cunningly writes, is delivered in "a slower tempo, because our guns were faster than theirs" (1929, 208–9).

Equally persuasive is Graves's account of the training accident that supposedly occurred during his instructorship at the "Bull Ring." Passing "the place where bombing instruction was given," he hears

> a sudden crash. An instructor of the Royal Irish Rifles had been giving a little unofficial instruction. . . . He had picked up a No. 1 percussion grenade and said: "Now, lads, you've got to be careful with this chap. Remember that if you touch anything while you're swinging it, it will go off." To illustrate the point he rapped it against the edge of the table. It killed him and another man and wounded twelve others more or less severely. (1929, 233)

Once again, the concrete details—the regiment of the instructor, the noticeably exact number of dead and wounded, even the technical description of the grenade—create a sense of plausibility. Like so much of the grotesque, Monty-Pythonesque farce in *Good-bye to All That,* however, this passage raises some intriguing questions. How, for example, can we account for Graves's characteristic specificity? Granted, he was near enough to hear the "sudden crash," but did he actually witness the accident? Moreover, why reconstruct this episode so impressionistically, opening with the explosion, then proceeding, Conrad-like, to the delayed cause, which is offered in the past-perfect tense? Given such ambiguity, it is not unreasonable to assume that Graves has relied on other witnesses, unacknowledged in the text, who were presumably closer to the accident than himself. Which, if true, raises still more questions: Who were these witnesses? And just how reliable were they?

In contrast with this fascinating anecdote, which, if I am right, deftly passes off a complex (re)construction with multiple sources as an innocent piece of firsthand observation, are the passages in which Graves concedes the limits of his knowledge, thus appearing to make sober and meticulous distinctions between fact and rumor. Again, Defoe employs the same technique in the *Journal*. Following a set of especially dramatic anecdotes, for example, Defoe's ultrascrupulous narrator tacks on a tongue-in-cheek admission of ignorance: "I could give a great many such stories as these . . . which are very certain to be true, or very near to the truth; that is to say, true in general: for no man could at such a time learn all the particulars" (*Journal,* 71). Likewise, after detailing the abandonment of a plague victim by her family, the narrator concedes that the wrongdoers' ultimate fate remains a mystery: "whether sick or sound, that I could never learn; nor, indeed, did I make much inquiry after it" (69). In much the same way, Graves admits that his account of Bumford and Bunford's deaths may be inaccurate: "Bumford was old enough to be sent back to the battalion in the later stages of the war, and was killed; Bunford was killed, too, in a bombing accident at the base camp. Or so I was told—the fate of many of my comrades in France have come to me mainly as hearsay" (1929, 119). Graves's more subtle acknowledgments of secondhand information or hearsay include the ambiguous phrase "they say" ("*They say* that a certain Captain Haggard first used [the battalion rallying-cry] in the battle of Ypres" [139, emphasis mine]) and its even foggier passive-voice form ("There was only one officer in France who *was ever said* to have refused to go on leave when his turn came around" [175, emphasis mine]).

Far from destroying the reader's initial confidence in the text's representational accuracy, such passages work in concert with the presumably exact and trustworthy "eyewitness" information presented elsewhere. In other words, by intentionally fostering doubts about some portions of his narrative, Graves buttresses the appearance of truth created in others. Here, the innocent, firsttime reader may conclude, is a narrative that scrupulously distinguishes between first- and secondhand information. Yet the line between the two—

between direct observation and material provided by additional sources (or perhaps simply invented)—is, as we have already seen in Graves's account of that bizarre grenade accident, frequently blurred. Moreover, the passages whose factual authenticity Graves himself calls into question are no less rhetorically forceful than the sections of supposedly firsthand observation. Thus, Graves's text cancels out its own claim to having meticulously sorted the evidence. If we return, for example, to the description of the only officer "who was ever said to have refused to go on leave," we find that Graves has counterbalanced the appearance of rumor with characteristic specificity, detailing both the name of the officer and his unit: "Cross of the Fifty-second Light Infantry." Then, to establish further the sense of concreteness, Graves provides a section of impossibly exact dialogue:

> Cross is alleged to have refused on these grounds: "My father fought with the regiment in the South African War and had no leave; my grandfather fought in the Crimean with the regiment and had no leave. I do not regard it in the regimental tradition to take home-leave when on active service." (1929, 176)

Within several sentences, a man whom Graves apparently never met is transformed from the vague subject of a wartime rumor to a tangible character, complete with his own memorable voice. Thus, this anecdote achieves two contradictory objectives: by drawing the reader's attention to the secondhand nature of Cross's story, through phrases like "was said to have" or "is alleged to have," Graves presents himself as a trustworthy narrator; the wealth of detail, on the other hand, gives the passage an air of factual authenticity in spite of the narrator's qualifications. In effect, Graves has it both ways: passing himself off as a meticulous historian *and* establishing hearsay as reality.

Suffice it to say, then, that in terms of their sources, or basis in first- or secondhand observation, the anecdotes in *Good-bye to All That* present an insolvable conundrum. Firm distinctions between fact and fiction, reportage and rumor, dissolve—or deconstruct— before the reader's eyes. More surprising, and unnerving, is the extent to which Graves's documents participate in this instability. The practice of substantiating narrative experience with interpolated documents was introduced to the novel by Defoe. In the *Journal,* for instance, Defoe's narrator interrupts his account with everything from weekly bills of mortality, numbingly presented in full, to the Lord Mayor's orders for the London populace. The symbols and charms of sham magicians are reproduced, together with advertisements posted by medical quacks. As Defoe no doubt realized, this tactic both creates the impression that a fragment of the event signified by the narrative has been literally incorporated into the text and helps to bolster the reader's confidence in the authenticity, whether factual or mythic, of the material that flows around these outcroppings of historical "reality." Yet despite their use in the service of a fictional narrative, Defoe's documents in the *Journal* are comparatively innocent, since they have been appropriated from historical accounts considered factual and authoritative in Defoe's day; as Anthony Burgess points out, the text *London's Dreadful Visitation* (1665), for example, provided Defoe with his impressive bills of mortality (Burgess 1986, 15). Graves's manipulation of documents in *Good-bye to All That*, on the other hand, represents less an appropriation than a deconstruction of historical "facts."

A revealing exercise in this regard is to read Graves's original 1929 edition beside his revised version published in 1957. Remarkably, discrepancies appear not only in the details of the anecdotes—the German reply to the imaginary British machine-gun message, for instance, is significantly different in the later edition—but also in the language of passages which Graves claims, in both versions, to have left unedited. Upon close examination, the collection of wartime letters in chapter 13, for example, proves to be subtly reworked in the 1957 edition; Graves has converted passive-voice constructions to the active, made new paragraph breaks, inserted commas, and, in some places, inexplicably removed or added entire sentences. Granted, such modifications fall within what Graves calls, in the 1957 preface, "the general editing of my excusably ragged prose"; however, the opening of chapter 13, in both editions, implies that the letters constitute genuine wartime discourse, unadulterated by later revision. In the 1957 version, for instance, Graves retains the original one-sentence opening—"Here are extracts from letters that I wrote at this time"—and then explains the inclusion of place names "which we were forbidden to mention" (1957, 106). The alterations, however, go far beyond the restoration of geographical details. As Seymour-Smith points out, the wartime letters by Graves included in his father's autobiography, combatively titled *To Return to All That* (1930), are "more youthful" in style than the cynical correspondence in *Good-bye*. Seymour-Smith further indicates (though without establishing any specific sources) that Graves "edited" his letters before presenting them in the original 1929 edition, "doubtless to cut out any "wetness"" (35). Thus, the purportedly "original" documents in chapter 13 may have *twice* undergone extensive revision!

This may seem like excessive scrutiny. Yet Graves's revisions are important because they indicate the extent to which *Good-bye to All That* subordinates literal authenticity to the interests of mythic authenticity, as well as structural coherence and style. Norton Cru and Falls would likely consider the edits in chapter 13 as tampering with historical evidence, as lying under oath; I, however, see them as evidence of Graves's irreverent skepticism toward the retrievability of history (personal or private) and as part of an elaborate parody which serves up endless documentary "evidence," all the while subverting it from within. Indeed, the outrageousness of these subtle modifications becomes clear when one recalls the photograph of Graves's personal memorabilia included in the original edition: featuring military forms, a notebook page, ration book, and other wartime paraphernalia, the photograph bears the Gravesean caption, "Various Records Mostly Self-explanatory." But are these so-called records really self-explanatory? This cluttered montage, which few readers are likely to examine carefully, serves little function other than suggesting that everything in Graves's text—including the letters in chapter 13!—can be substantiated through actual artifacts.

Nor, I suspect, does the fun end there. Most scholars, including the otherwise skeptical Paul Fussell, have tended to regard Graves's other documents, such as the field dispatches, newspaper editorials, and Egyptian student essays, as factual gems unearthed in the author's personal archives of the absurd. Graves's confidence-inspiring, deadpan delivery has even taken in military historian John Terraine. Impressed by the wartime press clippings that Graves assembles in chronological order (these conclude, you will recall, with an outrageous image of Hun depravity: heroic Belgian priests strung up as "living clappers" for church bells [1929, 89]), Terraine describes the collection as a "fascinating demonstration of how myth is born, and how evil is injected into it" (Terraine 1980, 32). A "fascinating demonstration" indeed, but a demonstration comprised of actual documents or Gravesean concoctions? I would argue that virtually all of the documents in *Good-bye to All That* are of dubious factual authenticity, with the exception of items easily confirmed elsewhere, such as Sassoon's "A Soldier's Declaration." The infamous "Little Mother's Letter," for example, is especially suspect. Not surprisingly, the only corroborating evidence that I have found for this document appears in "A Postscript to *Good-bye to All That*," where Graves quotes from a diatribe allegedly sent to him by a former soldier: after attacking Graves as a "discredit to the service," the letter reads, "The only good page [in *Good-bye to All That*] is that quoting the beautiful letter of the Little Mother, but even there you betray the degenerate mind by interleaving it between obscenities" (Graves 1930, 35). This sounds convincing enough, as if the belligerent veteran knew of the "Little Mother's Letter" before seeing it in Graves's text. But is this second document any more reliable than the first? Both letters, one begins to suspect, may derive from Graves's formidable talents as a mimic.

Detailed research into Graves's "sources" remains to be done; however, his cavalier revisions in chapter 13 warn, at the very least, against *automatically* regarding the documents as scattered outposts of fact amid a no-man's-land of myth and rumor. Moreover, if I am correct in my assumption that Graves's autobiography contains more rewritten or invented documents than previously suspected, then we confront a text that radically defies the assumptions of critics like Norton Cru or Falls by asserting, as Defoe's novels do, the primacy of myth through the trappings of factual discourse, a discourse that Graves, a celebrant of imagination masquerading as an historian, ultimately rejects and deconstructs from within.

3. CONCLUSION

Both Defoe and Graves wrote during periods of profound literary confusion and reorientation. As indicated by his endless equivocation and duplicity, Defoe avoided openly defining the nature of novel—the "new"—as a referential text. Such a definition comes later in the eighteenth century, with Fielding, one of the first English writers to present his novels as novels—that is, as narratives openly different from those aspiring to the status of factual accounts. Thus, works such as *Robinson Crusoe* or *A Journal of the Plague Year* reflect Defoe's uncertainty as he experimented with an unprecedented and problematic variety of literature, one filled with conscious invention yet also claiming, through its specificity, a higher degree of correspondence with reality than that achieved by traditional forms. Even the titles of Defoe's works point to the instability and amorphousness of this new "formal realism," especially the original title of *Robinson Crusoe*, which reads in part: *The Life and Strange Surprizing Adventures of Robinson Crusoe, of York, Mariner: Who Lived Eight and Twenty Years, all alone in an uninhabited Island on the Coast of America, near the Mouth of the Great River of Oroonoque; having been cast on Shore by Shipwreck.... Written by Himself.* As a modern critic has pointed out, this is less a title than an argumentative invitation, one which plays up the exotic— presumably fictive—appeal of Crusoe's adventures, and, simultaneously, anchors the narrative in the familiar and the specific (Richetti 1987, 52). Moreover, the claims of a text "written by [Crusoe] himself" are, to put it mildly, unclear. Was this denial of the true author's existence merely, as most modern readers assume, a tongue-in-cheek prank recognized by Defoe's audience? Was it simply understood, in other words, that the artifice of the fictional narrative began on the title page? Or did Defoe genuinely intend to fool his readers, at least in the early editions? Just what kind of contract, if any, does this title page establish between writer and audience? If nothing else, such questions suggest that Defoe's narratives appeared at a time when the relationship of the novel to the realms of fact and myth had yet to be charted clearly—when, in effect, any kind of claim went.

Graves's *Good-bye to All That* appeared amid an equally chaotic milieu, one left shaken and disorientated by the debacle of the Great War. Paradoxically, the conflict set into motion two contradictory movements in interwar historiography, both of which influenced the literature of the period. For some historians, the war suggested, through its incomprehensible enormity and horror, that history had stopped, that human events were no longer open to exposition through empirical study. Hence, as Modris Eksteins has argued, the skepticism evinced by twentieth-century historians such as H. A. L. Fischer, who in 1934 wrote, "Men wiser than I have discerned in history a plot, a rhythm, a predetermined pattern. These harmonies are concealed from me. I can see only one emergency following another as wave follows wave" (Eksteins 1989, 291). The more chaotic war books, like Henry Williamson's *The Patriot's Progress* (1930) (in which horrific events merely happen, without any clear causality or meaning), reflect this nihilistic perspective. At the same time, however, the cataclysmic nature of the Great War made its (re)construction through supposedly factual discourse all the more urgent—and the epistemological confidence of some historians that much greater. As a result, historians who doubled as literary critics, like Falls, insisted that the real war could be retrieved, by historians and autobiographers alike, through the disciplined recording of facts which were self-apparent.

Graves, I contend, not only rejected this assumption, he turned it on its head, using what appears to be factual discourse in order to invent and mythologize with abandon. Thus, Graves's admission, in the final sentence, that he has "learned to tell the truth—nearly" is highly suggestive. For *Good-bye to All That* reflects, I believe, Graves's prophetic realization that the literal truth of one's own life, or of a titanic historical event such as the Great War, can never be captured in writing. "Nearly" is as close as we can come. It is only as an expression of myth, and as a product of the creative imagination, that Graves's autobiography can be said to tell the truth completely.

Works Cited

Burgess, Anthony. 1986. Introduction to *A Journal of the Plague Year*, by Daniel Defoe. London: Penguin.

Cru, Jean Norton. 1976. *War Books: A Study in Historical Criticism*. San Diego, Calif.: San Diego University Press.

Davis, Lennard. 1983. *Factual Fictions: The Origins of the English Novel*. New York: Columbia University Press.

Defoe, Daniel. 1986. *A Journal of the Plague Year*. London: Penguin.

———. 1994. *Robinson Crusoe*. New York: Norton.

Eksteins, Modris. 1989. *Rites of Spring: The Great War and the Birth of the Modern Age*. New York: Doubleday.

Falls, Cyril. 1930. *War Books: An Annotated Bibliography of Books about the Great War*. London: Davies.

Fussell, Paul. 1975. *The Great War and Modern Memory*. London: Oxford University Press.

Graves, Richard Perceval. 1990. *Robert Graves: The Years with Laura, 1926–1940*. London: Weidenfeld.

Graves, Robert. 1929. *Good-bye to All That*. London: Cape. Rev. 2nd ed. New York: Doubleday, 1957.

———. 1930. "A Postscript to *Good-bye to All That*": *But It Still Goes On*. London: Cape.

Hynes, Samuel. 1990. *A War Imagined: The First World War and English Culture*. London: Bodley Head.

Remarque, Erich Maria. 1929. *All Quiet on the Western Front*. Boston: Little.

Richetti, John J. 1987. *Daniel Defoe*. Boston: Twayne.

Seidel, Michael. 1991. *Robinson Crusoe: Island Myths and the Novel*. Boston: Twayne.

Seymour-Smith, Martin. 1982. *Robert Graves: His Life and Work*. New York: Holt.

Terraine, John. 1980. *The Smoke and the Fire: Myths and Anti-Myths of War, 1861–1945*. London: Sidgwick.

Watt, Ian. 1957. *The Rise of the English Novel: Studies in Defoe, Richardson, and Fielding*. Berkeley: University of California Press.

Williamson, Henry. 1930. *The Patriot's Progress*. London: Bles.

Robert Graves, W. B. Yeats, and Dylan Thomas: Poetry, Sex, Religion, and Feud

JOHN PRESLEY

> A laughing, crying, sacred song,
> A leching song . . .

T. S. ELIOT, IN HIS ESSAY ON YEATS, SAYS THAT ONE OF YEATS'S MOST IMPORTANT contributions to English literature is his influence upon the younger British poets who were able to observe a master in their own time. The influence of Yeats upon the poetry of Dylan Thomas is proof of Eliot's insight. But other poets, perhaps of an intermediate generation, rejected Yeats's influence—the most notable such example being Robert Graves.

Of course, W. B. Yeats was a familiar figure to Robert Graves and the Graves family, with less than a generation separating Graves and Yeats. Robert's father, Alfred P. Graves, had met Yeats, "then still in his teens, but full of promise," in the later 1880s when he met in Dublin some of the people associated with the Irish Literary Renaissance, including the painter John Butler Yeats. Later, in 1893, when Alfred P. Graves served as Secretary of the Irish Literary Society, Robert's mother Amy remembered seeing "the young poet Yeats" at a garden party at Edenhurst (Graves 1987, 18, 47).

Robert Graves's saturation in Irish culture, via his father's antiquarian and folklore interests, can hardly be overstated. As John Kelly has pointed out, "Red Branch House," where Robert was born, was named for the Red Branch Cycle of Celtic folktales; A. P. Graves was "by no means an insignificant writer" on Celtic folklore and traditions. Both Robert Graves and W. B. Yeats were to follow their interests in Celtic folklore, though to different ends; this despite the similarity between Graves's White Goddess and Yeats's Celtic Banshee. True to their social class—both poets' families were represented among the clergy of the Church of Ireland, for example—both Yeats and Graves were traditionalists and perpetual revisers of their works. It is natural that Robert Graves might follow his father's literary interests, even if to some odd distinction; it is just as natural that he might feel great "anxiety of influence" in his father's shadow. A. P. Graves was "an accomplished writer, and his work may well be the swan song of his class and his generation of Anglo-Irish."

In 1941 Louis MacNeice made the point that as members of two poetic generations before his, Yeats's and Graves's careers had certain similarities, though Graves was in no sense influenced by Yeats.

> Where Yeats began in the Celtic twilight, then moved on to a period of occasional and disillusioned poetry, and finally took to expressing an esoteric philosophy in verse that is symbolic but hard, Graves began with the romanticism of the nursery, moved on to a period of occasional and disillusioned poetry, and is now writing poetry that is bleakly metaphysical. The chief difference is that, whereas Yeats' poetry became increasingly human, Graves's poetry has moved further and further from humanity. (190–91)

Where Yeats finally exalted the most human, Graves attempted to show the ritual and mythic meaning of the most human acts; one finally reveled in the human, the other in the mythic.

Dylan Thomas once remarked to W. Y. Tindall that the three artists he admired most were Yeats, Joyce, and Valéry; many critics find allusions or even borrowings from Yeats in Thomas's poetic diction. As Keith Selby in his 1990 essay "Hitting the Right Note: The Potency of Cheap Music" points out, "Rage against the dying of the light" seems a clear echo of Yeats's "raging in the dark," for example, and the "be gay" in the third tercet of Thomas's villanelle echoes the advice in "Lapis Lazuli" (107).

Selby argues that Yeats was Thomas's favorite poet because Thomas was drawn by the Celtic tradition of the poet as prophet and seer (see Thomas's school essay "Modern Poetry") and further, that the "pose" of the poet which Yeats "manufactured" is particularly significant to the development of Thomas's own poetic posturings. Interestingly, it is probably the public persona and the stance adopted by both Yeats and Thomas that led Robert Graves to dismiss both Yeats and Thomas as poets; Graves had a lifelong dislike of both *men,* a dislike which led him to discount the poetry of both, often in scathing terms. The first public evidences of this dislike occurred when Graves refused Yeats permission to reprint any of his poems in the 1936 *Oxford Book of Modern Verse,* following up on his critical attack on "The Lake Isle of Innisfree" in the 1928 *Pamphlet against Anthologies.* Here Graves's criticism of "Innisfree" centered on Yeats's inaccuracies of observation. For example, Yeats's linnets fly about in the evening; linnets are, in reality, day feeders. Graves similarly thought it inadvisable to keep the beehives in the "nine bean rows," rather than at a safe distance from the cabin. In a letter to Lady Dorothy Wellesley, Yeats described Wellesley's own anthology as "ultra-radical," but after Lady Dorothy praised Laura Riding, Yeats changed his opinion of Riding's poetry, admitting that "I had rejected her poetry in a moment of stupidity, but . . . I re-read her . . . and delighted in her intricate intensity" (Wellesley, 37). Yeats decided that "as a matter of honor" he should ask permission to quote three of her poems. He knew, however, that she would refuse, "as Graves has" (49). In fact Riding agreed, but specified conditions Yeats would not meet (58–60). (At least Yeats's poetry was not subjected to the odd sort of analysis to which e. e. cummings is subjected in *A Survey of Modernist Poetry*. In justifying—finally—Cummings's dislocated syntax, grammar, form, and punctuation in his poem "Sunset," Graves and Riding "rewrite" it as a conventional poem.)

Graves's comments about the poetry of Dylan Thomas—and about Thomas himself—were even more scathing, and they are based on Graves's disdain for the Yeats-Thomas notion of the public "role" of the poet, and possibly on Graves's special disdain for those who idolized Yeats. In a 1941 letter to Alun Lewis, Graves wrote that "to admire Yeats as strongly as you do may be a sign of immaturity. . . . [S]ee whether his glamour is really the reflection of poetic fire and not a piece of post-druidic magic, cast by a little man, over young minds." Lewis had written that he placed Graves's poems "second to Yeats." He apparently thought this was a compliment to Graves (Graves 1988, 304–6). However, Graves's most vitriolic statement—probably—was reserved for Dylan Thomas, whom he called "a Welsh demagogic masturbator who failed to pay his bills," according to Martin Seymour-Smith, in his *Robert Graves: His Life and Work*, (373).

The influence of Yeats is plain to trace in Thomas's form and technique, borrowed phrases, and themes, and, most clearly, in his echo of the peculiar mixture of religious, sexual, and aesthetic imagery Yeats perfected in his later poetry. Both poets, in creating "substitute religion" for themselves, use sex as an analogy for human and divine creativity, and the fusion of art with this analogy gives positive self-affirmation for poets contemplating—and creating—the public role of the poet (and each term in this equation was offensive to Robert Graves).

While Thomas was able to see in Yeats's work the mature treatment of these themes by a mature artist, Yeats had no such model for this theme; he arrived at this analogy of sex and art after long years of work with these themes.

Yeats's own treatment of sex as subject matter undergoes a radical change during the course of the poet's career. In the earlier poems, the erotic is present only symbolically and is often presented as a threat. Most of the poems about Helen, or Maud Gonne, express a frustrated, traditionally romantic view of sexual love, but during the writing and revision of his "myth," *A Vision,* Yeats began to see the place of sex as a point of contact between the great opposites, between the natural and supernatural, between time and eternity. During this period, according to J. Hillis Miller, Yeats characteristically expresses this conjunction [between time and eternity] as sexual union. Eternity wants to incarnate in matter in all its forms, and . . . Yeats sees this as a procreative drive:

> The stallion Eternity
> Mounted the mare of Time
> 'Gat the foal of the world.
>
> (89)

The early poems insist that all life is not one—that all things do not remain in God—and Yeats insists upon viewing the world Platonically, separating spirit from flesh. It is important to note that neither extreme is completely good or bad; Yeats never, in fact, actually retreats to Innisfree. In these "dichotomy" poems, one can see the figure of the dance beginning to take on its later meanings of artistic and sexual activity. But the "faeryland" described in "The Stolen Child" is a land in which the faeries

> foot it all the night
> Weaving olden dances
> Mingling hands and mingling glances.

This rather genteel temptation is quite different from the later nymphs and satyrs copulating in the foam, but even this genteel display of sexuality is ambivalently threatening or tempting: in "The Stolen Child," the sexy faeryland is not really desirable. In choosing the faeryland, the child loses the comforts of the positive images in the last stanza, the calves, the mice, and the oat-meal chest. "Who Goes With Fergus?" is quite similar; the invitation is to go with Fergus "and pierce the deep wood's woven shade." The dual meaning of the verb is followed closely by a mention of the dance—"And dance upon the level shore." But this dance is not alluring either, upon close examination: Fergus "rules the shadows of the wood," his sea is "dim," and the wandering stars are "dishevelled." In "Fergus and the Druid," Fergus was warned that the spirit world causes a loss of vitality, both social and sexual:

> Look on my thin grey hair and hollow cheeks
> And on these hands that may not lift the sword,
>
> This body trembling like a wind-blown reed.

Though in the early poems the contraries are incompatible, later the sexual "sword" will become for Yeats the means of uniting opposites.

The result of sexual activity is sharply contrasted with the results of artistry in another early poem, "The Dolls." Man-made dolls, perfect like Pythagorean statues, are insulted by the doll maker's infant child.

> The man and the woman bring
> Hither, to our disgrace,
> A noisy and filthy thing.

The child certainly brings no comfort or reconciliation to his parents, one set of unreconciled opposites. The poem ends with the wife protesting, "It was an accident."

Yeats's distrust or fear of sex is combined with a new sense of its potential in "Solomon and the Witch." The potential lies in the transfiguring power of sex; the witch reports,

> "Last night, where under the wild moon
> On grassy mattress I had laid me,
> Within my arms great Solomon,
> I suddenly cried out in a strange tongue
> Not his, not mine."

A cock crows, but is mistaken: "Yet the world stays." If the lovers were perfect, time would have ended. The lovers must try again to purify both themselves and their images of each other: "Maybe an image is too strong / Or maybe is not strong enough." Sex is still threatening, even though now Yeats begins to broaden its uses as artistic subject.

The first of the Byzantium poems, "Sailing to Byzantium," continues to exhibit the characteristics of the earliest poems. Here, art is associated with some spiritual realm away from the "young in one another's arms," and the flesh must be discarded or conquered by will before the artist can be "gathered" into eternity. Several things are noteworthy about the expression of the poem. The first stanza, in which the old man describes the country he has forsaken, creates a division between art, the "monuments of unageing intellect," and sexual life:

> the young
> In one another's arms, birds in the trees—
> Those dying generations—at their song,
> The salmon-falls, the mackerel crowded seas,
> Fish, flesh, or fowl, commend all summer long
> Whatever is begotten, born, and dies.

In rejecting the physical, Yeats relies upon an old conceit, the sexual death metaphor which Dylan Thomas later exploited so successfully, and which has a history in English poetry reaching back at least to the metaphysical poets. The speaker wants to be completely free of the body, which he sees as dross:

> Consume my heart away; sick with desire
> and fastened to a dying animal
> It knows not what it is; and gather me
> into the artifice of eternity.

The faeryland of the early poems has now become an eternal "artifice" made by the God-artist. The speaker escapes into eternity, where he sings of "what is past, or passing, or to come," by abhorring the body; "Once out of nature I shall never take/my bodily form from any natural thing." The poet will become a prophet in Byzantium, but even this faeryland will not be perfect, as Yeats's diction implies. The emperor is "drowsy" and inattentive to prophet or to artifice.

Poems written after "Byzantium," beginning with those of 1932, reflect Yeats's search for this transcendence in personal terms, a quest which seeks moments of intensified perception, or wholeness of being. In the poems written before this group, Yeats had proposed personality and devotion to art as successful approaches to reality, reflecting perhaps, as James H. O'Brien suggests, the influence of his father or the theories of the Aesthetes (361–71). After 1932, however, Yeats turns more concretely toward the "fury and mire" of human existence. In these last poems, images of art combined with images of sex attempt to show that artistic and sexual creation are one, and that transcendence of self begins with acceptance of self. Crazy Jane, like Yeats, sees love as "a conflict of opposites but also as an escape from them to unity, wholeness, or, to use a word which she would not have used, to beatitude" (Ellmann, 268).

Laura Riding and Robert Graves's attack on Yeats in *A Survey of Modernist Poetry* has been described as "an elaborate piece of special pleading by Laura Riding in favor of the type of poetry written by herself" by Richard Perceval Graves (1980, 43). In fact, this biography downplays Graves's role in the production of *A Survey* to that of a stylistic editor of Riding's prose; nonetheless, this piece of special pleading savages both W. B. Yeats and the several poetic movements that influenced his work (and which influenced Graves, too, for that matter). "Twentieth-century dead movements" included Imagism, the Anglo-Irish movement, Georgianism—all seekers of novelty for novelty's sake. Sassoon, Eliot, Williams, Pound are all criticized for various attempts to be "new." But Yeats is dealt with most severely and most personally. Yeats, "who, observing that his old poetical robes have worn rather shabby, acquires a new outfit," is guilty of a certain poetic dishonesty. It is precisely the growth and change in Yeats's work that Graves consistently interprets as dishonesty.

Yeats is one of the "five living idols" Graves later pulls down in "These Be Your Gods, O Israel." His criticism of Yeats remains personal, and exaggerated. Behind it seems to be Riding's earlier charge that Yeats was insincere and changed styles too easily. But on the way to making that point, Graves accuses Yeats of "greed, impatience, and a lack of proportion, or humour . . . the early poems fall short of the pathetic only by their genuine feeling for Ireland and their irreproachable anvilcraft . . . the work of a negligently-dressed, misty-eyed, murmuring Dubliner, living in the Fenian past" (131). He accuses Yeats of lacking the courage of Vachel Lindsay and quotes Yeats's letter to Sturge Moore preferring "the violent expression of error to the reasonable expression of truth which corrupts by its lack of pugnacity."

Thomas's poetry is similar to Yeats's later poetry in many respects. Like Yeats, Thomas sees art as the reconciliation of opposites. In a letter to Charles Fisher in 1935, Thomas writes, "I like things that are difficult to write and difficult to understand; I like "redeeming the contraries" with secretive images." (1966, 51). Again in 1938, in a letter to Henry Treece, Thomas describes his technique in terms of reconciling opposites:

> I make one image—though "make" is not the word, I let, perhaps, an image be "made" emotionally in me and then apply to it what intellectual and critical forces I possess—let it breed another, let that image contradict the first, make of the third image bred out of the dangling over the

formal limits, and dragged the poem into another . . . a poem of mine is, or should be, a watertight section of the stream that is flowing all ways, all warring images within it should be reconciled for that small stop of time. (1966, 190–91)

The phrase "redeeming the contraries" embedded in this Yeatsian—and Joycean—image is of course from Blake's *Milton,* in which Blake explores the poetic and religious doctrine of synthesizing opposites. Yeats was also familiar with this doctrine: from 1889 to 1893 he had helped publish a three-volume edition of Blake's works.

That Thomas, too, accepted the reconciliation of opposites in poetry as an essentially holy act is demonstrated in the "Author's Prologue" to the *Collected Poems.* Here, a drunken Noah, the poet, is gathering his animals into his ark of poetry (the similarity to Yeats's central metaphor in "The Circus Animals' Desertion" is obvious). W. S. Merwin, the American poet, draws the point directly: in Thomas' poem, "the creative act, in this case the creation of the imagination, is seen as holy:

> song
> Is a burning and crested act
> The fire of birds in the world's turning wood

It is triumphant over death:

> I build my bellowing ark
> To the best of my love
> as the flood begins.
>
> (Brinnin, 67)

With his central themes of art, life, and death, Thomas constantly uses sex as both subject matter and metaphor in his poetry. Eventually he comes, like Yeats, to use sex as an analogy for all creation, divine or artistic: all creation, whether literary, procreative, or cosmic, whether by man or artist or deity, eventually is fused, for Thomas, into one act. Thomas found occasion in his poetry to express his kinship with Yeats many ways: Thomas says, for example, he is "shut, too, in a tower of words," and over and over he uses the tower as symbol of art and of sex, as in "I, in my intricate image," or "Ears in the turrets hear."

"In My Craft or Sullen Art" shows Yeats's influence most clearly in its form and, to some extent, in its subject matter. The lines are three-stress lines, except for the feminine endings, as in "The Fisherman." Thomas has approximated Yeats's tone of cold passion, and the poet pursues his craft under a Yeatsian raging moon, writing "on these spindrift pages" only

> for the lovers, their arms
> Round the griefs of the ages
> Who pay no praise or wages
> Nor heed my craft or art.

Though the lovers "pay no praise or wages," Thomas dedicates his poetry to them, because they have, against all rational assessment, embraced reality. In "Our eunuch dreams" Thomas rejects the world of "eunuch dreams, all seedless in the light" and motion pictures—"the gunman and his moll"—in favor of heterosexual sex:

> This is the world: the lying likeness of
> Our strips of stuff that tatter as we move
> Loving and being loth.

Thus embracing, the lovers are holding "the griefs of the ages" because, in Thomas's world, reality, with its finitude, is deadly—"I saw time murder me." Many of Thomas's poems present this juxtaposition or combination of artist and lovers in league against death. In "Once it was the colour of saying," Thomas describes his childhood haunt, Cwmdonkin Park,

> Where at night we stoned the cold and cuckoo
> Lovers in the dirt of their leafy beds.
> The shade of their trees was a word of many shades
> And a lamp of lightning for the poor in the dark.

Here the poet recognizes his kinship with the lovers: their protective, camouflaging shade is similar to the many-shaded word; the last line combines two common symbols of art and inspiration in describing the lovers' trees and their act.

"Unluckily for a death" shows that Thomas had assimilated the Laurentian version to the Yeatsian version of the gospel of love's holiness; the poem abounds in phoenixes and stars in holy balance. Even the least derivative imagery shows how Thomas reveres the love he is pleading for in this "Caitlin" poem, one of a series written on the troubles of marriage. A catalog of the religious metaphors in stanza one includes saint, choir, cloister, order, nunnery, and, in stanza two, hosts, wound, ceremony, celebrated, communion, and breviary. Just as the poetic art is holy in "Author's Prologue," here sex is holy.

> Blessed by such heroic hosts in your every
> Inch and glance that the wound
> Is certain god, and the ceremony of souls
> Is celebrated there, and communion between suns.

Aneiran Talfan Davies's comparison of the earlier version of this poem in *Life and Letters Today* (October 1939) and the *Collected Poems* version shows that most of the religious images were added during the revision, along with most of the tortured syntax (1964, 37–39). In 1976 R. B. Kershner Jr. produced in his *Dylan Thomas: The Poet and His Critics* an excellent critical summary of explication that had focused on Thomas's religious images, most frequently attempting to trace the development of his faith, or his lack of faith, or to claim the Welshman as this or that type of religious or heretic (66–105). I would suggest that, as for Yeats, the great themes of poetry for Thomas were themes inherently mysterious and religious, thus making the vocabulary of religion one more vocabulary he could borrow, blend, and pun with in generalizing his meaning. His religious "thought" is seldom more specific than the consistently presented view that life is in its totality a sacrament.

Increasingly, though, Thomas displays his celebrated "pantheism," or his sacramental view of nature, in a near obsessive fashion; the religious is expressed in sexual terms, and the sexual in religious terms (Maud 1963, 94–101). Sex becomes "a way of attaining the fountains of origin through the woman as mediator (Miller 1965, 205)." In woman's "every inch and glance"—body and spirit—the poet sees "the globe of genesis spun." In embracing woman, the poet draws nearer to reality and nearer to divine creativity:

> the phoenix' bid for heaven and the desire after
> Death in the carved nunnery
> Both shall fail if I bow not to your blessing
> Nor walk in the cool of your mortal garden
> With immortality at my side like Christ the sky.

"Where once the waters of your face," a celebration of fertility, includes a direct allusion to the "dolphin-torn" sea in Yeats's "Byzantium." Thomas' poem is an elaborated version of the Yeatsian image; "waters of your face" is a reversal—Thomas's favorite device—of "face of the waters," the sea in Genesis which waits for the Word of creation. The diction and images of the poem indicate that Yeats's spirits, in another guise, may also be present:

> There round about your stones the shades
> Of children go who, from their voids,
> Cry to the dolphined sea.

In "From love's first fever to her plague," Thomas uses an even more direct allusion to Yeats's work:

> One womb, one mind, spewed out the matter,
> One breast gave suck the fever's issue;
> From the divorcing sky I learnt the double,
> The two-framed globe that spun into a score;
> A million minds gave suck to such a bud
> As forks my eye;
> Youth did condense; the tears of spring
> Dissolved in summer and the hundred seasons;
> One sun, one manna, warmed and fed.

Notice the image of the globe that spins into twenty globes, like interpenetrating gyres.

The sexual, religious, and aesthetic are joined in the "three-eyed, red-eyed spark, blunt as a flower" (buds and blooms are consistently phallic for Thomas), which is the central image of "In the beginning." This is a poem about the Word, and its three analogous products, cosmos, child, and poem; the Word appears in metaphysical and mystical incarnations: cipher, signature, sign, imprint, characters, letter, breath, and star. In Thomas's view the Word is sexual; "In the 1933 manuscript at Buffalo the creative instrument, neither spark nor Word, is the three-eyed 'prick' (Tindall 1962, 59–62). Here, in Thomas's most metaphysical poem, he comes closest to Ribh's description of divinity: "Godhead on Godhead in sexual spasm begot Godhead."

"Ballad of the Long-Legged Bait," Thomas' most obscure and surrealistic poem, is a narrative of a young man's sexual experience. The young man puts out to sea—the ground of all creation—and fishes for a poem, using a girl as bait. A word repeated continually is "rod," phallic or literary (as pencil), the fisherman's rod, the magician's wand or, as in Psalms, the tool of God. The fish sought by the fisherman may even be the traditional symbol for Christ. W. Y. Tindall draws the Yeats-Thomas connections even closer in this context: "Since the fish is the Word, it can be the word, as Yeats suggests in 'The Fish'; and the fisherman, as he suggests in 'The Fisherman,' can be the poet" (249–54). God is an artist in "Incarnate devil," a poem about Eden. Here, while Satan, "the incarnate devil in a talking snake," is shaping "the bearded apple," God is resting after creation.

"And God walked there who was a fiddling warden / And played down pardon from the heavens' hill."

The "fiddling" suggests tinkering, standing idly by, or making music (poetry) while bringing—or maybe minimizing—salvation.

If all creation is one, the poet is like God. In "When I woke," the poet's activities are likened to divinity, even though the bells ring, "No God."

> Every morning I make,
> God in bed, good and bad.
> After a water-faced walk,
> The death-stagged scatter-breath
> Mammoth and sparrowfall
> Everybody's earth.

Like God, the speaker makes a new world every morning (cf. "Fern Hill," where the farm comes wandering back every morning, with the cock on its shoulder). There are other possibilities—the speaker may be writing a poem, a microcosm of "everybody's earth," and the making may be a sexual making. But the last lines are periodic: "I drew the white sheet over the islands / And the coins on my eyelids sang like shells." Now we learn that the speaker is either dead, with coins on his eyes and a sheet over his head, or he is reaching for "the white sheet" on which poetry is written. If the god in bed is a poet, then the coins on his eyes are the foreknowledge of death, the poet's Muses, singing like shells in defiance of death. Tindall's early work on Thomas points out that these ambiguities were also added as afterthought, subsequent to original publication of the poem in *New Poems* (234–35).

Interestingly, given the similarities of Thomas's poetic themes to those of Yeats, Robert Graves's comments on Thomas seem to be comments only on Thomas's poetic technique. But on further analysis, these criticisms of technique may also be aimed at the Yeats-Thomas notion of the public "role" of the poet.

Graves's most specific criticism of the poetry of Dylan Thomas involve the opening lines of "If My Head Hurt a Hair's Foot."

> If my head hurt a hair's foot
> Pack back the downed bone.
> If the unpricked ball of my breath
> Bump on a spout let the bubbles jump out.
> Sooner drop with the worm of the ropes round my throat
> Than bully ill love in the clouted scene

Henry Treece, in *Dylan Thomas: "Dog among the Fairies,"* has called this specific passage "a verbal compulsion, almost a psychopathic phenomenon, musical-rhythmic automatism" (1956, 131).

In "These Be Your Gods, O Israel," Graves takes these lines as his text for discussing Thomas. Graves, before addressing these lines, has already characterized Thomas and his poetry for the reader, in a sort of preamble to specificity. "Dylan Thomas was drunk with melody, and what the words were, he cared not." Graves says that he had told the sixteen-year old Thomas, after reading a sheaf of his poems, that "they were irreproachable, but that he would eventually learn to dislike them." Graves claims that "to conceal" what he had concluded was a "defect in sincerity," Thomas had decided to maintain "musical control of the reader without troubling about the sense." Whatever the terms in which he couches his criticism, referring to "Dylan's golden voice" and so on, clearly Graves considers this technique a cheap trick. "But professionally-minded poets ban double-talk, except in satire, and insist that every poem must make prose sense as well as poetic sense on one or more levels" (1968, 148–49). (My Irish friends point out that this is almost a stereotypical English reaction to Celtic art; cf. James Wright's *Paris Review* interview [summer 1975]: 38–41, 54–55, in which he connects "being Irish" with the poet's negative capability, and an "irritable reaching after fact and reason" with British criticism.)

In a public lecture, Graves offered a one pound note as a prize to anyone who could explicate the opening lines of "If My Head Hurt a Hair's Foot." Graves himself attacked the lines as "typical . . . nonsense" (149).

A brave member of the Cambridge faculty in English, M. J. C. Hodgart, offered a reading of the lines (paraphrased here by Graves):

> The child cries out that if he is about to cause her any pain by his birth, let him not be born at all. He suggests that the child about to be born is here addressing his mother. . . . Birth . . . is represented here as a violent movement like a bouncing ball; and the child's breath before birth is compared to an unpricked bubble. Therefore: "If ever this soft bubble of breath should hurt you by bouncing on your spouting blood, prick it and let my life run out in bubbles." And: "I would sooner be born hanged with my navel string coiled around my throat than bully you when I appear on a scene made wretched by baby-clouts, or clouts on the head." (Graves, 1968 149–50)

The reading of the poem by Treece has been characterized by William T. Moynihan in *The Craft and Art of Dylan Thomas* (1966) as "shock and dismay." Hodgart's reading Moynihan characterizes as "one which accepts the lines on their own terms and tries to make them intelligible." Graves's reading of the lines is, in Moynihan's terms, "one of apparent hostility to Thomas's methods and temperament" (74).

Graves points out "the flaws" in Hodgart's reading:

> The hair's foot, misleadingly identical in sound to hare's foot, is not a hair's root. Also, the physical situation is blurred by the apparent contact of the baby's downy head with the mother's hairy one, and by the description of the navel-string as "the worm of the ropes"—why "ropes" in the plural? And by the metaphor of an unpunctured ball bouncing on the top of a spout—as in pleasure fountains; how the bubble of breath could bounce on the flow of lochial blood is not easy to see (blood is not mentioned in the poem). And why should the unpricked bubble become "bubbles?" And is the infant experienced or ignorant? If ignorant, how can it anticipate baby-clouts, and balls bouncing on fountains? If experienced, how can it make so absurd a suggestion as that the mother should push its head back to relieve her labour pains? And if it is so considerate and saintly as Mr. Hodgart suggests, why should it ever turn bully? (1968, 150)

Needless to say, Graves kept his one-pound note, conceding only that Hodgart "may have identified the thin thread of sense on which the enormous and disgusting hyperboles of the child's address are strung." Graves concluded "the five lines taken as a whole remain nonsensical" (1968, 150).

Graves was not alone in his dislike for Thomas's obscurity by any means. Lord Samuels, making an award to John Betjeman in 1955, had denounced poetic obscurity in his address, taking a few lines of "A grief ago" as illustration. The first public interchange on the subject was a series of letters—reprinted in Treece—between Edith Sitwell and Thomas himself, where Thomas maintained that he did have a "literal meaning" in mind for his poems. Julian Symons, in "Obscurity and Dylan Thomas," in the *Kenyon Review*, had classified Thomas among those poets who obscure simple thoughts and ideas with difficult, and sometimes irrelevant, language. Some of the poems, according to Symons, simply are "not about very much" and display "no story, no continuity." A simple subject appears in an overworked poem with complexity and obscurity "imposed from outside," the poem "has too many meanings." John Press, in *The Chequer'd Shade: Reflections on Obscurity in Poetry*, had complained "the profusion of heady images blurs the clarity and the coherence of the poetic argument" in Thomas's work. These and other attacks on

Thomas's techniques are summarized in *Dylan Thomas: The Poet and His Critics,* by R. B. Kershner Jr. (1976, 203–11).

A third critic, William York Tindall, offered this explanation of the opening of the disputed poem in his *A Reader's Guide to Dylan Thomas:*

> Hair and foot, anatomical extremes, find reconciliation in "hair's foot" at the pubic middle. Promising no harm to this, the embryo, still "unpricked" in several senses, also promises no interference with father's "spout." The imagery is at once familiar and extravagant—but so, after all, [sic] a speaking embryo. Compare the "bubbles of unpricked breath" with the "swag of bubbles in a seedy sack" (76). The "worm of the ropes" seems umbilical, phallic, and deathly. Better polite death than playing the bully to parental loving, however "ill" or ill-timed. "Clouted," which echoes "out," involves amatory striking and, by anticipation, swaddling. (1962, 173–74)

"Nothing by Thomas could be plainer," Tindall maintains. Treece characterizes Tindall's reading, however, as at times "over-imaginative and over-ingenious." Nonetheless, he considers Tindall's reading, Hodgart's and his own—which merely corrects the other two—to be successful explications, and claims they are so for several simple reasons. Tindall, Treece, and Hodgart are "familiar with Thomas's use of voices" and are "exploiting common knowledge of Thomas's verbal devices." Here Treece means the substitution of other words for the usual words in a cliche, for example; "hair's breadth" becomes "a hair's foot." These three critics, too, "understand certain of Thomas's metaphorical practices." In other poems, a "ball" may mean life, so a "pricked bubble" eventually loses its air, its life—Treece points out that Yeats uses this same image in "In Memory of Major Robert Gregory" (74–75).

But in his conclusion to the comparison of these readings, Treece comes very close—though Kershner considers Treece a critic sympathetic to Thomas—to the positions of Graves and Symons. Treece admits, at first, no quarter: "it is not justified to exalt Thomas's verbal play . . . nor is it justified to see this kind of craftsmanship as a low-grade entertainment, one rank below detective stories and crossword puzzles." However, he finally admits, "it would seem to be that there is a marvelous abundance of imagination in Thomas, but its obscurity often mars our esthetic appreciation of it."

How familiar must the successful reader be with a poet's themes and techniques, with a poet's "system?" In considering themes—rather than techniques—it is only reasonable to attempt to link Graves's *White Goddess* with Yeats's *A Vision,* as does John B. Vickery throughout his study, *Robert Graves and the White Goddess*. But he makes a distinction between two types of poems which is, finally, a specious distinction. Graves's love poems are mostly all lyric poems, Vickery argues, relating "fertility or phallic myths, deities, and rituals." But the White Goddess poems "extend beyond the lyric mode." Poems dealing with the Goddess, her consort, roles, and rituals "have epic aspirations." These poems "endeavor to make some larger, more inclusive statement about man, his place in the world and society, and the particular character of his cultural history." These poems, Vickery maintains, have aims similar to Yeats's poems that allude to "a Vision." "Both Graves and Yeats have written fragments of an epic whose outlines are sketched in workbooks entitled *The White Goddess* and *A Vision* respectively" (Vickery 1972, 130–31).

On the other hand, with the systems of *A Vision*, its cycles, its incarnations, Yeats began to see the sex act in mythical terms, giving intercourse the glory of contact with the world of spirit. *A Vision* gives Yeats an overview of the great cycles of history, and his view of sex changes as a result; Yeats now believes that the start of each new age is engendered by an Incarnation, whether the unwitting victim is Mary or Leda (cf. "The Mother of God"). In "Leda and the Swan," Yeats first portrays coitus concretely in his poetry—though the meaning of the act is explored, one must admit, by means of rhetorical questions:

> Being so caught up,
> So mastered by the brute blood of the air,
> Did she put on his knowledge with his power
> Before the indifferent beak could let her drop?

Graves's own treatment of the same subject, in "Leda," shows one very critical contrast with Yeats's mature treatment of sexual subjects. Where Yeats's Leda is caught up in a sexual act that is "primarily a mystical or religious experience," as Douglas Day contends, and his poem "is an attempt to portray her mystification and bewilderment during the event," Graves, on the other hand, does not concern himself with the meaning of the "ugly occurrence."

> Then soon your mad religious smile
> Made taut the belly, arched the breast
> And there beneath your god awhile
> You strained and gulped your beastliest.

For Graves, the sex act is "a graceless and even bestial expression of lust" (Day, 134).

Day follows this view through many of the major poems of Graves's pre-Goddess period, in "Ulysses," in "The Stranger," and in "Succubus." Typical is the treatment of physical love in "Sandhills," where, according to Day, "Graves rejects physical love as a pointless striving by the lovers for unity—pointless because sexual union results only in an endless and meaningless multiplication (136–37)." Graves has a contempt for sensuality, as shown by his use of the word filthy to describe Ulysses with Circe in "the lotus garden's filthy ease" (138).

In stark contrast, another poem in Yeats's *The Tower* which illustrates his mature thinking is "Among School Children." Here the moment of union is less concrete but more personal; the poem is a narrative of a moment of penetrating insight. Yeats is inspecting schools, one of his duties as a member of the Irish Senate, when he sees a girl who reminds him of an incident in which Maud Gonne told him of some childish tragedy. This is the launching point for a long argument which culminates in the very un-Platonic last stanza, where, in some of Yeats's most memorable lines, he argues that the image and the real are, if not one and the same, at least of equal importance. Yeats has embraced the phenomenal world and its fusion with the eternal (in his scheme of things now, images and divinity are of the same realm). "A living man is blind and drinks his drop. / What matter if the ditches are impure?" Yeats's speaker has realistically accepted sexual life, even "if it be life to pitch / into the frog-spawn of a blind man's ditch." The image of the dance has become specifically associated with the union of the sexes and with art in "Among School Children;" and in "A Dialogue of Self and Soul," Yeats accepts the fury and the mire as a condition necessary to perceiving the universe as sacramental:

> I am content to follow to its source
> Every event in action or in thought;
> Measure the lot; forgive myself the lot.
> When such as I cast out remorse
> So great a sweetness flows into the breast
> We must laugh and we must sing,
> We are blest by everything,
> Everything we look upon is blest.

The very fact that "Self" wins the argument indicates that this poem represents a reversal of values for Yeats. From this point onward, he increasingly "praises sexual experience as a means of reaching divine fusion. He is obsessed by the notion of a kinship between the erotic and the divine. Sex, which seems least like the holiness of heaven, is actually the human experience which most intensely combines the opposites and therefore is nearest to God" (Miller 1965, 128). Sex becomes the artistic analogy of God's creation.

In "Crazy Jane Talks with the Bishop," Jane speaks of the necessity of sex for wholeness of being: "For nothing can be sole or whole / That has not been rent." Another of Yeats's later characters, Ribh the Hermit, comments upon the importance of this fusion of art and sex and makes the images of "Byzantium" analogous to God's creation:

> My soul had found
> All happiness in its own cause or ground
> Godhead on Godhead in sexual spasm begot
> Godhead.

Another of the "Supernatural Songs" describes this point of divine sexual activity:

> There all the barrel-hoops are knit,
> There all the serpent tails are bit,
> There all the gyres converge in one,
> There all the planets drop in the Sun.

In these poems, "eternity is passion," both "sexual joy" and the artistic "passion-driven exultant man" who "sings out / sentences that he has never thought."

In the face of such achievement, most baffling, perhaps, of Graves's criticisms is that Yeats lacked "grace," or the presence of the Muse Goddess, that Yeats "had a new technique, but nothing to say." And with nothing to say, "instead of the Muse, he employed a ventriloquist's dummy called Crazy Jane." Graves then goes on to describe in "These Be Your Gods" many of the sources for Yeats's borrowings, from his spiritualist wife, Rosicrucianism, Blavatsky, and so on. He criticizes Yeats's technique in "The Chosen," with its off-rhyme of astronomer with sphere (Graves criticizes Yeats on the very technical ground that the single stress word should come first in the poem) and what Graves sees as an ambiguous modifier:

> If questioned on
> My utmost pleasure with a man
> By some new-married bride

Graves even criticizes Yeats's understanding of Macrobius, from whom Yeats claimed to have borrowed the line, "The Zodiac is changed into a sphere." Graves concedes that many of Yeats's Irish readers might be familiar with some of these sources; Gaelic Revivalists might know *The Three Sons of Usna*. "But . . . to publish a poem strewn with references to which not one reader in ten million has the key, is regarded as impudence by Dame Ocupacyon. The case becomes worse when the poet misquotes" (Graves 1968, 135–36). It might, perhaps, be an academic point, but as Peter Ure pointed out in a letter to the *Times Literary Supplement,* 12 June 1959, Graves is himself guilty of sloppy or hasty reading: he assumes the speaker of "The Chosen" is a man, and thereby causes the ambiguity for which he criticizes Yeats.

Whatever Yeats's errors in his reading, in the "Crazy Jane Poems," the images of art, sex, and eternity are joined; the dance becomes sexual with the borrowing of the orgasm-as-death metaphor of the metaphysical poets: "Did he die or did she die? / Seemed to die or died they both?" The interdependence of the profane and sacred, hinted at in the image of the burning candle in "Solomon and the Witch," is given direct statement by Crazy Jane, with a borrowing from Blake.

> "Fair and foul are near of kin,
> and fair needs foul . . ."
> . . . .
>
> "But Love has pitched his mansion in
> the place of excrement."

If the interpenetrating gyres of *A Vision* were a sexual symbol (Ellmann, 229), Yeats is now stating things more directly. "All things remain in God," even the extended metaphor for sex and fertility, the "great battle . . . in the narrow pass" and the house "suddenly lit." With this vision, Yeats finally sees wholeness of being and offers up, for younger poets following him, a treatment of human love and passion as artistically compelling as the vision of the Metaphysicals. The holy imagery in Yeats's and Thomas's poetry does not signify belief, but is used as metaphor or analogy, first to attempt making the poet's profession holy, and finally to attempt making all things holy.

Graves's criticism of other poets is also notoriously idiosyncratic. Thomas and Yeats are only two of a long list of poets whose work Graves derided, a list that includes Milton, Dryden, Pound, and Eliot, among others. There are many possible explanations for his hostility to these two in particular. Unlike Skelton, Thomas and Yeats seemed, to Graves, to have their own names, rather than the Muse's name, woven into their mantles, seeking self-aggrandizement rather than devotion to the Goddess. And Graves's antipathy may well be the jealousy of a poet on whom little public acclaim fell until late in his career.

In the case of Thomas, I believe, Graves's motivation is clear: Graves refused to grant to the stylistic techniques of surrealism the leading role in English poetry. And, of course, Thomas publicly proclaimed himself a follower of Yeats and used Yeatsian themes and images in his work.

With Yeats, the sources of Graves's hostility are more difficult to locate. We may simply take Graves at his word—he finds Yeats's devotion to the Muse less thorough than Yeats's devotion to his own reputation and fame. The possibility of jealousy is not to be dismissed, nor is the possibility that Yeats's devotion to Irish subjects was, even for a poet who was familiar with psychoanalysis, simply too close to the enthusiasms of Alfred Perceval Graves.

It is, I believe, an error to equate *A Vision* and *The White Goddess* very closely at all even though both systems gave their authors "metaphors for poetry," and even though, as Daniel Hoffman has shown, Yeats and Graves are frequently working the same field. Yeats called the White Goddess Aoife, and Cuchulain was her mortal lover; what are *The Death of Cuchulain, A Full Moon in March,* and *The King of the Great Clock Tower* if not the "one story only" of a mortal lover ritually sacrificed to an immortal female (Hoffman, 199–200)? Yeats's spiritualism may not have its obvious counterpart in *The White Goddess* (though I would argue that it does), but his Celtic material certainly has its counterpart; Graves, the son of an Irish Man of Letters, simply went to the other Celtic source, the Welsh, to localize his knowledge of Classical and Bronze Age worship. Graves never acknowledged that at least one of Yeats's themes was identical with his one great theme. When he attacked Yeats and one of his followers "with more ire than accuracy" to arrive at what Hoffman calls his "preposterous judgment" that Yeats was using "a ventriloquist's dummy" because "he had nothing to say" (Hoffman 1967, 201) was he attacking his father, or himself, or an image of the public poet, the man of letters, more successful than either himself or his father?

"Yeats in his seventies could reconcile the divisions that Graves could but grimly endure," Hoffman says, and continues, "Yeats is not compelled to mix masochism and punishment with his imagination of delight" (201). Yeats finally reveled in, and exalted, the utterly human; Graves exalted the mythic and metaphysical dimensions of the same. Beneath his criticism of Yeats lies Graves's sincere belief that Yeats was thus in error, even in working the same materials as Graves.

Works Cited

Brinnin, John Malcolm, ed. 1960. *A Casebook on Dylan Thomas*. New York: Crowell.
Davies, Aneirin Talfan. 1964. *Dylan: Druid of the Broken Body*. New York: Barnes and Noble.
Day, Douglas. 1963. *Swifter than Reason*. Chapel Hill: University of North Carolina.
Ellmann, Richard. 1948. *Yeats: The Man and the Mask*. New York: Dutton.
Graves, Richard Perceval. 1987. *Robert Graves: The Assault Heroic, 1895–1926*. New York: Viking.
———. 1990. *Robert Graves: The Years with Laura, 1926–1940*. New York: Viking.
Graves, Robert. 1968. *On Poetry: Collected Talks and Essays*. New York, Doubleday.
———. 1988. *In Broken Images: Selected Correspondence*. Edited by Paul O'Prey. Mt. Kisco, N.Y.: Moyer Bell.
Henn, T. R. 1950. *The Lonely Tower*. London: Methuen.
Hoffman, Daniel. 1967. *Barbarous Knowledge: Myth in the Poetry of Yeats, Graves, and Muir*. New York: Oxford University Press.
Kershner, R. B., Jr. 1976. *Dylan Thomas: The Poet and His Critics*. Chicago: American Library Association.
MacNeice, Louis. 1941. *The Poetry of W. B. Yeats*. New York: Oxford University Press.
Maud, Ralph. 1963. *Entrances to Dylan Thomas' Poetry*. Pittsburgh: University of Pittsburgh Press.
Miller, J. Hillis. 1965. *Poets of Reality*. Cambridge: Harvard University Press.
Moynihan, William T. 1966. *The Craft and Art of Dylan Thomas*. Ithaca: Cornell University Press.
Selby, Keith. 1990. "Hitting the Right Note: The Potency of Cheap Music." In *Dylan Thomas: Craft or Sullen Art*, ed. Alan Bold, 89–113. New York: St. Martin's.
Seymour-Smith, Martin. 1982. *Robert Graves: His Life and Work*. New York: Holt, Rinehart, and Winston.
Thomas, Dylan. 1957. *Collected Poems*. New York: New Directions.
———. 1966. *Selected Letters of Dylan Thomas*. Edited by Constantine Fitzgibbon. London: Dent.
Tindall, William York. 1962. *A Reader's Guide to Dylan Thomas*. New York: Noonday.
Treece, Henry. 1956. *Dylan Thomas: "Dog among the Fairies."* London, Benn.
Ure, Peter. 1959. Letter. *Times Literary Supplement*, 12 June.
Vickery, John B. 1972. *Robert Graves and the White Goddess*. Lincoln: University of Nebraska.
Wellesley, Dorothy. 1964. *Letters on Poetry from W. B. Yeats to Dorothy Wellesley*. New York: Oxford University Press.
Yeats, William Butler. 1962. *Selected Poems and Two Plays of William Butler Yeats*. Edited by M. L. Rosenthal. New York: Collier.

The Pastoral Vision of Robert Graves
Robert Davis

THE ARGUMENT I WISH TO ADVANCE IN THIS ESSAY SEEKS TO ESTABLISH LINKS between the writings of Robert Graves and that ancient and influential body of poetic doctrine we have come to know as the pastoral. I believe that reading the work of Robert Graves as essentially a modern—not to say modernist—inflection of the pastoral tradition not only helps reveal the underlying unity of his art, but also enables us to revisit the pastoral itself with an enhanced understanding of its central meanings and its once-potent mythic language. Graves, I would venture to suggest, can be approached as both a distinguished representative of the pastoral tradition and also as possibly one of its last and best modern interpreters. In his combination of poetic learning, romantic primitivism, and lyrical watchfulness, Graves not only drew sustenance from the narratives and motifs of the pastoral, he sought also to penetrate some of its most abiding mysteries, and may perhaps point us towards the solution to its final, most complex enigma. If, as many have suggested, (Pugh 1988) the cultural and ecological upheavals of modernity spell the demise of the pastoral as an enduring source of imaginative replenishment, then it may be that the Orphic voice of Robert Graves has given to us one of the final expressions of its legacy.

Any account of the key principles of pastoral thought as it was anciently understood resonates immediately and ironically with the pattern of Robert Graves's life and writings. Beginning in the ritual laments for the dead Adonis, of the fifth and fourth centuries BC, pastoral poetry rapidly became the dominant form of classical escape literature, celebrating the pleasures of rural simplicity, bucolic love, and the carefree joys of poetic song. Its position within classical civilization drew it very quickly into the structural relationship between nature and culture, the center and the periphery, and the succession of binary oppositions this relationship frequently generates for complex preindustrial societies. Hence the celebration of the innocent joys of the countryside assumed the character of an implied critique of the values of the city and the state, especially those which derived from the enthronement of politics, war, money, and law as sovereign forces in human affairs. The politicization of the pastoral arose as the inevitable consequence of its resistance to influences hostile to the pieties of the merely natural man. It thus became, ineluctably, a poetic of exile. The clamant call of the classical pastoral poet—and of his Renaissance successors—was for a return to the symbolic order of nature, and the remembered innocence of a Golden Age and a golden place: Arcadia (Halperin 1983).

Philippe Borgeaud (1988: 9–10) has drawn a crucial distinction between what he terms a "pre-Selenic" or primitive pastoral and the civic arcadias of the later classical poets. The pre-Selenic pastoral maintains its vital, atavistic links with the urgent voices of the ritual elegists, its landscape dimmed by the shadow of sacred murder. Its version of Arcadia is receptive both to aesthetic Platonism and its daemonic antecedent, the poetic theology of the poet-victim Orpheus, priest of Dionysus-Adonis, who, in this view, is the pastoral's true presiding genius (West 1983). Inscribed with the narrative of Orpheus's erotic adventures, including betrayal, death, and rebirth, the pastoral landscape becomes a metaphor for the vicissitudes of love. Orpheus's dismemberment and subsequent elevation to oracular status supply a paradigm of the poetic vocation. In one of the finest flowerings of his later poetry, the trilogy *Man Does, Woman Is*, Graves assumes the persona of this Orpheus, desperately questing for release from the cycle of death and resurrection.

> 'I am oppressed, I am oppressed, I am oppressed'—
> Once I utter the curse, how can she rest:
> No longer able, weeping, to placate me
> With renewed auguries of celestial beauty?
>   ("Eurydice", Graves 1975, 264)

Set against the pre-Selenic is an alternative, more ornate pastoral in which the dangerous values of Arcadia are recuperated by the decorum of classical civic humanism. The champion of this mode is Graves's bête noire, Virgil Maro, the "suave hexametrist" (Graves 1927, 174), one of the figures Graves blamed for the repudiation of true poetic values (Graves 1949, 51).

Virgilian pastoral formalizes and redefines the protest of the bucolic imagination, domesticating its subversive possibilities. Innocence becomes artifice and Orpheus the mystagogue is replaced by Apollo the god of reason. The adversarial tones of exile are muted by assimilation to the pattern of the Virgilian poetic career, which moves sequentially through pastoral panegyrics to the composition of the epic, and its celebration of precisely those urban and martial values the pastoral had originally sought to question.

The classical hierarchy of genres thus established provides the basis of Graves's quarrel with the "anti-poet" Virgil and his principal English successor, "monstrous Milton" (Graves 1961, 28; 1917, 36): that each self-consciously renounced the virtues and poetics of pastoral love in order to assume the mantle of the epic poet. In so doing, they helped reinforce a deterministic pattern of the poetic career which was to have an enormous—and, in Graves's view catastrophic—impact on Western literature. Its influence, charted most recently by Simon Schama, (1995, 517–79) is evident everywhere as a cultural and literary paradigm, from the gardens of the Renaissance to romantic visions of the sublime and the terrible. Throughout its history, a tension is visible between the idealized idyll of simplicity, the "ironical acceptance of aristocracy" as Empson called it (1935, 75), and the wilder, more archaic summons from the sacred grove where Adonis lies bleeding. It was to the poetry of this darker Arcadia that Robert Graves found himself heir.

It would appear that a peculiar interaction of the pressures of heredity and environment first drew Graves into the aesthetics of the pastoral realm. The infantile anxieties induced by his complex parentage and nightmare experience of school drove him, initially, into that ambiguous pastoral of childhood, the nursery, with its "funny muddling mazes, / Each rounded off into a lovely song" ("The Poet in the Nursery," Graves 1916, 4), where fear and escapism dwelt in uneasy proximity (Kohli 1975). His attachment to the themes and imagery of nursery pastoral made Graves, for a time, the perfect Georgian, but the horror of trench warfare exhausted the resources of his juvenile Arcadia and sent shadows looming large and ominous across the landscape of the idealized England into which his injured psyche had fled:

> The fruit between my lips to clotted blood
>   Was transubstantiate, and the pale rose
> Smelt sickly, till it seemed through a swift tear-flood
>   That dead men blossomed in the garden-close.
>   ("The Morning Before the Battle," Graves 1916, 21)

Violence, destruction, the malevolence of tormented natural elements too frequently invade the pastoral retreat from the adjoining epic conflagration in Flanders for it to function effectively as the warrior's sanctuary :

> It's pleasant here for dreams and thinking,
>   Lolling and letting reason nod,
> With ugly, serious people thinking
>   Prayer-chains for a forgiving God.
> But a dumb blast sets the trees swaying
> With furious zeal like madmen praying.
>
> ("A Boy in Church," Graves 1917, 29)

The recourse to pastoral, however inadequately formulated, was a more widespread response to the experience of the Great War than is commonly recognized. Graves's contemporary, Edmund Blunden, renewed himself for the fight by donning the robes of the artless shepherd. More importantly, the words of Wilfred Owen's famous preface to the volume of verse he intended to call English Elegies ("not about heroes . . . nor anything about glory, honour, might, majesty, dominion, or power") represent a direct moral rejection of the epic sensibility because of its complicity in the worst outrages of warfare (Stallworthy 1985, 192). If experience of the war prompted in many of his literary associates a deep questioning of their martial and imperial heritage, for Graves himself it began a revision of the archetypal poetic career and the artistic values which had traditionally underpinned it.

A growing horror of the conflict, and increased alienation from the civilization which had produced it, were pressures intense enough to bring about a subtle restructuring of the aesthetics of the body of pastoral verse Graves was writing during and shortly after the war: sunny cornland where / Babes lie tickling, and where tall white horses / Draw the plough leisurely in quiet courses (Graves 1916, 22) was compelled to yield to the darkly symbolic landscapes of "Rocky Acres":

> This is a wild land, country of my choice,
> With harsh craggy mountain, moor ample and bare.
> Seldom in these acres is heard any voice
> But the voice of cold water that runs here and there
>
> (Graves 1975, 7)

The country of Graves's choice was no longer the sequestered grove of childhood fancy and war time escapism, but a landscape dominated by images of violence and the omniscient gaze of the predator.

Many of Graves's poems of this period are haunted by a nostalgia for a realm of being in which the feudal, the archaic, and the prehistoric are associated with the instinctual and the automatic, with a brutal realm of primary responses which, as as in the brief poem "Outlaws," is identified with the most ancient and abiding recesses of the psyche (Graves 1975, 8). Here "Old gods, almost dead, malign" stalk the boundaries of rational consciousness, liminal figures who menace the stability of the pastoral by recalling its once-fluent intercourse with the chthonic terrors of the wilderness, night, prehistory, and the distant reaches of the unconscious mind, where "These aged gods of power and lust / Cling to life yet." The fascination of this territory lies in the challenges it makes to the vain claims of technological civilization, and the access it affords to a vast fund of mythological motifs where poetry, power, and religion converge.

In a very meaningful sense, then, I think it can be argued that the immense ritual belief system in the light of which, Graves insisted, his poems were to be interpreted, can be seen as, essentially, a pastoral myth. From his experience of cultural crisis and personal trauma, Graves emerged with a renovated pastoral vision in which the threat of violence has been sublimated, and the self confirmed in the difficult demands of its own solitude and isolation. It is from this stance that the shape of Graves's mature work starts to emerge, beginning with his favorite, obsessive image—that of a man walking alone on hills:

> To go in no direction
> Surely as carelessly,
> Walking on the hills alone,
> I never found easy.
> ("In No Direction," Graves 1975, 41)

A leading theoretician of the pastoral, Renato Poggioli, has shown that its "psychological root is a double longing after innocence and happiness, to be recovered not through conversion or regeneration but merely through a retreat" (Poggioli 1975, 1). The vocabulary of Graves's verse, and its growth towards myth, is deeply rooted in this aesthetic.

With his emigration to Majorca as its biographical manifestation—emblematized in the typically pastoral maxim "Here is escape then Hercules from empire"—Graves's exile took him to a place where his inner conflicts, and the pursuit of reconciliation, could be dramatized in a confrontation with nature; nature, it must be said, preferred as a wild infinity, rather than an orderly bounded vista. There, anxiety and guilt could be subsumed into an enlarged myth of pastoral love, the coherence of which derived from the increasingly ritualized relationships between the poet and a visionary procession of lovers:

> Weather we knew, not seasons in the city
> Where, seasonless, orange and orchid shone
> Knew it by heavy overcoat or light,
> Framed love in later terminologies
> Than here, where we report how weight of snow,
> Or weight of fruit, tears branches from the tree.
>   (Graves 1975, 130)

The structure of oppositions in "Language of the Seasons" serves to separate an account of nature where distinctions are determined by the calculus of rational measurement from one where they are signifiers of sensory experience. The "heavy overcoat or light" represents a narrowed awareness of seasonal change, where the encounter with nature is distanced and deflected, routinized to the point of uncomprehending reflex. The "weight of snow, / Or weight of fruit," by contrast, expresses a direct alignment of the human point of vision with the revered and unfathomable forces of seasonal change. Thus released from the "urban" and rational ambition to "know" and master nature, the registering consciousness of the poet is required merely to "report"—and hence celebrate—the violence and beauty of nature's unfolding process. The language of the seasons is, in a sense, a reproach to the rational designs of language itself. We know such ambivalence of feeling towards the cool web of language to be an abiding feature of Graves's poetry. It is also, historically and generically, a recurring preoccupation of the pastoral imagination, which instinctively harbors a regressive suspicion of the totalizing claims of language and reason, yet which faces the dilemma of harnessing language to the moral and erotic imperatives of poetic song.

Nature becomes in many of Graves's pastoral poems the context for what Frye has termed "expanded consciousness" (Frye 1951, 301). By transforming an untamed landscape into its central metaphor for the intractable awareness of the affective self, Graves's version of the pastoral initiated an ironic reversal of the paradigm of the Virgilian or Miltonic poetic career. Recoiling in pain and horror from the martial experience recorded in *Good-bye To All That*, Graves fled the domain of the city and its gods of technology and war, and sought a new background for his poetry in the rejuvenated pastoral of his Majorcan oasis, making of his exile an ethical and artistic stance. For this was to be no mere temporary respite. The setting for the development of his creative talents was destined to remain the scene of his life's work, where an ancient mythology of love came to be revived in the figure of a barbaric Lunar Muse who animates the natural world and takes up all of the poet's offerings of love and suffering:

> The seven years' curse is ended now
> That drove me forth from this kind land,
> From mulberry-bough and apple-bough
> And gummy twigs the west wind shakes,
> To drink the brine from crusted lakes
> And grit my teeth on sand.
> (Graves 1975, 43)

The perspective revealed by "Return" completed Graves's individuation and inversion of the inherited pastoral model. Exile is interpreted not as temporary withdrawal, but as release, and, in consequence, the polarity of the city and the country is reversed, rendering the values of Arcadia a constant reproach to the failures of civilization.

This particular version of the pastoral makes clear a separation between what Barthes once said was the classical view "that Nature ... can be possessed, that it does not shy away and cover itself in shadow, but is in its entirety subjected to the toils of language," and the modern sense that nature is "a fragmented space, made of objects solitary and terrible, because the links between them are only potential" (Barthes 1956, 49–50). Graves's poetry, sometimes so modern in its sense of disintegration, establishes an eloquent commerce with that ancient shamanistic awareness of nature as the shadowy female whose mystery and caprice resist comprehension by the cool web of language.

> Nature is always so: you find
> That all she has of mind
> Is wind
> ("Nature's Lineaments," Graves 1975, 79)

To the topographical arcadian metaphors, Poggioli suggests, can be added temporal figurations, because,

> To restore at least ideally its own moral balance, the pastoral turns back to the myth of the Golden Age and claims that in prehistoric times there existed a state of perfect equality and absolute justice, which lasted as long as the goddess Astraea graced the earth with her presence. (Poggioli 1975, 26–27)

Whether as symbolic landscape or as imagined history, Graves's pastoral assumes an individualizing force through the healing ceremonial eros of poetic love. "Pale at first and cold," the experience of love passes over the pastoral terrain in "The Finding of Love," as a "blaze" of energy, at once both purging and quickening the scene, the imagery of the poem modulating from gloom to light and from cold to heat. Poetic love is presented as an overpowering force cognate with the life-giving properties of spring and nature's seasonal self-renewal. Under its influence, the pastoral landscape rises to a fresh vitality with far-reaching benefits to the poet's emotional, life: "With end to grief, / With joy in steadfastness" (Graves 1975, 6).

The discovery of love did not bring to Graves's pastoral a self-satisfied, unequivocal peace. Just as love can be found more authentically in this charged landscape, so also it can be lost as unpredictably, its "grief" suggesting a perversity beyond the poet's understanding. Many of Graves's most convincing love lyrics are devoted to explorations of "love's defeat" (Graves 1975, 46), which, repeatedly, is alleged to originate in the vanity of the male ego, the inscrutable inconstancy of the female, and the inability of men and women properly to understand the desires which motivate them. Fragments of a drama of love found and abandoned, of deceit and murder, of dark trysts and fearful compacts, are spoken by a series of voices and personae who pass over the haunted vista, propelled by some still unresolved conflict at the heart of the poet's vision. "Who was it said "I love you?" asks one voice, intruding into some undisclosed act of betrayal and receiving no reply. The enlargement of the poet's senses afforded by the pastoral realm may be "godlike," but it turns the poet into a driven figure, traversing the landscape "Without relief seeking lost love" (Graves 1975, 17).

The emergence in his pastoral domain of the story Graves was to term "the single poetic theme" (Graves 1961, 21) drew substantially upon the resources and the imaginative traditions of Arcadia. Its narrative structure is derived from the seasonal and cyclic patterns of pastoral myth, with which both the fluctuations of poetic inspiration and the fortunes of love are compared. Images of snow, springtime, winter, animals, birds, the moon spangle the poems, valorized by the insights and sentiments to which Graves so frequently returns. The consistency of the symbolism over dozens of poems is such that an organized system of associations and perceptions can be seen gathering shape and form in the texture of the verse. The "tyrannous queen above / Sole mover of their fate," of "Full Moon" becomes a lunar "Queen Famine" in "A Love Story," and the poet is both her lover and servant (Graves 1975, 46, 121). The beloved whose embrace restores springtime and inspiration in "Mid-Winter Waking," yet whose departure appears motiveless, unreasonable comes to be regarded with a devotion bordering on religious reverence in poems such as "Like Snow" and "She Tells Her Love while Half Asleep" (Graves 1975, 130, 111, 135). One critic has compared the static formality of Graves's best love poetry to a Book of Hours (Carter 1990, 129). If my hypothesis is correct, it is perhaps more accurately described as a Shepherd's Calendar, dedicated to woman as the Center, and striving to restore to the exchanges of heterosexual love a ceremonial gravity of purpose and meaning. Arcadia, it transpires, affords the poet the ideal symbolic landscape in which to invest his verse with the unity of form we associate with myth.

At the outset of this paper it was proposed that Graves's mythopoeic revision of Arcadia took us to the core of the pastoral mystery and addressed one of its most puzzling conundrums. Graves's mature mythology is, essentially, a myth of memory, summed up in the Orphic formula "Do not forget," or "remember / What you have suffered" (Graves 1975, 138, 159; 1961, 140). In the shamanistic doctrines of the Orphics, the primal sin of humanity was the slaying and eating of the boy-god Dionysus by our accursed ancestors the Titans. The pre-Selenic pastoral traditions confused the cult of Dionysus the kid with other animal sacrifices, including those of Zagreus, Actaeon, and Adonis, slain by "the great boar" (Burkert 1987). The officiating priest at these rituals was, according to Graves, a primitive form of the poet-priest-victim Orpheus, revered by his adherents as an incarnation of the god he represented: "This Orpheus did not come in conflict with the cult of Dionysus; he was Dionysus, and . . . because he was the principal in the Dionysian rites, is said to have suffered the same fate as the god" (Graves 1960, 1.114)).

The rites to which Graves refers are those commemorating the birth, marriage, and killing of the year-god, consort and victim of the Goddess or Triple Muse. From the dramatic highlights of his sacred story comes the inspiration of all true poetry, and the origins of poetry run back, therefore, to the primal scene of exaltation and defeat.

Stamped on all of the trappings of the pastoral is the riddling motto *Et in Arcadia Ego,* so beautifully elucidated for us a generation ago by the great art historian Erwin Panofsky (1936, 295–320), and now recognized as an ironic emblem of the peculiarly English pastoralism of the Great War: And I, too, am in Arcadia (Fussell 1975: 245–46). The sudden, shocking discovery of death in the bowers of Arcadia, memorably depicted in the famous Poussin canvas of the shepherd's tomb, uncovers the ritual secret concealed at the heart of the landscape: the bloody sacrifice of Dionysus-Adonis, in the elegies for whom the pastoral, Orphic voice was born (Berg 1965).

To many modern readers, shaped by the Virgilian principles Graves sought to throw off, it may seem that the formality of pastoral writing is too stilted, too operatic a genre to accommodate the expansive rhetoric of the White Goddess. In one sense, then, my explorations in this essay seek to cooperate with the project of Graves's revisionism. For behind the literary traditions of the poet-victim Orpheus, behind Dionysus and Adonis, and his Semitic forebear Tammuz, lie those ancient Sumerian laments for the shepherd-god Dumuzi, chosen one of the Mother Goddess Inanna. The ur-myth of the pastoral—a haunting echo of Graves's single poetic theme—tells the story of the passionate love affair and eventual marriage of the Great Goddess Inanna to the shepherd-poet Dumuzi; his tragic death, descent into the underworld and final rescue by Inanna (Kramer 1969, 132; Jacobsen, 1970, 100–101). It suggests, ultimately, that the primary task of the pastoral imagination may be defined as a remembering of, and return to, the mother. The goal of this immense feat of pastoral reconciliation is to place the experience of sympathy, connectedness, destiny, shared love, and suffering at the center of human subjectivity, and to unmask all those bogus values of orthodox poetics and "scientific-pluto-democracy" which threaten it (Graves 1961, 9).

Works Cited

Barthes, Roland. 1956. *Writing Degree Zero.* Translated by Anette Laver and Colin Smith. New York. Hill and Wang.

Berg, William. 1965. "Daphnis and Prometheus." *Transactions of the American Philological Association* 96:54–64.

Borgeaud, Phillipe. 1988. *The Cult of Pan in Ancient Greece.* Translated by Kathleen Atlass and James Redfield. Chicago. University of Chicago Press.

Burkert, Walter. 1987. *Ancient Mystery Cults.* Cambridge: Harvard University Press.

Carter, D. N. G. 1990. *Robert Graves: The Lasting Achievement.* London: Longman.

Empson, William. [1935], 1966. *Some Versions of the Pastoral.* Harmondsworth: Peregrine.

Frye, Northrop. 1951. *Anatomy of Criticism: Four Essays,* Princeton: Princeton University Press.

Fussell, Paul. 1975. *The Great War and Modern Memory.* Oxford: Oxford University Press.

Graves, Robert. 1916. *Over the Brazier.* London: The Poetry Bookshop.

———. 1917. *Fairies and Fusiliers.* London: Heinemann.

———. 1927. *Poems (1914–1926).* London: Heinemann.

———. 1949. *The Common Asphodel: Collected Essays on Poetry, 1922–1949.* London: Hamish Hamilton.

———. 1960. *The Greek Myths.* 2 vols. Harmondsworth: Penguin.

———. 1961. *Oxford Addresses on Poetry.* London: Cassell.

———. 1961b. *The White Goddess: A Historical Grammar of Poetic Myth.* 2nd ed. London: Faber and Faber.

———. 1964. *Man Does, Woman Is.* London: Cassell.

———. 1975. *Collected Poems.* London: Cassell.

Halperin, David. 1983. *Before Pastoral: Theocritus and the Ancient Tradition of Bucolic Poetry.* New Haven: Yale University Press.

Jacobsen, Thorkild. 1970. "Toward the Image of Tammuz." In *Harvard Semitic Studies 21,* ed. W. L. Moran. Cambridge: Harvard University Press.

Kohli, Devindra. 1975. "Dream Drums: Child As an Image of Conflict and Liberation." *Malahat Review,* 35:75–100.

Kramer, Samuel Noah. 1969. *The Sacred Marriage Rite: Aspects of Faith, Myth, and Ritual in Ancient Summer.* Bloomington: Indiana University Press.

Panofsky, Erwin, ed. 1936. "Et in Arcadia Ego." In *Philosophy and History: Essays Presented to Ernst Cassirer,* 295–320. Oxford, Clarendon.

Poggioli, Renato. 1975. *The Oaten Flute: Essays on Pastoral Poetics and the Pastoral Ideal.* Cambridge: Harvard University Press.

Pugh, Simon. 1988. *Garden, Nature, Language:* Manchester: Manchester University Press.

Stallworthy, Jon, ed. 1985. *The Poems of Wilfred Owen.* London: The Hogarth Press.

West, M. L. 1983. *The Orphic Poems.* Oxford: Oxford University Press.

Contributors

JOHN BENNETT lives in Berkeley, California, with his wife and daughter. He graduated from Pomona College, Claremont, California.

SIMON BRITTAN has taught renaissance and twentieth-century English literature at the universities of East-Anglia and Essex, and was visiting professor of English language and literature at the University of Michigan-Dearborn, where he taught renaissance drama, twentieth-century British literature and modern criticism and theory. He also teaches at the Department of Continuing Education, University of Oxford. He has written on the drama and poetry of the sixteenth and twentieth centuries, as well as on Robert Graves and his interpretation of John Skelton. He is currently working on *Renaissance Criticism & Theory: A Reader* for the University of Michigan Press. His collection of poetry, *The Light Ages,* is to appear with Festival Books.

ROBERT A. DAVIS is Director of Inservice Education and Lecturer in Language and Literature at St. Andrew's College, Glasgow. He was educated at the Universities of Strathclyde and Stirling, where he completed a doctoral study of Robert Graves, and worked as a school teacher for several years. In addition to ongoing research in education, he has written and broadcast widely on literature and myth, literature and religion, Romanticism, and on the cultural history of childhood. He has contributed recently to *Sons of Ezra* edited by J. McGonigan and M. Alexander (Rodopi, 1995), and *Romantic Dreams* edited by S. Dickson and M. Ward (Edinburgh University Press, 1998) He is currently preparing a literary-critical study of the English lullaby. Robert Davis is vice-president of the Robert Graves Society.

DEVINDRA KOHLI was educated at the Universities of Panjab and Delhi in India, and Leeds in Britain, where he took his Ph.D. on Robert Graves. Professor of English at the University of Kashmir, Srinagar, since 1986, he has been from 1992 a Visiting Professor at various Universities in Germany, including the Universities of Frankfurt, Essen, Munich, and Bonn. He teaches at present at Martin Luther University, Halle. His publications include two books on the poetry of Kamala Das, *Indian Writers at Work* (ed.), and papers on nineteenth and twentieth century British, American, and Commonwealth Literatures. He is a founding co-editor of the journal The Indian Literary Review, and is currently co-editing The Oxford Book of Commonwealth and Postcolonial Poetry.

IAN FIRLA received his first degree (B.A. Honors) from the University of Toronto in 1994 and his doctorate from the University of Leicester in 1998. His doctoral dissertation was on the historical novels of Robert Graves and the paper included here is based upon a chapter of that work. He has recently assumed the editorship of *Gravesiana: the Journal of the Robert Graves Society*, a journal he helped to found together with Patrick Quinn and has co-organised three international conferences on Robert Graves, two to celebrate the centenary of Graves' birth (St. John's College (Oxford) and Palma, Majorca) and most recently at the University of Manchester to celebrate the 50th anniversary of the publication of The White Goddess. After teaching for three years at Nene College, Northampton, he moved to Poland to take up a professorship of 20th Century English Literature at the Adam Mickiewicz University in Poznan.

NICK GAMMAGE was born in Northampton, England. He studied English Literature at the University of Bristol, where he wrote his dissertation on the poetry of Ted Hughes. He began his career in journalism and currently works in public relations. He has published numerous articles on poetry and theater, and is currently editing a tribute to mark the seventieth birthday of Ted Hughes, which will be published by Faber and Faber in August 2000.

CHRIS HOPKINS is a Senior Lecturer at Sheffield Hallam University, where he is Course Leader for the B. A. in English Studies. His research is mainly on the British novel in the 1930s, on Anglo-Welsh writing, and on representations of modernity in the twentieth century. He has published on these topics in journals including *Critical Survey, Literature and History, Focus on Robert Graves and his Contemporaries, Notes and Queries, The Journal of Gender Studies, The Review of Irish Studies, English Language Notes* and *Style*. He has contributed chapters to books on the Thirties and on the writing of the Great War, and is currently working on a book for Macmillan: *Thinking About Texts—An Introduction to English Studies*.

IAN MCCORMICK is Senior Lecturer in English Studies at Nene University College, Northampton. He is the author of Secret Sexualities: Seventeenth and Eighteenth-Century Writings; a four-volume sequel, Sex and Sexualities 1750–1850 will be published in 1999. He has published on Locke, Fielding, and British eighteenth-century satire. Ian is editing Robert Graves's *Antigua, Penny, Puce and They Hanged My Saintly Billy* for Carcanet and is also completing a book called *Grotesque Enlightenment* based on his doctoral thesis.

PATRICK MCGUINNESS is a fellow of St. Anne's College, Oxford, and a university lecturer in French. He is the editor of *T. E. Hulme: Selected Writings* (Carcanet Press, 1998), and Paul Adam's *Petit Glossaire des Auteurs Decadents et Symbolistes* (Exeter University Press, 1998). He has written widely on modern French and English literature, and is working on a study of the theater of Maurice Maeterlinck. He won an Eric Gregory award for his poetry in 1998.

JOHN WOODROW PRESLEY began working with the manuscripts and letters of Robert Graves in 1973, when he started to inventory the Graves collection at Southern Illinois University. His book, *The Robert Graves Manuscripts and Letters at Southern Illinois University*, was published in 1976. Since that time, Presley has written dozens of articles and notes on Robert Graves and reviews of works on Graves. His work on Robert Graves has been mostly bibliographical or stylistic studies, or, like Presley's work on other modern writers—most recently D. H. Lawrence and James Joyce—has examined the boundaries between popular culture and high culture. He has also written, co-written or edited over a dozen textbooks and a collection of his poetry. Presley is Dean of the College of Arts, Sciences, and Letters at the University of Michigan-Dearborn.

PAUL O'PREY has edited the two volumes of Robert Graves's selected letters, *In Broken Images, 1914–1946* (1982) and *Between Moon and Moon, 1946–1972* (1984), in addition to his *Selected Poems* (Penguin 1986) and *Collected Writings on Poetry* (1995). O'Prey's other publications include *The Reader's Guide to Graham Greene* (1988) and a translation, with Lucia Graves, of Emilia Pardo Bazán's *Los Pazos de Ulloa* (1990). He is Director of Research Development at the University of Bristol.

DIONYSIOUS PSILOPOULOS earned his Ph.D. in English literature from the University of Edinburgh in 1995. His dissertation, *A Conspiracy of the Subconscious: Yeats, Crowley, Pound, Graves and the Esoteric*

Tradition, traces the influence of the occult on modernist poetics. Focusing primarily on the works of Graves and Yeats, he has presented papers on the subject of modernism and the occult at several international conferences. He has taught composition at Southern Illinois University, Carbondale, where he received his M.A. in English literature in 1992, and at a number of academic institutions in Athens, Greece. Since 1995 he has been a lecturer of English literature and composition at The American College of Greece, Athens.

STEVEN TROUT received his M.A. (1987) from the University of Missouri-Kansas City and his Ph.D. (1993) from the University of Kansas. An assistant professor of English at Fort Hays State University, he teaches undergraduate and graduate level courses in Victorian writers, modern British fiction, and twentieth-century war literature. His articles—on such writers as Evelyn Waugh, H. G. Wells, Joseph Conrad, and Willa Cather—have appeared in numerous journals, including *Twentieth Century Literature, War, Literature, and the Arts,* and *Journal of Commonwealth and Postcolonial Studies,* and he is coeditor of an essay collection devoted to World War I literature (forthcoming from Macmillan and St. Martin's Press).

PATRICK QUINN is Professor of English Literature at University College Northampton and general editor of the twenty-four volume Robert Graves Programme currently being released by Carcanet Press in Manchester. He is author of *The Great War and Missing Muse: The Early Poetry of Robert Graves and Siegfried Sassoon* and editor of *Recharting the Thirties* and *The Dictionary of Literary Biography Documentary Series* volumes on English Great War poets. He is the former editor of *Gravesiana: The Journal of the Robert Graves Society* and *Focus on Robert Graves and His Contemporaries.* His current literary projects include studies of American Great War literature and the English Decadent writers of the 1890s.

Index

Adams, Barbara, 101
Adonis, 209, 211, 217, 218
Albigenses, 161, 166
Aldridge, John, 97
Alexander the Great, 42
Amis, Kingsley, 55, 58
Aphrodite. *See* Venus
Apollo, 210
Aracdia, 210, 211, 215, 216, 217
Astarte, 154
Auden, W. H., 46, 47, 48, 53, 55, 58, 61, 92–93, 95, 97, 123

Bacon, Francis, 138 f
Bakhtin, Mikhail, 145
Barbusse, Henri, 177
Barthes, Roland, 215
Bennett, John, 11, 19–35
Bentley, Phyllis, 129, 130, 133; *Farewell Freedom*, 129, 130, 133
Betjeman, John, 201
Blake, William, 156, 195, 206; *Milton*, 195
Blunden, Edmund, 112, 113, 115, 212
Borgeaud, Philippe, 210
Brittan, Simon, 11, 84–93
Brook, Peter, 157
Brown, Dennis, 124; *The Modernist Self*, 124
Buffalo, University of, 198
Brutus, Marcus Junius, 135
Burgess, Anthony, 183
Byron, George Gordon, 123

Caesar, Julius, 130
Caligula, Gaius Caesar, 114
Cambridge University, 27, 46, 60, 149
Cameron, Norman, 97
Carter, D. N. G., 11, 99, 102; *The Lasting Poetic Achievement*, 11, 99
Castor (son of Zeus), 98
Charterhouse School , 67, 71

Chaucer, Geoffrey, 39, 66
Christ, Jesus, 41, 163–64, 166, 167, 170, 198
Clark Lectures, 19, 46, 47–48, 53, 56, 58, 60, 61
Clytemnestra, 98
Coleridge, Samuel Taylor, 154
Conquest, Robert, 55, 60
Corinth, 161
Cohen, Joseph, 169; *Robert Graves*, 169
Cru, Jean Norton, 177–78, 184, 185; *War Books: A Study in Historical Criticism*, 177
Cummings, E. E. 46, 50–55, 60, 190; "Sunset," 50–52, 190
Cyprus, 167
Czechoslovakia, 95

Daily Mail, 42
Davie, Donald, 55, 58–61. Works: "Impersonal and Emblematic," 58; *Poet in the Imaginary Museum*, 58–59; "The Toneless Voice of Robert Graves," 58
Davies, Aneiran Talfan, 197
Davis, Lennard J., 176
Davis, Robert, 13, 209–19
Day, Douglas, 68, 203–4; *Swifter than Reason*, 68
Defoe, Daniel, 12, 175, 179–86; *A Journal of the Plague Year*, 12, 175, 179–85; *Robinson Crusoe*, 185–86
Deia (Deya), Majorca, 10
De la Mare, Walter, 39
Dickens, Charles, 29
Dorchester, 39
Druids, 24
Dryden, John, 206

Eksteins, Modris, 186
Eliade, Mircae, 165–66, 169; *A History of Religious Ideas*, 166

224

INDEX

Eliot, T. S., 30, 33, 46, 47, 48, 53, 59, 60, 61, 66, 73, 123, 188, 194, 206; *Four Quartets*, 30; "Ash Wednesday," 73
Ellidge, Mary, 97
Empson, William, 211
English Studies, 10
Enright, D. J., 46, 55–56, 57, 58, 59–60; *Conspirators and Poets*, 46, 55–56

Falls, Cyril, 178, 179, 184, 185, 186; *War Books: An Annotated Bibliography of Books About the Great War*, 178
Faust, Elfriede, 97, 98
Fielding, Henry, 185
Firla, Ian, 12, 107–27
Fischer, H. A. L., 186
Fish, Stanley, 40
Fisher, Charles, 194
Focus on Robert Graves and His Contemporaries, 10
Fox, Ralph, 131
France, 26
Frazer, James George, 67, 162, 167; *The Golden Bough*, 162, 167
Freemasonry, 161, 165, 166
Freud, Sigmund, 38, 157
Frost, Robert, 66, 71
Frye, Northrop, 214
Fussell, Paul, 110, 175, 180, 184; *The Great War and Modern Memory*, 110

Gammage, Nick, 12, 149–58
Gay, Karl (Kenneth; formerly Goldschmidt), 114
Gielgud, John, 158
Gnosticism, 159, 163–64, 165–66
Gonne, Maud, 191
Graves, Alfred P., 188–89, 207
Graves, Amy, 188
Graves, Beryl (Pritchard), 100, 102
Graves, Diana, 65
Graves, Lucia, 26
Graves, Richard P., 9, 95, 97, 98, 101, 116, 118, 120–21, 194; *Robert Graves and the White Goddess 1940–1985*, 9
Graves, Robert von Ranke.
—Autobiography: *Good-bye to All That*, 10, 12, 36, 38, 41–42, 67, 72, 74, 107, 110, 112, 113, 115, 117, 120, 121, 122–23, 124, 125, 135, 151, 175, 176, 177, 179, 180–82, 183–85, 186–87, 214

—Critical studies: *The Crowning Privilege*, 44, 58; *The Greek Myths*, 88, 118; *The Hebrew Myths*, 118,120; *Mammon and the Black Goddess*, 162; *The Meaning of Dreams*, 38, 108; *The Nazarene Gospel Restored*, 163–64; *On English Poetry*, 22, 38, 39, 40; *Poetic Unreason*, 38–40, 44; *Steps*, 71; *A Survey of Modernist Poetry*, 44, 46, 48, 50, 52, 53, 60, 190, 194; *The White Goddess*, 12, 26, 32, 44, 68, 74, 76, 80, 136, 141,142, 144, 145, 149–52, 154, 155–56, 157, 159, 161, 164, 165, 166–67, 168–69, 202–3, 207
—Essays: "The Anti-Poet," 166; "The Bible in Europe," 162–63, 164; "The Case for Xanthippe," 24, 32; "Centaur's Food," 19; "Dr. Syntax and Mr. Pound; 123; "Genius," 23; "The Ghost of Mr. Milton," 19; "Legitimate Criticism of Poetry," 19–20, 22, 25, 30, 32, 56; "The Making and Marketing of Poetry," 22,59; "The Poet and His Public," 25; "A Postscript to *Good-bye to All That*," 184–85; "Rationality," 21; "Some Instances of Poetic Vulgarity," 123; "These Be Your Gods, O Israel," 46, 194, 200, 205; "Tyger, Tyger," 123; "Uses of Superstition," 161; "What Has Gone Wrong," 164–65
—Novels: *Count Belisarius*, 12, 124–25; *The Golden Fleece*, 118; *I Claudius*, 12, 31–32, 34, 114, 116, 118, 120–21, 128, 129, 131–135; *King Jesus*, 120, 167; *My Head! My Head!*, 107; *The Real David Copperfield*, 29; *Wife to Mr. Milton*, 12, 27, 28, 31, 33, 136
—Poems: "Acrobats," 81–82; "Around the Mountain," 76;"Attercop: The All Wise Spider," 75–76, 81;"Between Dark and Dark," 81; "Big Words," 67; "A Boy in Church," 211–12; "Brother," 67; "Certain Mercies," 68; "The Christmas Robin," 79–80; "The Clipped Stater," 42; "Cock in Pullet's Feathers," 67; "Country Sentiment," 37; "The Co-Walker," 76–77; "Cry Faugh!,"80; "The Devil's Advice to Story-Tellers," 117, 118; "Down," 37; "Down, Wanton, Down," 97; "Endless Pavement," 74; "A Face in the Mirror," 67; "The Fallen

Tower of Siloam," 94; "Familiar Letter to S.S.," 36; "The Feather Bed," 167–68; "The Finding of Love," 216; "Finland," 66; "Fire-Walker," 81–82; "Free Vesrse," 71; "Full Moon," 216; "Galatea and Pygmalion," 87, 91–93, 95, 100–02; "General Bloodstock's Lament for England," 76; "The Gnat," 109; "The God Called Poetry," 37; "The Gorge," 78; "The Hills of May," 68–69; "The Homecoming," 78; "In Broken Images," 67; "In No Direction," 74–75, 213; "In the Wilderness," 66; "In Trance at a Distance," 78; "Language of the Seasons," 214; "The Laureate," 95–97; "Leda," 95, 98–100, 203–4; "The Legs," 68; "A Letter From Wales," 40–41; "Like Snow," 217; "Lost Love," 66; "Love in Barrenness," 11, 84–86, 88, 91; "A Love Story," 216; "A Lover Since Childhood," 66; "Lyceia," 78; "Mid-Winter Waking," 216–17; "The Miracle," 79; "The Morning Before the Battle," 211; "My Ghost," 76–77; "Nature's Lineament's," 68, 215; "Nobody," 139f; "No More Ghosts," 102; "Not Dead," 68; "Oh, Oh!," 66; "The Oleaster," 80–81; "On the Ridge," 11, 86; "Outlaws," 37, 212–13; "Over the Brazier," 36; "The Pier Glass," 37; "The Poet in the Nursery," 211; "The Portrait," 79; "Purification," 78; "Pygmalion to Galatea," 11, 78, 87–91, 100; "Reassurance to a Satyr," 67; "Records," 79; "Return," 215; "The Ridge Top," 86; "Rocky Acres," 37, 212; "She Tells Her Love While Half Asleep," 217; "Sick Love," 81; "Son Altesse," 78; "Song: The Promise," 78–79; "The Stranger," 204; "Succubus," 204; "The Sweet-Shop Round the Corner," 79; "Theseus and Ariadne," 79; "To be in Love," 74, 81–82; "To Bring the Dead to Life," 117, 121–22; "To Walk on Hills," 68, 69–70, 81; "The Traditionalist," 74; "Trudge, Body!," 68, 70, 73–74, 81; "Ulysses," 204; "The Undead,"77; "Wanderings of Christmas," 79–80; "Your Private Way," 79
—Poetry collections: *Collected Poems (1938)*, 79–80, 86; *Collected Poems (1959)*, 61; *Collected Poems (1975)*, 68; *Fairies and Fusiliers*, 41; *Goliath and David*, 68; *The Green-Sailed Vessel*, 76; *Man Does, Woman Is*, 13, 210; *Mock Beggar Hall*, 75, 81; *More Poems 1961*, 66; *Over the Brazier*, 41; *Poems 1914–1926*, 87; *Poems 1929*, 81; *Poems 1968–1970*, 76; *Whipperginny*, 86
—Short stories: "Epics are out of Fashion," 107, 111–12, 113, 114–15, 117, 118, 122, 123, 125–26; "The Shout," 34, 107–110, 113, 116, 117, 126; "A Toast to Ava Gardner," 21; "The Tenement," 118–19, 121

Graves, William, 9, 65–66; *Wild Olives*, 9, 65–66
Gravesiana: The Journal of the Robert Graves Society, 10
Greece, 85, 111
Guardian, The, 56
Guernica, Spain, 95
Gunn, Thom, 55

Hale, Robin, 97
Hardy, Thomas, 37, 39, 55, 66
Harlech, Wales, 68, 69
Hatch, Edwin, 159
Helen of Troy, 98, 191
Hemingway, Ernest, 178; *A Farewell to Arms*, 178
Henderson, Philip, 131
Henry I, King of England, 143
Hermeticism, 159
Hodgart, M. J. C., 200–201, 202
Hodge, Alan, 26, 29, 34; *The Reader Over Your Shoulder*, 26, 29, 34
Hoffman, Daniel, 68, 86, 87, 207; *Barbarous Knowledge*, 68
Hoffpauir, Richard, 99
Holloway, John, 60
Homer, 161
Hopkins, Chris, 12, 128–135
Hughes, Ted, 12, 149–58; Works: "Bride and Groom Lie Hidden For Three Days," 154; *Cave Birds*, 154; *Choice of Shakespeare's Verse*, 156; *Crow*, 154; "Esther's Tomcat," 153; *Gaudete*, 153; "The Harvesting," 155; *The Iron Woman*, 153–54; "Macaw and Little Miss," 153; *Moortown*, 153, 154, 157;

"The Rain Horse," 155; *River*, 153; *Shakespeare and the Goddess of Complete Being*, 156; "Song," 149–50; "The Wound," 154
Hulme, T. E., 47, 48–49
Hynes, Samuel, 43; *A War Imagined*, 43

Imagists, 47, 49–50, 52, 54
Islam, 165

Jackson, Schuyler, 33
James, St., 164
Jehovah, 164
John the Baptist, St., 168
Josephus, 162
Joyce, James, 123–24, 180, 189. Works: *Dubliners*, 180; *Finnegans Wake*, 123–24; *Ulysses*, 180
Jung, Carl, 150, 154, 156, 157, 159; *Psychological Types*, 150

Kazin, Alfred, 65; "The Open Street", 65
Keats, John, 165
Kelly, John, 188
Kemp, Harry, 102
Kenner, Hugh, 40; *A Sinking Island*, 40
Kenyon Review, 201
Kershner, R. B. Jr., 197, 202; *Dylan Thomas: The Poet and His Critics*, 197, 202
Khayaám, Omar, 10; *Rubáiyat*, 10
Kirk, Edward, 76; *Secret Commonwealth*, 76
Kirkham, Michael, 68, 75, 108
Kohli, Devindra, 11, 65–83
Koike-Ferrick, H., 11; *Robert Graves: The Poet and the Muse*, 11

Larkin, Philip, 55, 56–57, 58; "Graves Superior," 56
Lawrence, D. H., 149, 196
Lawrence, T. E. (T. E. Shaw), 31, 40, 42, 129, 135
Leavis, F. R., 20, 53
Lewis, Alun, 190
Lindsay, Jack, 129, 131. Works: *1649*, 131; *Caesar is Dead*, 129; *Rome for Sale*, 129
Lindsay, Vachel, 194
London, 97, 183
London's Dreadful Visitation, 183

Lucan, 114, 122; *Pharsalia*, 114
Lucifer, 30, 167–68
Lukács, Georg, 130–31; *The Historical Novel*, 130–31

MacNeice, Louis, 189
Macrobius, 205
Majorca, 9, 22, 101, 213, 214
Mallory, George, 71–72; "The Mountaineer as Artist," 71–72
Malraux, André, 58–59
Marduk, 154
Martin, Wallace, 113; *Recent Theories of Narrative*, 113
Marxism, 128
Mary, Blessed Virgin, 166–68, 169
Masefield, John, 39, 95
Mason, Ellsworth, 10
Massey, Gerald, 159
Matthews, T. S., 25, 33; *Under the Influence*, 33
McCormick, Ian, 12, 136–45
McGuinness, Patrick, 11, 46–61, 123
Mead, G. R. S., 159
Merwin, W. S., 195
Miller, J. Hillis, 191
Milton, John, 19, 24, 26–28, 29, 32–33, 66, 123, 136–144, 206, 211, 214. Works: *Comus*, 137; "L'Allegro," 24, 26–28, 33; *Paradise Lost*, 19, 144
Mitchell, Leslie (Grassic Gibbon), 129
Mitchison, Naomi, 129; *The Blood of Martyrs*, 129
Modernism, 46–61, 124, 177
Mommsen, Theodor, 130
Moore, Marianne, 55, 60
Moore, Sturge, 194
Mount Holyoke College (USA), 20
Movement, The, 47, 55–60
Moynihan, William T., 200–201; *The Craft and Art of Dylan Thomas*, 200–201
Mussolini, Benito, 129

Neoplatonism, 159, 166
Nero, 122
Neurasthenia, 36, 108, 110
New Criticism, 24, 52
New Lines, 55
Nicholson, Nancy, 36

O'Brien, James, H., 193
Odyssey, The, 90
Opie, Iona and Peter, 80

O'Prey, Paul, 11, 36–45; *Between Moon and Moon,* 11; *In Broken Images,* 11
Order of the Knights Templar, 161, 165, 166
Orpheus, 209, 210, 217, 218
Ovid, 87–88, 90, 92, 100; *Metamorphoses,* 87–88, 90
Owen, Wilfred, 42, 43, 72–73, 212; "Smile, Smile, Smile," 42
Oxford Poetry (1921), 86
Oxford University, 123

Panofsky, Erwin, 217
Paphos, Cyprus, 167
Paris Review, The, 31, 33
Patai, Raphael, 120
Paul, St., 162–64
Perseus, 90
Pelasgians, 85
Peter, St., 162
Plath, Sylvia, 154; *The Bell Jar,* 154
Platonism, 31, 92, 191, 210
Podro, Joshua, 163; *The Nazarene Gospel Restored,* 163
Poggioli, Renato, 213, 215
Pollux, 98
Pope, Alexander, 19
Poulet, George, 29–30
Pound, Ezra, 19, 21, 24, 30, 33, 34, 46, 47, 48, 49, 53, 56, 59, 60–61, 123, 160, 161, 162, 164, 165, 169, 170, 194, 206. Works: "Ballad of the Goodly Fere," 53; *The Cantos,* 21, 169; *Hugh Selwyn Mauberly,* 30, 123
Poussin, Nicolas, 217
Presley, John, 12, 13, 107, 188–208
Press, John, 201; *The Chequer'd Shade: Reflections on Obscurity in Poetry,* 201
Procopius, 125
Propertius, Sextus, 24
Propoetides, 88
Proteus, 90
Psilopoulos, Dionysious, 12, 159–171
Punch, 114

Quennell, Peter, 24
Quinn, Patrick, 11, 12, 86–87, 94–103, 108, 109; *The Great War and the Missing Muse,* 12, 86–87

Ranke, Leopold von, 131–32
Ransom, John Crowe, 65

Reitzenstein, Richard, 159
Remarque, Erich Maria, 178; *All Quiet on the Western Front,* 178
Richard I, King of England, 166
Riding, Laura (Jackson), 12, 41–42, 43–44, 46, 48, 54, 70–71, 73, 87, 93, 94, 95–102, 110–11, 116–17, 122, 123, 190, 194. Works: "Christmas 1937," 101; *Collected Poems,* 101; "The Covenant of Literal Morality," 94; *Epilogue,* 87, 96; "The Left Heresy," 102; "Love as Love, Death as Death," 95; "Politics and Poetry," 96; "A Prophecy or a Plea," 43; *A Survey of Modernist Poetry,* 44, 46, 48, 99, 107, 123; *The Telling,* 70–71; *A Trojan Ending,* 116; *The World and Ourselves,* 94
Rimbaud, Arthur, 53
Rivers, W. H. R., 40, 108
Roberts, Eirlys, 118
Rome, 111, 118, 129, 130

Samothrace, 161
Samson, 140
Sassoon, Siegfried, 38, 39, 41, 112, 113, 115, 125, 184, 194; "A Soldier's Declaration," 184
Satan, 140, 198
Schama, Simon, 211
Selby, Keith, 189; "Hitting the Right Note: The Poetry of Cheap Music," 189
Seneca, 157–58; *Oedipus* (adapted by Ted Hughes), 157–58
Seutonius, 122
Seymour, Miranda, 9, 101; *Robert Graves: Life on the Edge,* 9
Seymour-Smith, Martin, 9, 68, 73, 95, 107, 108, 116, 118, 128, 183, 190
Shah, Idries, 165; *The Sufis,* 165
Shakespeare, William, 39, 99, 156, 157; "Sonnet 129," 99; *The Tempest,* 157
Sherriff, R. C., 179; *Journey's End,* 179
Sisson, C. H., 37
Sitwell, Edith, 201
Skelton, John, 30, 39, 206
Somme, The Battle of the, 36, 178
Song of Amergin, 68
Spain, 166
Spender, Stephen, 23–24, 97, 124; *The Struggle of the Modern,* 124
St. John's College, Oxford, 9, 36, 114

Suficism, 161, 165–66
Surette, Leon, 159, 160; *The Birth of Modernism: Ezra Pound, T. S. Eliot, W. B. Yeats and the Occult*, 159, 160
Swinburne, A. C., 39, 47
Symons, Julian, 201, 202; "Obscurity and Dylan Thomas," 201

Tacitus, 32, 132
Tennyson, Alfred, 47
Terraine, John, 184
Thomas, Dylan, 13, 21, 34, 46, 47, 48, 53, 55, 61, 188, 189, 190, 193, 194–201, 206, 207. Works: "A Grief Ago," 201; "Author's Prologue to Collected Poems," 195,196; "Ballad of the Long-Legged Bait," 198; *Collected Poems*, 197; "Ears in the Turrets Hear," 195; "Fern Hill," 199; "The Fisherman," 195, 198; "From Love's First Fever to her Plague," 198; "I, in my Intricate Image," 195; "If My Head Hurt a Hair's Foot," 199–200; "In my Craft or Sullen Art," 195; "In the Beginning," 198; *Life and Letters Today*, 197; "Modern Poetry," 189; *New Poems*, 199; "Once it was the Colour of Saying," 196; "Our Eunuch Dreams," 196; "Unlucky for a Death," 196; "When I Awoke," 199; "Where Once the Waters of Your Face," 197
Tiamat, 154
Times (London), 179
Times Literary Supplement (London), 206
Tindall, W. Y., 189, 198, 199, 202; *A Reader's Guide to Dylan Thomas*, 202
Tiresias, 136, 139–40
Treece, Henry, 194–95, 200, 201, 202; *Dylan Thomas: "Dog among the Fairies,"* 200
Trout, Steven, 12, 175–87
Tryphonopoulos, Demetres. P., 159; *The Cantos, The Celestial Tradition*, 159
Tyndareus, king of Sparta, 98

University of Toronto Quarterly, 10
Ure, Peter, 206

Valéry, Paul, 189
Venus, (Aphrodite), 88, 100, 154, 166–67

Vers Libre, 39
Vesta, 170
Vickery, John B., 167, 202–3; *Robert Graves and the White Goddess*, 202–3
Virgil, Maro, 210, 211, 214, 218

Wallace, Anne, 11, 65; *Walking, Literature, and English Culture*, 65
Warner, Sylvia Townsend, 129
Watt, Ian, 176
Waugh, Evelyn, 129
Wellesley, Dorothy, 190
White Goddess, 12, 41, 57–58, 59, 66, 69, 75, 77–78, 99, 118, 149, 150, 157, 159–70, 188, 203, 207, 217, 218
White, Hayden, 177
Williams, William Carlos, 194
Williamson, Henry, 186; *The Patriot's Progress*, 186
Wordsworth, William, 24, 28–29, 33, 66, 144; "Lucy poems," 24
Worth, Irene, 158

Yeats, John Butler, 188
Yeats, W. B., 13, 44, 46, 47, 48, 53, 57, 59, 61, 66, 68, 98, 160, 161, 162, 169, 170, 188, 189, 190–94, 195–96, 197, 198, 199, 202, 203, 204–6, 207–8. Works: "Among School Children," 204; "The Chosen," 205–6; "The Circus Animals' Desertion," 195; "Crazy Jane Talks with the Bishop," 205; *The Death of Cuchulain*, 207; "A Dialogue of Self and Soul," 204–5; "The Dolls," 192; "Fergus and the Druid," 192; "The Fish," 198; "A Full Moon in March," 207; "In Memory of Major Robert Gregory," 202; "The King of the Great Clock Tower," 207; "The Lake Isle of Innisfree," 189–90; "Leda and the Swan," 98, 203; "The Mother of God," 203; *The Oxford Book of Modern Verse* (1936), 189; "Sailing to Byzantium," 192, 197, 205; "Solomon and the Witch," 192, 206; "The Stolen Child," 191; "Supernatural Songs," 205; *The Tower*, 204; *A Vision*, 169, 191, 202–3, 206, 207; "Who Goes with Fergus," 191–92

Zeus, 98, 164

821.912
NEW   New perspectives on Robert Graves

T0063745

821.912
NEW   New perspectives on Robert Graves

T0063745